Entrepreneurial Textile Communities

Entrepreneurial Textile Communities

A comparative study of small textile and clothing firms

Anna Bull

Martyn Pitt

Joseph Szarka

School of Modern Languages and International Studies and School of Management, University of Bath

CHAPMAN & HALL
University and Professional Division
London • Glasgow • New York • Tokyo • Melbourne • Madras

Published by Chapman & Hall, 2–6 Boundary Row, London SE1 8HN

Chapman & Hall, 2–6 Boundary Row, London SE1 8HN, UK

Blackie Academic & Professional, Wester Cleddens Road, Bishopbriggs, Glasgow G64 2NZ, UK

Chapman & Hall Inc., 29 West 35th Street, New York NY10001, USA

Chapman & Hall Japan, Thomson Publishing Japan, Hirakawacho Nemoto Building, 6F, 1-7-11 Hirakawa-cho, Chiyoda-ku, Tokyo 102, Japan

Chapman & Hall Australia, Thomas Nelson Australia, 102 Dodds Street, South Melbourne, Victoria 3205, Australia

Chapman & Hall India, R. Seshadri, 32 Second Main Road, CIT East, Madras 600 035, India

First edition 1993

© 1993 A. Bull, M. Pitt and J. Szarka

Typeset in Great Britain by University of Bath

Printed in Great Britain by T J Press, Padstow

ISBN 0 412 42720 6

A catalogue record for this book is available from the British Library

Library of Congress Cataloging-in-Publication data
Bull, Anna.
    Entrepreneurial textile communities : a comparative study of small textile and clothing firms / Anna Bull, Martyn Pitt, Joseph Szarka. —1st ed.
        p. cm.
    Includes bibliographical references and index.
    ISBN 0 412 42720 6 (alk. paper)
        1. Textile industry—Europe—Cross-cultural studies. 2. Small business—Europe—Cross-cultural studies. 3. Entrepreneurship—Europe—Cross-cultural studies. I. Pitt, Martyn II. Szarka, Joseph. III. Title
HD9865.A2B85 1993
338.4'7677'0094—dc20   92-38134
                                                                      CIP

Contents

Preface

This book has a number of themes, most prominent among them being entrepreneurship, the rejuvenation of mature industries in Europe, small firms, and inter-firm collaboration and network formation. Based on a cross-national study of entrepreneurship in small firms in the textiles and clothing industries, we have attempted to shed light on the formulae or 'recipes' for success in three well-established communities of small firms in Britain, France and Italy.

To this end, we have considered a range of units and levels of analysis, notably the individual proprietor, the firm, the cluster of firms and the sector. A major conclusion has been that the circumstances of each community are essentially distinct and that each is embarked on a developmental track which is largely particular to it, and therefore not replicable directly in other venues. That said, we are of the opinion that each community of firms has much to learn from others. Indeed future success will depend in large measure on the ability of each community to be open-minded to the possibility of 'importing' new ideas, new methods and new structures from outside. This lesson is more generally applicable.

As we see it, the work reported here tries to make a useful contribution to the growing literature on entrepreneurship and networking. On the basis of this and other work, we have little doubt that there is a significant linkage between effective network formation among firms and the strategic viability of an industrial sector. We think this theme will continue to be an important area for research, and it is one we are glad to have contributed to, however modestly. We would like to think that our work will prove interesting to readers and will stimulate them to advance the debate.

All three authors joined the University of Bath at the same time, and this is one reason why we had the opportunity to discover shared interests and a desire to work collaboratively. Our thanks, then, go to the university for providing us with this opportunity, and more especially we thank our respective Schools for supporting our efforts from the outset. In addition, a number of colleagues at the university have provided critical and insightful comments; of these, we would like especially to mention Charles Baden-Fuller and Bryn Jones.

The research on which this book is based began some five years ago. Fieldwork was facilitated by a modest research grant from the Twenty-third Directorate of the European Commission, which we acknowledge with thanks. The views expressed here are, of course, those of the authors and have not been presented as those of the Commission.

Writing is a time-consuming and, in some respects, a selfish activity, in as much as writers commit a good many hours especially during evenings and weekends to projects which are personally meaningful, but may lack immediate benefit for those around them. Thus we gratefully acknowledge the forbearance and encouragement of our respective partners and families. Though it is difficult for loved-ones to share the intrinsic satisfaction gained from the writing process, we hope they will nevertheless share our satisfaction in the completion of this book. To them all, we offer our heartfelt thanks.

Anna Bull
Martyn Pitt
Joseph Szarka

June 1992

1

Small firms and the survivability of mature industrial sectors

1.1 DEFINING THE FIELD OF STUDY

Europe and the world are in a state of flux. There can be few generations in this millennium who have witnessed ongoing political, cultural and economic changes with such an obvious sense of history in the making. Indeed for those of us in Europe the future seems paradoxical as,individually and collectively, we grapple with our evolving European identity and our place in a world struggling to cope with a multiplicity of politico-economic stresses.

Changing circumstances promote great uncertainty in respect of future outcomes and possibilities. Though dimensions of change cannot readily be isolated from one another, nowhere are the uncertainties more acute than in the economic sphere. In the Europe of the Twelve we have been fortunate since the 1950s to enjoy rising living standards, contingent in no small measure on a well-established and economically viable **manufacturing base**. Yet the historically strong international standing of European industries can no longer be taken for granted in the face of the growing competitiveness of the Japanese, of the newly industrialized countries of the Pacific Rim, notably Hong Kong, Malaysia, the Philippines, South Korea and Taiwan, and of the emerging economies of Brazil, India, Mexico and Pakistan, to name but a few. In the twenty-first century the list of strong competitors will surely grow to include a number of African states as well.

There is a well-trodden pattern of economic development: an emerging state seeks to take advantage of its plentiful, low-cost physical and human resources by attracting inward investment. Labour-intensive manufacturing sectors, such as textiles and clothing, are often regarded as ideal vehicles for industrialization, forming the vanguard of export-led, hard currency generation which then underpins economic development on a broader front. Subsidy and other forms of governmental assistance commonly reinforce this process. Europe and the USA are obvious targets for exports from newly industrialized countries as Hong Kong, notably, has demonstrated over the past two decades. But this example also demonstrates that long-run competitiveness is not sustained merely by producing cheap and inferior goods. Over time the quality and specification of Hong Kong's manufactured products – in sectors as diverse as garments and electronic watches – have risen inexorably, so that European producers of similar goods now face competition across the full spectrum of demand, save perhaps at the most sophisticated and costly end of the spectrum.

So it comes as no surprise that intense international competition from newly industrialized producers has driven many European producers out of business, despite the defensive intent of the various provisions of four successive Multi-Fibre Arrangements in textiles and clothing. Some producers in threatened but long-standing sectors have elected to stand their ground and fight, as exemplified notably by the Swiss in wristwatches and the Italians in textiles and clothing. None the less, official statistics clearly show that the European textiles and clothing sectors on which this book focuses have been steadily losing ground, as measured by share of world trade. Moreover, while some viable industrial responses undoubtedly exist in textiles, their scope to respond to competitive pressures and their potential in terms of accessible demand may in fact be quite limited.

The disinterested observer can, of course, shrug and say that this does not matter. Europe's industrial destiny, so the argument goes, lies in the advanced technologies and applications of the microchip and telecommunications, and by extension, increasingly in the service industries as opposed to manufacturing. In Britain this has occasioned talk of 'the post-industrial society'. We submit that such talk is premature and ill-advised. The evidence from other European economies is that relatively traditional sectors of industry can survive and prosper in advanced, high-wage economies, even in the face of potent international competition. Indeed many commentators would accept that there is a 'strategic necessity' for Europe to retain a capability in industries such as steel and microchips. To that end, investment in state-of-the-art manufacturing technology allied to non-traditional forms of organization structure and work practices may be imperatives. Whether textiles and clothing are widely regarded in Europe as a 'strategic necessity' is doubtful, though one should not underestimate their ability to generate wealth and sustain employment.

Much of the recent literature in English still construes these issues largely in terms of the problems and prospects of large, generally **vertically integrated** industrial concerns. The 'strategic logic' of large-scale mass production has been well documented by influential US consultants such as the Boston Consulting Group (e.g. Henderson, 1979) and the Strategic Planning Institute (Buzzell and Gale, 1987). This logic can be described simply: scale and relative standardization of output facilitates continuing cost reduction and quality enhancement. These, in turn, should lead to competitive superiority, increased market share and high profitability, which then dictate the drive for increased scale of output and investment by a few dominant firms in the sector. The cycle of scale leading to market dominance which in turn elevates scale potentialities is – if such commentators are to be believed – virtually self-sustaining.

A more thoughtful strand of empirically grounded theorizing about industrial development recognized that the cycle does not generally continue indefinitely. Indeed many US firms in 'mature' industries, such as automobiles, have notably failed to sustain profitable growth. Abernathy and colleagues (Abernathy, 1978; Abernathy, Clark and Kantrow, 1983) advanced the notion of **industrial dematurity**. They argued that there was an evident need for innovative approaches to the management of mature industrial sectors; and they posited the concept of **industrial renaissance** associated with a paradigm shift from the 'roadblock' of standardization and inflexibility inherent in the prevailing 'Fordist' mass production methods of big firms. Piore and Sabel (1984) also supported the seminal, if controversial, argument that the Fordist paradigm was not inevitable and that it was entirely possible for industries of the future to organize in a largely fragmented or 'deintegrated' way. Their proposition was underpinned by the apparent ability of small units (whether subdivisions of larger legal entities or quasi-independent firms) to: (i) specialize in a limited range of tasks within the value-adding chain of production and (ii) combine efficiency with responsiveness **to market needs**, by applying advanced manufacturing technology to enhance productivity and flexibility. Further, the comparative ease with which information technologies of the future would facilitate remote or distributed communications among firms and individuals might be expected to encourage the adoption of post-Fordist practices.

Other academics have addressed the debate over managing in mature and declining industries in a European context, leading them to transmute the argument of the exit of firms into imperatives for strategic and structural rejuvenation (Baden-Fuller, 1989; Baden-Fuller, dell'Osso and Stopford, 1991; Grant, 1986). In general, increased flexibility to satisfy market needs appears to be a shared prescription of these and other writers, applying to the textiles and clothing sectors as elsewhere (e.g. Stopford and Baden-Fuller, 1990). One response to the need for flexibility has been a considerable interest in several examples of loosely integrated, collaborative organizational forms variously characterized as 'quasi-firms', 'mutual organizations' and industrial networks (e.g. Jarillo, 1988; Johannisson, 1986; Johanson and Mattson, 1987; Koenig and Thietart, 1990; Thorelli, 1986).

Yet whether these observed phenomena offer prototypical models for systematic industrial organization in the future remains an open question.

From within the 'Fordist paradigm' flexible operations may be accepted as necessary to cope with increasing variety in demand (a concomitant of maturing and sophisticating markets) but are not necessarily seen to challenge the paradigm itself so much as to require a reformulation of the most efficacious approach within it, as witness 'lean production' concepts. A number of highly successful Japanese industries including automobiles lend credence to this assessment.

In this paradigm of industrial development, the long-run place of small firms is problematic. To be sure, the emergence of new high technology sectors creates populations of small firms, but this (so the argument goes) is a transitory phenomenon. The implicit assumption is that over time sector evolution concentrates myriad small firms into much fewer numbers of large ones; the personal computer industry could be cited as an example. Some young start-up firms have grown to maturity (e.g. Apple, Compaq) and now thrive in competition with the giants of the industry such as IBM. Others thrived for a short period and then demised or were taken over (e.g. Acorn, Sinclair, Osborne). However, as dominant product design configurations emerged, a second wave of small firms has formed, competing not on technical superiority, but on excellent customer service and dedication to particular applications.

Traditional sectors such as textiles and clothing are no exception to this broad pattern of big firm/small firm coexistence: the pre-eminence of a few major firms like Benetton (scale-dominant via organic growth) and Coats Viyella (scale-dominant via acquisitive growth) has in no way precluded the continued existence of large numbers of quite small but relatively stable firms.

It was noted recently that small firms in Europe, Japan and the USA have actually increased their numbers and share of employment since the 1970s (Loveman and Sengenberger, 1990). For the most part, these trends have occurred in what we might call fully mature industries. Certainly attempts during the 1970s, notably in Britain, to create vast industrial organizations via merger and integration were not notably successful in terms of economic performance. Subsequent recession in the early 1980s then reversed the trend (Amin, Johnson and Storey, 1986; Shutt and Whittington, 1987). Elsewhere in Europe industrial organization manifests a similar trend to fragmentation, notably in Italy, where many small firms operate in a comparatively large number of quite localized industrial clusters which have become noted for their particular specialisms. These clusters are mostly found in the northern and north-central regions of Italy (Sforzi, 1987; Becattini, 1987, 1990), though a similar phenomenon also occurs elsewhere (Porter, 1990). Clustering has been noted as a particular feature of high-technology sectors, generally around acknowledged centres of scientific excellence, exemplified in the US 'Silicon Valley' near Stanford University and Boston's Route 128 near MIT, and around Cambridge University in England.

Recognition of the economic significance of firm clustering is by no means new. The term 'economic growth pole' dates back to Perroux (1950) and so-called 'industrial districts' have evidently existed since the birth of the nineteenth-century Industrial Revolution (Marshall, 1919). Yet the idea of **internationally competitive** localities of small firms sits uneasily with conventional theories associated with: (i) economies of scale and scope primarily exploitable by large firms; (ii) high levels of vertical integration within the 'value-chain' encapsulated in organizational hierarchies (Williamson, 1979); and (iii) concomitant oligopolistic competition. Indeed the 'intellectual capital' now invested in the theoretical exposition of the development of large-scale, integrated firms could help explain past reluctance to take seriously the phenomenon of localized, deintegrated industrial communities and their contribution to the innovativeness and the economic vitality of their host nations.

None the less, there has been growing interest in small firms and localized small firm communities, and it is in this stream of research and literature that we locate our own work. Thus we continue here with a brief explanation of our motives for the research reported in this book and how it was developed.

1.2 MULTIPLE 'WINDOWS' ON THE RESEARCH AGENDA

In 1987 our differing disciplinary backgrounds and experience found a convergent interest in the small firm as a relevant research theme not only in economic, but also in sociocultural terms. Stated briefly, this interest became focused on a research study with the following characteristics:

1. Small firms, witnessed in regional/local agglomerations and based on a mature industry context.
2. The textiles and clothing sectors as exemplars of mature industries in general.
3. A genuinely cross-national, cross-comparative and multi-perspectival methodology.

We were aware that the issue of small firm viability in mature sectors of manufacturing subject to intense international competition could be seen not just in terms of the survival of small firms *per se*, but to have a bearing on the survival of a European presence in so-called 'sunset' industries. The label should not, of course, be taken to imply that sector maturity is associated with imminent decline; rather the crucial question is whether, in general, small firms can make a significant contribution to sector survivability.

Yet we acknowledged too the need to avoid an unquestioning 'European' perspective. The cultures, traditions and industrial experiences of countries are patently as diverse within Europe as between Western Europe and other parts of the world. Conclusions with cross-national validity must be approached cautiously. To be most credible new research should address a particular sector and be cautious of generalizing its findings too broadly. Still, even if observed configurations of industrial structures, organizational forms and business practices are context-bound, this does not automatically negate the prospect of identifying underlying themes germane to small firms and survivability in mature sectors generally.

We chose textiles and clothing as exemplars of 'sunset' industries and of manufacturing sectors with a particular history of European pre-eminence. It is a sector in which small firms have always played a substantial part. Recently the textiles and clothing sectors have experienced marked secular decline in levels of output and employment in the countries of the European Community overall. None the less, they remain a significant employer and further decline would impact painfully on many EC countries. Our opening assumption, then, was that small firms in textiles and clothing will continue to be economically significant, though how much and in what ways is a matter for investigation.

Initial reviews of the literature confirmed that cross-national comparative studies constructed as parallel inquiries with common research agendas were quite rare. We chose to carry out a genuinely cross-national study of small firms and their proprietors in three countries, namely France, Italy and the UK. We wanted to describe and understand the nature of small firms in three separate local agglomerations and the circumstances, past and present, offered by these localities to constituent firms. Additionally, we wanted to consider the characteristics of the firms' proprietors and the nature of their relationships with their counterparts in other firms. Given the economic and other environmental changes anticipated in the EC from 1993 onwards, we chose to focus also on how well small firms were preparing for the decisive new stage in European integration associated with the Single European Market, hence what contribution they might make to future European economic prosperity.

Having defined briefly our sphere of interest and our reasons why, we can now address our concerns more specifically. From the outset, we were interested in the cross-national and, by inference, cross-cultural impact of small firm behaviours on performance and the ultimate survivability of a mature sector. Clearly a variety of levels and units of analysis present themselves for possible consideration. Most published studies have considered one or two such levels and scarcely acknowledge the impact of others. We were determined to consider a range of levels or 'windows' on the research agenda in the belief that we might thereby realize a fuller understanding of the issues, not least because different perspectives might generate new and otherwise inaccessible insights.

It is appropriate therefore to say a little more about the nature of these 'windows' and why they are important. Later chapters will then as it were look through each window, in turn, as we report our various findings.

1.2.1 The small firm and its strategic characteristics

A common and essential unit of analysis is the firm. Classical economists saw the interests of the (small) firm and the entrepreneur as synonymous. The former could therefore be treated as the well-known 'black box', the internal structures and processes of which were regarded as of little consequence, while entrepreneurial motives were assumed to be largely economic. But it is quite clear from a great variety of organization research that internal structures and processes and entrepreneurial motives all bear on the way firms develop.

Of direct relevance to the issue of industrial survivability are the type and range of strategic choices available to firms in an industrial sector and the degree of autonomy each firm enjoys in the implementation of these choices. The debate over so-called **environmental determinism** has become polarized, logically extreme positions being articulated by Child (1972) in respect of strategic choice, and by Hannan and Freeman (1977) on population ecology. Neither position can be ignored. Small firm proprietors are obliged to take account of external opportunities and constraints but they also have, in principle, considerable freedom as to the conduct of their firms. For example, individual proprietors make choices over the nature and scope of the value-adding activities of the firm within the competitive sectoral arena, the deployment of staff and other resources, and so on. But the very existence of such arenas impose more or less systematic limits, whether market-derived, technical, geographic or otherwise, on these choices. Thus in reality small firms will be constrained in what they do, and in what they become, by reason of prudence and feasibility. Indeed, given adequate prior knowledge of their progress to date, it may be possible for an informed observer to describe the evolution of small firms, either individually or collectively, in terms of fairly predictable development tracks (as we shall discuss in later chapters).

An important question for our research therefore was about the nature of the strategic choices open to firms in the study and the patterns of choice manifest within a given locality. Would there be **systematic differences** in these patterns of choice, and if so, how would these relate to the collective technological specialisms and idiosyncrasies of firms within and comprising (in whole or part) a locality? Also what differences, if any, would emerge as to the internal organization of firms, the contributions made by their proprietors, and the nature and extent of inter-firm contacts within and beyond the geographic locality?

The prevailing assumption in the mainstream strategic management literature is, curiously enough, shared with the population ecologists, namely that of unremitting inter-firm combat, meaning that only the 'fittest' survive and grow. Ecologists posit the survival of individual firms through the mechanism of natural selection, which firms cannot directly influence or control. Strategists posit the ability of firms to control their destinies through intelligent, anticipatory choices (strategies) with respect to the changing competitive environment. This view leads to the concept of generic strategic choices open to firms in competitive market environments. Expressed simply, the individual firm has but two generic choices. One is to control its destiny through the dominance it may achieve by scale of operation allied to low production cost per unit of output. This strategy leads to sectoral concentration as smaller and weaker firms demise. The other strategy is, in effect, to occupy a 'niche', a position of relative security, by virtue of its isolation from competitive predation. This is achieved either by differentiating what the firm does from what its closest competitors can do or by occupying a niche so tightly defined that would-be competitors cannot or simply do not wish to prise it out.

Differentiation and tight focus as means of niching in principle go hand in hand, though the potential for small firms to sustain truly differentiated positions is generally limited since emulation by competitors is usually possible. Indeed the 'perfect competition' of classical economics presumes no potential for advantage and security via any of these mechanisms, so firms compete on efficiency and price. In theory, competition depresses the equilibrium price to the level consistent with the cost-of-capital floor. In contrast, **sustained differentiation** can be a particularly effective mechanism for astute firms to decouple or isolate prices from the prevailing floor and thus achieve above-average returns. If the prospects of large returns either to scale or to differentiation are subverted by circumstances, sectoral concentration is discouraged and the competitive arena remains populated by many powerless small firms.

For this research, a salient question is the extent to which small firms can identify and exploit isolating mechanisms by which to enhance profit and growth prospects. The literature suggests that in general small firms are unable to do so, particularly in sectors where bigger firms occupy powerful positions. This raises questions about how the prospects compare in different countries, localities and sectors, as well as the existence of facilitating mechanisms and agencies such as government departments and industry associations aiming to compensate for the strategic weaknesses of individual small firms.

1.2.2 Entrepreneurial culture and the small firm proprietor

It is generally accepted that the personal and managerial characteristics of small firm proprietors vary in reasonably systematic ways. Their outlooks or identities depend – as one might expect – partly on traits of personality, and partly on the conditioning effects of their developmental and operating environments. Good reviews of these issues were provided by Carland *et al.*

(1984) and by d'Amboise and Muldowney (1988). Important characteristics, it has been argued, include: (i) personal traits and values, such as individualism, need-for-achievement and inwardness vs outwardness of outlook; (ii) attitudes towards risk-taking and growth (incorporating attitudes towards control, innovation and change); (iii) interpersonal and leadership qualities (the ability to organize and motivate others) and (iv) attainments in education and training.

A good many commentators distinguish small firm owner-managers from 'classic' entrepreneurs. Proprietors of the first kind tend to be comparatively inward-looking, concerned principally with the internal affairs of the firm and how it can be sustained in a rather narrowly defined product and customer niche. Typically, these small firm proprietors promote a strong 'craft culture' in their firms. Growth is almost certainly less important to them than stability and continuity in quality of output and in client relationships. 'Entrepreneurs', in contrast, are more outward-looking and opportunistic. They are generally more confident in their ability to cope with the demands of the world-out-there, to take calculated risks, to innovate and to promote growth and change. They are less concerned with craft-based activities *per se*, and they are likely to conceive their business purpose as to make money rather than to make things. Research principally from North America also suggests that classic entrepreneurs are often better educated than small firm craftsmen (e.g. Smith, 1967).

In fact the entrepreneurship literature reveals a strong North American and Anglo-Saxon orientation. As Thurley and Wirdenius (1989) have noted, the concept of managerial role was essentially American, and it has been for many years a source of considerable confusion and misuse in Europe. The possibility exists therefore that the foregoing characterizations of proprietor types are culturally bound, empirically and normatively, a view reinforced by the cross-cultural research reported by Hofstede (1980). A salient question for our own research was whether small firm proprietors in our three chosen countries would conform broadly to these archetypes, or whether they would manifest particular traits and evidence of idiosyncratic, local conditioning.

This question is important. Other work we have done and are aware of (Blim, 1991; Cento Bull and Corner, 1992) suggests that **sociocultural** conditioning, for instance, the influence of the family on the entrepreneur, has a significant bearing on the individual's behaviour. If so, the prospect of being able to generalize findings beyond the firm and its local environment is clearly reduced. Put in different terms, if proprietors' recipes for business success are determined locally, they are unlikely to be transferrable to, or work well in, other venues. Conversely, a transferrable managerial model would, as a minimum, require a pragmatic and pluralistic outlook based on learned skills and experience, as well as the local sociocultural and economic milieu of the entrepreneur. Given the widely varying histories and cultures of the European regions, the concept of a European Management Model (Thurley and Wirdenius, 1989), posited on scientific/rational as opposed to cultural/ideological assumptions, may have its attractions but is currently premature, however well-intentioned its proponents may be. In any event, a full exposition of proprietorial behaviour observed in the small firm context cannot afford to ignore either the individual proprietor or the contextual influences on him or her.

1.2.3 The community of small firms and inter-firm relationships

Given the wider constraints and opportunities already indicated in terms both of sectoral determinants and socioeconomic factors, it is important to understand the behaviour and outlook of individual firms not just in respect of the strategic choices they implement individually, but also in their patterns of action involving others in the local industrial arena. For this to be possible, one must consider issues at a more aggregate level than that of the individual firm. Issues to do with inter-firm relationships (including co-ordination and collaboration) have historically been ignored in the strategy literature though they are now increasingly noted. Likewise, this book emphasizes the community level, and we use the term 'community' to indicate a geographical agglomeration of firms.

Much recent interest has focused on the more obvious collaborative mechanisms for small firms, including firm-to-firm co-operation and information-sharing or networking (Schermerhorn, 1980; Johannisson, 1986). The emergence of quite systematic small firm **constellations**, often with the 'guiding' hand of a big firm acting as a prime contractor, was noted by Lorenzoni and Ornati (1988). Other mechanisms include technology licensing and transfer, usually from big to small firm (Lowe, 1986; Rothwell and Beesley, 1989), as well as traditional cooperatives (e.g. Hunt and McVey, 1984). We will argue that the distinction between information exchange and the physical exchange of goods and services is important, as is the distinction between exchanges having strategic, as opposed to purely operational, significance for collaborators.

Analysts of small firm communities in Italy have discussed local industrial organization using the concept of **industrial district** (Becattini, 1987, 1990), a term originated by the economist Alfred Marshall (1919). An accumulation of evidence now supports the view that industrial districts result from the alignment of particular social, cultural and economic circumstances over long periods of time. This observation is consistent with the notion of a 'trajectory of development' peculiar to a country, a locality or a firm.

Of course, one should be wary of over-stretching sociocultural or geographical explanations of industrial development. These factors help to explain the historical origins and formative evolution of an industrial community, yet once formed, communities may develop industrial structures which no longer necessarily depend on sociocultural underpinnings for subsequent survival and commercial development. Rather, later developments are determined largely by techno-economic considerations. Porter (1990) noted the existence of effective industrial clusters as a worldwide phenomenon, though he interpreted their significance largely in techno-economic terms. He argued that their effectiveness depends largely on two factors: (i) the emergence of shared (or related) technological competences and concomitant linkages among firms, both vertically in the value chain and laterally between similar or related activities, and (ii) local and national factor conditions supportive of long-run growth of the industrial sectors based on these technologies. None the less, shared culture and loyalties attributable to the family, to shared ownership, to influential trade associations and prevailing norms of behaviour facilitate information flows and sustain goal congruence within such clusters (Porter, 1990, p. 153).

In appearing to regard these non-economic aspects as a superficial overlay rather than as fundamental issues, Porter (an exemplar of English-speaking strategy commentators) may have understated the significance of relational or community mechanisms in the developmental process. This would likely be the view of various Italian commentators (Becattini, 1990; Brusco, 1986; Sforzi, 1987). For though he acknowledged that 'In Italy... effective mechanisms underlie the workings of clusters...[of which] the most important are the family...ties that frequently link firms together', and that 'Italian industry is also particularly concentrated geographically' (Porter, 1990, pp. 154–5), the positive association between locality, social structures and economic development was not emphasized. In this respect, the Italian community phenomenon patently differs from that of the clustering of British auction houses in a few London streets which Porter (1990, p. 155) seems to consider identical.

An important issue notwithstanding is the empirical balance between competitive and collaborative mechanisms and so forms an important research issue in our work in relation to the behaviour of local industrial communities. Was intra-community competition fierce and endemic? Would small firms invariably compete aggressively, or would there be evidence of *de facto* collaboration, co-ordination or other mechanisms pointing to enlightened self-interest among individual decision-makers? In down-to-earth terms, what kinds of inter-firm contacts, communications and shared actions might exist to suggest that individuals consider the best interests of the community of firms, as well as the best interests of their own firms? Finally (but importantly), to what degree might local attitudes and conditioning factors influence the developmental trajectory of the community, seen as an entity?

1.2.4 The industry sector

Consistent with our proposition about contextual singularity, our working assumption was that any community of firms will manifest a more or less distinctive configuration of strategic choices, core technologies, inter- and intra-community linkages, work organization practices and norms of behaviour within and among the indigenous firms. At the same time, we expected many observations to link directly to the character of the industrial sector in which the community participates. The sector is an influential level of analysis, determining in large measure the necessary skills and status of constituent firms. One must therefore understand something of the industrial characteristics of (in this case) the textiles and clothing industries to interpret micro-level phenomena. At a given point of time, however, we would not expect the development of the industry in three selected localities and countries to be at the same stage, nor even necessarily to be on the same developmental track. Such issues were properly a matter for investigation.

Economic differences among European countries should be located in a broad framework taking account of varying national factor and demand conditions in textiles and clothing and the particular strategies of the firms in the various textiles sectors, as well as those in related and supporting industries. It follows that particular configurations of dedicated equipment, skilled labour and know-how in local communities of firms, of whatever size, may prove to be intrinsically transient when examined over the long term. This clearly has implications for an assessment of the future viability of a particular locality. Textiles and clothing, for example, are mature industry sectors being subjected in the 1990s to the **dematuring** impact of automation and communications technologies.

Mature industries generally experience fragmenting demand as customers' needs become more sophisticated or discriminating. This works to the detriment of standardized, mass production methods, allowing small units to cater for specialized needs by differentiating themselves along relevant market and product dimensions. In textiles needs can be high fashion or technological (e.g. high-performance fabrics used in protective industrial garments). Market knowledge of fashion trends or specialized performance requirements become crucial variables for competitive success and survivability. But in consumer markets shifts in demand must be accurately and promptly relayed to the production unit. Computerized data relayed from point of retail sale to the factory (increasingly supported by 'lean production' methods) have become significant factors in reducing waste and enhancing competitive advantage in increasingly fickle, fashion-dictated markets.

These issues of market and technology indicate the need to appreciate the context imposed by the industrial sector under study.

1.3 RESEARCH FOCUS AND DESIGN

An important aspect of our agenda was to consider the extent to which small firms can play a major future role in sustaining wealth creation and employment in currently mature, 'sunset' industrial sectors. Many commentators have warned that developed economies cannot sustain positions in basic and, for the most part, low-technology industries. There are two kinds of justification for this assessment. First, there is a widespread view that to maintain a strong national position in a mature, traditional sector precludes the development of commensurately strong positions in emerging and ultimately more attractive sectors. This judgement rests either on limited resources to cope with both traditional and new technical and commercial demands, or on inertia or complacency. Secondly, it can be argued, despite the best endeavours of a mature economy, traditional sectors remain acutely vulnerable to low-cost producers from emerging economies on the other side of the world.

Yet traditional sectors may be amenable to an upgrading of their competitive status. In apparel production such moves include attention to materials, improving construction quality, fashion responsiveness, brand image, and so forth. In various product categories Italy, Germany and Sweden, to name but three developed European economies, have enjoyed some success in these various respects. Innovativeness in both marketing and production is thus a necessary if not always sufficient condition for underpinning and enhancing a strong traditional position. Our hypothesis is that small firms can play a significant part in this process. Whether and in what circumstances they do so is properly a matter for investigation and hence justifies new research.

We are not saying that big firms are unimportant in the upgrading process, merely directing our research question to the role of small firms in wealth and employment creation in a well-established, but threatened, sector. So we chose to focus on relatively homogeneous samples of small, apparently autonomous firms which were owned and operated by an independent proprietor as opposed to being a subsidiary of a larger firm or grouping. Given our assumptions about the contextual particularity of small firm behaviour, it was appropriate to study firms in a single, broadly based sector.

A number of selection criteria pointed to textiles and clothing. A long and evolving history was a relevant precondition for cross-national comparability. We were interested in a sector which manifested a variety of structural forms and possible paths to survival and growth in the face of external competition. There was also the desire to examine local industrial communities where small firms have historically always played a significant role. Finally, it was appropriate to consider a sector which other researchers had already shown was of widespread interest. Textiles and clothing is long-established, and still employs large numbers of people, many in relatively high-skill manufacturing jobs not supported by extensive mechanization. In addition, the industry manifests geographic localization in several countries.

Our agenda required us to take account of patterns of behaviour at a variety of levels, by means of the various 'windows' to which we have already referred. We are aware that any research design involves trade-offs. In this case, the richness we sought from opening these multiple windows would have a price, namely some loss of generalizability. But we have already argued that individual communities are likely to exhibit contextual singularity, so generalizability must be treated cautiously in any event.

A major plank of the research was to examine small firms in different European Community countries in a genuinely comparative way. The choice of France, Italy and the UK was predicated on their histories in the textiles and clothing industries, meaning that each has evolved characteristic patterns of structuring over the long term. Although multi-country publications are increasing in number, a majority rely either on secondary data or attempt to marry a variety of empirical findings from only partly comparable methods and/or contiguous research agenda. From the outset, we intended our findings to have greater comparability than this.

From this reasoning we selected one locality for study in each country. We were particularly interested in localities with evident **community characteristics**. Because these communities long ago established specialisms in respect of raw material types, fabric construction methods, etc., it would have been unrealistic to expect to find three localities with complete comparability in all respects. The localities we chose were Como, in Italy (principally silk-based woven textiles manufacturing); Lyon, in France (garments, woven and knitted fabrics in a wide variety of fibre types); and Leicester, in England (knitted fabrics and garments, also with a variety of natural and synthetic fibre types).

We chose a range of complementary data collection methods, mindful of practical resource constraints. The principal source was a detailed questionnaire sent to small firm proprietors, supported by direct contacts with industry associations, Chambers of Commerce, etc. A selection of respondents were also contacted in person and by telephone. The development of the questionnaire instrument was an iterative process extending over several months, including pilot testing in Britain, which allowed us to amend content and format prior to large-sample mailing. After the questions were substantially confirmed, they were translated by the authors into French and Italian. Before printing, these documents were inspected by local commentators to ensure idiomatic validity.

In all three localities the sample of firms was selected from the entire local population of relevant manufacturing firms, defined by industry association membership lists, trade directories, telephone listings, and so forth. Publicly quoted companies were eliminated from the sample frame. Within Como Province areas with a high concentration of textiles firms and employees were found in Como itself and in the surrounding villages. Within Rhône-Alpes Region the firms were located within the Lyon conurbation and in outlying towns. Within Leicester County firms were selected in roughly equal numbers from the city environs and from within the county. As far as we are aware, there were no substantial biases in the construction of the sample frames, although the emphasis on visible, legally constituted, firms effectively eliminated marginal, submerged units and homeworkers. However, in terms of responses received there may be some bias to older, larger or otherwise more established firms whose proprietors may have found the time to reply more easily.

In contacting firms we invoked the forthcoming impact of '1993' as a focal theme of the study to stimulate their interest. Of the 1200 questionnaires sent out (400 to each locality), 151 fully completed, usable returns were received. The findings reported in this book derive from these returns, from follow-up interviews and from extensive literature searches in the three countries.

1.4 THE STRUCTURE OF THIS BOOK

The research questions of the research have been addressed in a number of stages. In Chapter 2 we first consider the textiles and clothing industries at a macro-level, detailing recent international developments and pointing up the structures and strategies which have characterized textiles–clothing production and distribution in Britain, France and Italy. We then consider the situation within each of the three localities of Leicester, Lyon and Como and describe the distinctive profile of the textiles and clothing industries in each.

We then change level to consider the small firm and the entrepreneur. In Chapter 3 we examine the role of the small firm in mature Western economies and present comparative findings on the firms in our study. While the findings are broadly supportive of the current literature about the nature of small, independent firms, differences begin to emerge among the three localities, indicating that small firms (even within a single sector) cannot be considered as a homogeneous category and that the differences require further explanation.

In Chapter 4 (still at the level of the firm) we consider the nature of entrepreneurship and the problems of small firm development. We note the major influences on entrepreneurial behaviour, both personal and environmental, and we explore a number of role-identities derived from the relevant literature. We apply these in the discussion of our findings on the proprietors in our study. Once again, we note differences among our three localities, this time in terms of typical entrepreneurial profiles. This directs us to a more explicit context-sensitive treatment of entrepreneurship in Chapter 5.

Specifically, in Chapter 5 we consider entrepreneurship no longer at the level of the firm, but of the locality, treating it as an industrial community-based endeavour. This necessitates a consideration of the development of entrepreneurs as conditioned by their milieu, implying systemic, evolutionary aspects to the process. We look at a variety of collective mechanisms and models and invoke biological analogies, notably the 'population ecology' model to assist theoretical elaboration, leading to an exploration of the sociocultural as well as economic history of each community. From these observations we argue that each community has pursued a distinctive evolutionary track of entrepreneurial development over time. Overall development patterns are determined in part by the backgrounds and behaviours of the proprietors, and in part by the local environment or milieu in which proprietors operate (and ultimately come to influence). Patterns of business behaviour and firm strategies are deeply ingrained in a particular sector–locality context.

Having demonstrated the relevance of the community basis of development, we build on this base in Chapter 6 by using the concept of **industrial district**, a form of local industrial organization for which we present a theoretical archetype against which we carefully compare each of the three localities. We analyse firms in terms of structural/functional strata within a local production cycle, as well as reflect on the evolving dynamics of small-firm community development. The discussion will reveal that the three communities are individual in character not only in sociocultural terms, but also in terms of industrial structuring and organization within each. Thus effective organisational practices are not easily transferable, though it does not mean that communities cannot learn from one another.

Because the industrial district concept stresses the local production cycle, it cannot cover all the aspects germane to a discussion of an internationally effective clustering of firms. Thus in Chapter 7 we turn to the notion of network development; in particular, we explore the evidence for the emergence of what have been called **strategic networks**, in which particularized and specialist resident know-how can be defended, elaborated and enhanced by the actions of so-called 'leading' firms. We explore the nature of leadership in this context and discuss two aspects in some detail, namely activity co-ordination and the encouragement of innovation. We argue that one important criterion for an effective community is that 'leading' firms participate actively in promoting the community, and preferably reside within it. For when influential, 'leading' firms have their headquarters outside the locality, the community's interests may be too readily subordinated to opportunistic actions contrary to the locality's long-term interest.

In the final chapters of the book we look to the future. In Chapter 8 we consider the EC dimension and project potential developments in the post-1993 era of full market integration. More specifically, we consider the readiness of the three localities to compete in their respective sectors of textiles and clothing after 1993. In Chapter 9 we expand the discussion to review a range of global developments which have the potential to modify drastically the operating environment of European textiles firms and so impact on their medium- to long-term viability. Against this background of thoroughgoing change, we assess trends towards convergence of strategies both at the level of firms and at the industrial community level in Leicester, Lyon and Como in order to bring current and future development trajectories into sharper focus. Success will continue to require market-directed innovativeness in order to enhance and upgrade competitive performance. This, in turn, will require effective firms to draw heavily on regional know-how and resources. As such, the best prospect for continuing success lies with regional industrial communities with strong backgrounds in particular specializations.

The book's general conclusions address emergent policy issues. Successful local industrial communities clearly deserve encouragement, though there is no question that funds be directed either to 'lame ducks' or to those communities without either the initiative or infrastructures to benefit from investments – a stance consistent with EC thinking on regional policy. Localities with a wealth of small firms have demonstrated considerable market responsiveness, allied to genuine technical expertise, specialization and professionalism. The issues for the future will be how to ensure greater internal structuring of the more innovative communities, and greater innovativeness in the more structured ones.

2

Internationalization and specialization in the textiles and clothing industries

2.1 INTRODUCTION

In this chapter we provide an overview of the international industrial context in which the small textile and clothing firms surveyed in Leicester, Lyon and Como are situated. We will first indicate salient characteristics of the textile and clothing industries, then review the recent international trends, leading on to discussion of responses at national level in Britain, France and Italy. Finally, we discuss the specific profiles of the textiles and clothing sectors in the Leicester, Lyon and Como localities. Overall, in this chapter we will argue that the key features of the textile and clothing sectors are product variety, process specialization and internationalization of markets: firms large and small in a great variety of locations have to find successful ways to adapt to the implications of each of these sets of variables.

2.2 KEY CHARACTERISTICS OF THE TEXTILES AND CLOTHING SECTORS

The textile and clothing industries are frequently referred to by terms such as *filière*, value-chain and 'textile complex' (Toyne *et al.*, 1984). All of these terms convey the notion of an interconnected production and processing chain in which goods produced at the upstream end (fibres, yarns and cloths) are passed on to downstream producers for conversion into garments. Indeed, given the generic similarities in their products, the textiles and clothing sectors are sometimes subsumed under the heading of 'textiles'.

For example, the first Multi-Fibre Arrangement of 1974 defined 'textiles' as: 'tops, yarns, piece goods, made-up articles, garments and other manufactured products of cotton, wool, man-made fibres, or blends thereof.' Although this broad usage of 'textiles' has become largely a matter of terminological convenience in the English-language literature, it can lead to the inaccurate perception of the textiles and clothing industries as forming a single, seamless whole. In reality, textiles and clothing comprise a series of variegated subsectors which are frequently heterogeneous in terms both of processes and products.

Variegation is evident first in the range of raw materials that go into textiles. These principally include cotton, wool, flax, silk, artificial and synthetic fibres, as well as an enormous range of composite materials. (In common with most analyses of textiles–clothing, leather working will be excluded.)

To turn these basic materials into finished goods requires the manufacture of a number of intermediate products, namely fibres, yarns and fabrics. Production processes involved include (depending on the base material used) opening and cleaning, carding, combing, drawing and roving, yarn spinning, weaving or knitting. Finishing processes can occur at a number of points (particularly at the yarn, fabric and, of course, the garment stages) and include texturizing, dyeing and printing.

The major end markets for textiles are clothing, home furnishings and industrial goods. However, clothing accounts for only approx. 50% of all textile end-uses – a further indication that the amalgam often made between textiles and clothing is only partly accurate. The remainder of upstream textiles production goes principally into household textiles and technical textiles used in industry. Industrial applications vary, for example, from car upholstery to high-technology applications in satellite technology. Household textiles include curtains and furniture covers, as well as carpets and flooring. Thus the vast range of end-markets for textiles products, each of which breaks down into discrete subcategories, indicates the inappropriateness of viewing 'textiles–clothing' as a single sector.

Garment production is itself a vast and complex sector; processes include cutting, trimming and sewing. Product ranges are subdivided into men's, women's and children's clothing, produced in a variety of sizes, with each range having its own characteristics. Apparently similar products – such as shirts and blouses or trousers and jeans – represent quite different markets in reality and require different types of industrial and commercial expertise. Further, consumer preferences for clothing fluctuate greatly depending on social occasion, type of activity (leisure wear, sportswear, formal wear), fashion and season. Clothing products are also distinguished by market position (i.e. down-market, middle-market, up-market) and by brand names (or their absence). Stress must be placed on the importance of creativity in fashion goods, on creating an attractive 'look' for consumers and on developing a strong image for producers and distributors by means of publicity, promotion and brand enhancement.

The diversity of output which characterizes the textiles and clothing sectors is further reinforced by the marketing strategies of producers. Generally speaking, as markets mature they tend to segment into distinct pockets of demand as end-users become more sophisticated and selective. Producers seek to increase their competitive advantage by adjusting their output to precise demand trends. This frequently involves specializing in terms of both products and processes. Market-focused differentiation has increased the complexity of the textile and clothing industries in recent years.

Crucial differences relating to capital and skill requirements exist between subsectors of textiles and clothing. In general, fibre, yarn and fabric production are more capital intensive than garment manufacture. The minimum scale required for efficient production is much higher in the former, whether expressed absolutely or as a percentage of total market size. The clothing sector is still extremely labour intensive, frequently with limited capital investment in ageing machinery, and its workforce is generally unskilled or semi-skilled. Short to medium sized runs are the norm for a majority of product items. Because of the accessibility of capital and labour inputs, barriers to entry in clothing are low. Setting up a clothing firm either in the developed or developing world is relatively easy, but long-run survival is considerably more difficult. In the absence of differentiated positions based on distinctive products and strong brands, fierce price competition rages, with a large number of firms quitting or going bankrupt each year.

On the other hand, opportunities for specialization allow large numbers of small firms to trade successfully. Save for a limited number of specific cases (including man-made fibre production and tee-shirt manufacture), substantial economies of scale from mass production are hard to realize. Thus the textile and clothing sectors in most countries are largely composed of a myriad of small to medium sized firms which seek simultaneously to be distinctive in terms of their specialization(s) yet generate sufficient business for efficient production.

Specialization in narrow product ranges or in limited types of industrial application tends, however, to require close linkages between firms in adjacent activities since their livelihood depends on communicating product specifications upstream and receiving essential material inputs downstream. Commentators such as Boudon and Boss (1976) have argued that because of such interdependencies between upstream and downstream elements, developments in almost any subsector can have repercussions elsewhere. However, this interpretation is correct in some but not all cases. As Jacomet (1989, pp. 7–29) has indicated, to consider the textile and clothing industries as forming a single *filière* glosses over a number of complexities. For example, firms specializing in fibre or fabric types (cotton, silk, man-mades, etc.), or in types of clothing (suits vs shirts, etc.), may have little or nothing to do with each other in terms of intra-industry sales. Only when products reach the distribution system is there a mix and match of elements.

Moreover, when considered from a national or regional perspective, the textiles–clothing value-chain often contains gaps. First, the developed nations (with exceptions such as cotton in the USA and Greece) tend to import their raw materials. Secondly, a country can be short of a central component of the value chain. For example, Hong Kong imports many of the fabrics it uses in garment production (Anson and Simpson, 1988, p. 333).

The actual level of interdependence within a national or regional 'textile complex' is partly attributable to factor endowments (such as the local presence of particular raw materials or other inputs), but it is partly the result of strategic choices as firms seek to maximize their competitive advantages while minimizing their weaknesses. Any strategy carries opportunities and disadvantages. Opportunities arise where factor inputs can be mobilized from the cheapest sources available. The practice of 'outward processing', which involves subcontracting labour-intensive, intermediate processes to firms in low-wage countries, is extensively used by producers in developed countries (and is particularly associated with German firms) to preserve their competitiveness, so overcoming the disadvantage of expensive, indigenous labour. However, there are disadvantages too. The lack of a home production base leads to loss of flexibility due to slow shipments and reduced control over quality. Sourcing abroad leads to employment losses at home and runs the risk of a balance-of-trade deficit.

In summary, product and process variegation in the textile and clothing industries provides significant opportunities for effective specialization, particularly to small firms. Conversely, intra-industry linkages have to be assured, leading to different patterns and levels of interdependence within regional and national *filières* and in the international market-place. Linkages can be ensured by a number of different strategies, each of which has conduct and performance implications. The wide mix of potential industrial and commercial strategies introduces further elements of variegation into a complex picture in which local, national and international comparative advantages constrain in-firm strategy formulation and lead to discrete geographical patterns of specialization. Thus we now consider the issue of internationalization in order to provide the context for later discussions of the characteristics and strategies of particular national and regional textile and clothing industries.

2.3 INTERNATIONALIZATION IN THE TEXTILES AND CLOTHING INDUSTRIES

A number of factors explain a high level in internationalization in textiles trades. First, within the EC non-tariff barriers to trade in textiles and clothing have been low and European producers have been operating in a context of relatively high market integration (Cecchini *et al.*, 1988). Secondly, the various Multi-Fibre Arrangements (MFAs) have contained but not halted expansion in international trade in textiles. The MFAs have a long history: their roots are to be found in the so-called Short Term Arrangement of 1961, which was quickly transformed into the Long Term Arrangement of 1962. The first MFA as such came into effect on 1 January 1974 and was renewed in 1978, 1982 and 1986. Each of these arrangements has a number of features in common. They were concluded within the GATT framework, yet depart radically from GATT principles. Thus whereas GATT promotes free trade and non-discrimination among trading nations, the MFAs (and accompanying bilateral agreements) have constructed a complex palisade of trade barriers (especially tariff and quota restrictions) which discriminate by product categories and trading partners. In each case, the effective aim has been to minimize 'market disruption' (i.e. severe damage to producers) in the developed countries due to cheap imports from developing countries. The textile and clothing industries have been considered politically sensitive because of the essential nature of their output, and because employment is geographically concentrated, often in the regions that have been hardest hit by recession. Thus trade regulation by the various MFAs has sought to curb import peaks and to provide a breathing space in which to manage structural decline. Despite these protectionist barriers, imported garments and textiles from developing nations and the newly industrialized countries (NICs) have made increasing inroads into the markets of the developed world, in some cases decimating indigenous production.

Thus the textile and clothing industries of the developed nations were still experiencing a period of modest expansion until the first oil shock of 1973, but thereafter relative boom turned to gloom. In the period between 1963 and 1973, textiles and clothing production in all industrialized countries increased 4.5% by volume; in the EC it increased by only 2%. Over the 1973–9 period, textiles output was stagnant in industrialized countries and declined by 0.5% in the EC. The situation worsened at the start of the 1980s. In 1981–2, there was a decline in textiles output in *all* industrial countries. The situation was particularly difficult in the EC, where the recession lasted longer. Whereas the US and Japanese textile industries increased output in 1983, EC production again fell by 3.5%, exactly as it had done both in 1981 and 1982. The story for clothing is very similar (GATT, 1980, p. 79; GATT, 1985, p. 65).

In terms of national developments within the textiles sector, clear contrasts exist. For the three countries featured in this study – Britain, France and Italy – the contrasts are dramatic. In the decade up to 1973, textile production in the three countries had increased by between 10% and 15%. Yet between 1973 and 1980 output fell by 11% in France and 30% in Britain, but in Italy it increased 15% by 1980 (Shepherd, 1983, p. 30).

When the economic upturn came in the mid-1980s, the textile and clothing industries benefited from increases in output. Measured in constant prices, EC output increased yearly through the remainder of the decade. In millions of ECU, EC textiles output rose from 75 735 in 1983 to 86 691 in 1988; figures for clothing were 38 340 in 1983 and 42 432 in 1987 (*Panorama of EC Industry*, 1990).

However, the EC's share of world trade in textiles fell from 23.4% in 1963 to 15.7% in 1980, and in clothing from 22.1% to 14.4% in the same period (OECD, 1983). Further, measured in terms of employment, European textile and clothing industries have been in continuing contraction. As a broad indication, EC employment in textiles and clothing stood at approx. 2.6 million people in 1988, whereas in 1980 it was close to 3.2 million – a fall of some 19% (*Panorama of EC Industry*, 1990). However, employment falls taken in conjunction with increases in output during the latter part of the 1980s can be taken as a positive development inasmuch as they indicate increasing labour productivity. This, in turn, should have had a salutary effect on the international competitiveness of the sector.

Yet many European producers have found that they have had to 'run faster to stand still' because non-European producers have also improved their competitive position. The net result has been that the EC currently runs major deficits on its balance of trade in clothing, although trade in textiles has been close to equilibrium. Whereas in 1973, the EC ran a relatively small deficit (0.95 billion dollars) on trade in clothing products with developing countries and had a small surplus (0.11 billion dollars) in textiles, by 1984 the EC ran a modest deficit of 0.12 billion dollars in textiles, but the deficit in clothing amounted to 4.09 billion dollars (GATT, 1980, 1985). In 1988 total EC deficits grew to 0.89 billion dollars in textiles and 6.14 billion dollars in clothing (*Panorama of EC Industry*, 1990).

These growing trade deficits are the result of rapid yearly increases of textiles and clothing exports from a number of non-EC competitors, coupled with far slower rates of growth in EC exports. Over the 1980–8 period, a number of countries achieved very fast average yearly growth rates in textile exports. Principally, these were Hong Kong (+17.5%), Taiwan (+12.5%), China (+12%), Republic of Korea (+10.5%) and Pakistan (+9.5%). The principal end-markets of these goods were the developed countries. Yet over the same period the slowest yearly export growth rates were in the USA (+0.5%), the UK (+1.5%) and France and the Netherlands (+4%).

In clothing exports the fastest average yearly growth rates over 1980–8 were even more stark: 43.5% for Turkey, 27% for Thailand, 17.5% for Portugal, 15% for Greece, 14.5% for the Republic of Korea, 14% for China, 13% for India, 11.5% for Hong Kong and 9% for Italy. Meanwhile average yearly clothing exports growth in Britain, France and the USA was 3–4% (GATT, 1990). Thus at least three strong growth areas can be discerned: India and Pakistan, the Far East and the Mediterranean basin.

The general cause of low competitiveness in textiles, and particularly in clothing, of developed nations has been the effects of high raw-material and labour costs. The labour input into clothing production is especially high, hence low-wage countries have a major advantage. Anson (1991) reported that average EC hourly wage rates in the industry were seven times those of ten leading suppliers to the EC. Exporters such as China, Thailand, India and Pakistan have exploited a significant comparative advantage in textiles, largely due to the cheapness of their labour input and the proximity of raw materials.

The textile and clothing sectors in industrialized countries have been forced to undertake drastic restructuration and develop new strategies in a bid to retain competitiveness. Structural adjustments have been particularly dramatic for the small firms that predominate in many stages of the value-adding chain since they are least able to influence the direction of change.

2.4 MAJOR DEMAND TRENDS

To understand the constraints and opportunities for small textile and clothing firms recent international trends in trade have to be linked to changes in demand. The long-term trend has been towards a flattening of demand. In the EC consumer spending on clothing increased by a mere 0.3% in the 1980–5 period, with a slightly larger increase of 2% over 1985–90 (*Textile Outlook International*, 1991). Particularly as regards clothing, patterns of consumption have changed over the course of this century. While the purchase of clothes remains a necessity for all, clothing expenditure as a proportion of household budgets has steadily fallen (Herpin, 1986). Across the EC, spending on clothing as a proportion of total household spending fell from 8.6% in 1979 to 7.5% in 1990 – though Italy in 1990 had the highest per capita rates of spending in the EC at 9.3%, while in the UK the figure stood at 5.9% (*Textile Outlook International*, 1991).

Types of purchase have changed significantly. Basic 'heavy' and costly items, such as overcoats and suits, have become less popular, while the popularity of lighter, fashionable items, such as leisure wear and sportswear, has increased (Herpin, 1987). Moreover, the trend towards purchases on whim rather than need has allowed consumers to be much more selective in their rates of purchase. In times of recession consumers have tended to make cuts in the clothing budget rather than in other outgoings. A rapid compression of consumer demand in the late 1970s led to crisis in the clothing industry. In turn, clothing firms reduced their purchases from the upstream textiles firms and so aggravated the problems of the industry as a whole.

The 1980s was a period of fragmentation and multiplication of European life styles. As clothing and furnishing are among the vehicles by which these life styles are expressed, the result was a massive increase in the range of styles, patterns and colours of textile goods made available during the 1980s. While this process has generally been a demand-led phenomenon, European textile producers have been keen to promote its development because an acceleration of fashion-cycles generates increased sales. There are several reasons for this.

The first is that a high rate of fashion change reduces the tendency to market saturation. Instead of buying no more than they need, consumers buy as much as they can afford: the multiplying of 'alternative' life styles has reinforced consumerism. The second reason is that highly variegated demand is more easily satisfied by local producers than those several thousand miles away. The local producers' competitive advantages include: (i) lower transportation costs; (ii) speed of response to changes in demand; and (iii) lower inventory costs. In the past, the sale of an item of clothing in a retail store commonly required a production cycle of some 66 weeks, of which only eleven weeks corresponded to production activities. Thus roughly a year was spent as inventory due to 'waiting-time' between production processes (Tuloup, 1987, p. 95). During the 1980s producers aimed to reduce the cycle to 46 weeks, thereby cutting inventory costs. Fast response is particularly important in fashion markets where the aim is not simply to keep pace with demand, but to anticipate the next trend. The ability to anticipate requires in-depth familiarity with final markets, hence the marketing importance of being 'on the spot'.

Thirdly, highly variegated demand places a premium on creativity, originality and, frequently, on quality. Consumers have increasingly come to associate goods bearing a brand name with style and quality. This marginalizes 'unknown' producers whose primary competitive advantage is based on low wage costs and/or long production runs. Additionally, the problem of purchasing in the right quantities, particularly for non-average sizes, is more easily solved by purchasing locally rather than internationally.

Yet as the industry became increasingly demand-led and fashion orientated, crucial strategic knowledge derived more from market contacts than from production know-how. Textile and clothing producers became ever-more reliant on distributors, particularly on retailers in the case of fast-moving fashion goods. By the start of the 1980s distribution channels had become dominant in the textiles–clothing sector (Weisz and Anselme, 1981): they became the eyes and ears of the trade. At the centre of the operations of both Benetton and Marks and Spencer are Electronic Point of Sale systems. Not only do these facilitate the mechanical aspects of stock

control, they also keep up-to-the-minute track on how markets are moving
– in the case of Benetton, all around Europe. This type of sales information
has clearly become a strategic asset. Companies guard it jealously, and
release as little as possible in order to maximize their own advantage. In the
highly concentrated UK distribution system (see below), information
hoarding has tightened the stranglehold of distributors over producers.

Once fashions became more variegated, and as distributors refused to
hold large stocks, producers have come to enjoy fewer opportunities to
manufacture in long runs. Yet large firms geared to standardized mass
merchandise proved slow in adjusting to short-term changes in demand.
Their bureaucratic organizations militated against the promotion of the
entrepreneurial culture required for fast-moving markets. On the other
hand, small firms proved more nimble in adapting to rapidly changing
markets. Simultaneously, the need for frequent provisioning made recourse
to distant suppliers more problematic for distributors in the case of non-
standard products or in conditions of fashion dynamism. Producers have
therefore needed to develop multifaceted competitive strategies in relation
both to demand trends and to the behaviour of national distribution
systems.

2.5 NATIONAL STRATEGIES IN TEXTILES AND CLOTHING

Firms faced with an evolving array of choices must identify the combinations
of products, distribution channels and end-markets most likely to generate
success. Textiles and clothing consumer products must simultaneously be
designed for specific (sometimes very tightly defined) social groups and be
commercially attractive to the appropriate distribution channels. The
permutations are endless: this open-endedness and unpredictability drive
the fashion world and award a premium to creativity at every stage of the
value-adding process.

Yet the options of individual producers are limited by a number of
factors, including their design, marketing and production capabilities,
available capital resources and the structure of the distribution sector which
affords differential opportunities of access. For example, selling into the
concentrated UK distribution sector is a vastly different proposition to
selling into France's fragmented retail trade. Furthermore, the small
producer is particularly influenced by national or even local demand
characteristics. As Stopford and Baden-Fuller (1990) have indicated, it
remains extremely difficult in textiles–clothing to identify 'mass-customized
segments' – i.e. exact cross-border correspondences among national demand
segments allowing aggregation of international sales. Although the existence
of local and national differences in demand by no means eliminates the
scope for exporting, producers must find ways to link into international
distribution networks and tailor their products to foreign markets.

While variations in strategy clearly exist between firms in any one country, distinctive national strategies to maintain competitiveness can nevertheless be discerned. The characteristics of particular national textile production systems have resulted in differing levels of performance among nations and regions. Accordingly we now review some characteristic types of adjustment to demand within the textile and clothing industries of major producing nations, with particular attention to Britain, France and Italy.

Table 2.1 Major market positions in textiles and clothing

| Fashion positioning | Quality positioning | | |
	High	Medium	Low
High	1	2	3
Low	4	5	6

For the sake of clarity, Table 2.1 synthesizes the major permutations in product/market positioning. The archetypal example of high-fashion/high-quality products (segment 1) is *haute couture,* an area in which the French have traditionally been strong, though now experiencing greater competition from European and Japanese designers. In itself, this is a tiny market characterized by very limited production runs and a high degree of expertise in design, cutting and sewing up, but astronomical prices make it lucrative. It also launches some (though far from all) mass merchandising fashions. Closely allied is the luxury goods market, where Italy has also held strong positions. But much of the Italian textiles–clothing industry was characterized in the 1980s by a relatively high fashion content coupled with medium construction quality, investment in mechanization and medium runs (segment 2). These strong features allow competition on the price–quality relationship rather than price alone. The prices of Italian producers are relatively high, but considered affordable by the more affluent social groups in Europe and beyond.

Disposable fashion or *prêt-à-jeter* (segment 3) was enormously popular in the 1980s as fashion cycles accelerated and increasing consumerism made one-season purchases seem normal. Clearly this type of fashion favoured small local producers who were fast enough to catch the vagaries of fickle demand; it also corresponds to a wide-spread British view of what fashion is. Conversely, the British have historically associated quality with low fashion content: segment 4 represents the market situation of up-market outlets which trade in 'classic' handmade clothes such as Saville Row for men's suits, while segment 5 includes the major UK merchandizer in textiles–clothing for middle-market products, Marks and Spencer.

Finally, the low quality/low fashion segment (segment 6) covers a variety of producers, including large integrated firms trading on economies of scale and backstreet sweat-shops, in Europe and the Third World alike. However, it is worth noting that although segments 5 and 6 have accounted for the bulk of import penetration into European markets, third-party producers are increasingly attacking other segments. This can occur in association with European producers who provide the design, marketing and distribution expertise, while the third-party producer provides labour and sometimes materials. Germany is particularly associated with this strategy. As competitive pressures increased, the Italian response lay in further improving the quality and increasing the added value of products offered (Unioncamere-Istituto Tagliacarne-Censis, 1991).

Table 2.2 Trade balances in textiles and clothing for France, Italy and the UK 1980 and 1989 (millions US dollars)

		Imports		*Exports*		*Exports/ imports*	
		1980	*1989*	*1980*	*1989*	*1980*	*1989*
France	Textiles	4119	6151	3432	4967	0.83	0.80
	Clothing	2637	6406	2294	3626	0.86	0.56
Italy	Textiles	2618	5235	4158	7966	1.58	1.52
	Clothing	797	2028	4584	9449	5.75	4.66
UK	Textiles	3560	6171	3108	3605	0.87	0.58
	Clothing	2857	5799	1878	2362	0.65	0.40

Source: GATT (1990) *International Trade,* pp. 63, 67.

These different national product/market positions are associated with variations in performance as measured by trade balances. As indicated in Table 2.2, Italy has succeeded in maintaining large surpluses, whereas France and particularly Britain have accrued major deficits. These performance differentials indicate that low-cost imports represent only a partial cause of the difficulties of the textile and clothing industries in some EC countries. To comment further on their causes, the cases of Britain, France and Italy will now be considered separately.

2.5.1 Britain

Overall, the textiles industry in Britain has suffered from low competitiveness in international markets since the economic recession of the mid-1970s. As Table 2.3 illustrates, although the value of textiles exports has increased, the acceleration in imports has been even more rapid, causing a significant trade imbalance. A number of factors can be put forward to explain this situation.

Table 2.3 UK balance of trade in textile products (millions pounds sterling)

	Exports (fob)		Imports (cif)		Exports/ imports
	Value	Index	Value	Index	
1975	699	100	682	100	1.02
1980	1363	1951	545	227	0.88
1985	1708	244	3032	445	0.56
1988	1935	277	3636	533	0.53

Source: Central Statistical Office (1975–88) *Monthly Digest of Statistics*, tables 15.2 and 15.3.

From the 1960s increasingly fierce competition was experienced from Hong Kong and other Far Eastern producers. Since the UK joined the EC in 1973, Italy too has figured strongly as a competitor, particularly in fashion outerwear. More recently, Portugal has also increased its exports to Britain.

In Britain high productivity and competitiveness have frequently been considered to be linked to (large) company size and vertical integration. The salient trait of UK textiles–clothing has been the high level of concentration in textiles and clothing, both in production and in distribution. The tendency to industrial concentration by the formation of massive textiles corporations was already well developed in Britain by the 1960s. By 1970, the top five firms accounted for 52% of textiles output (Toyne *et al.*, 1984, pp. 86–7). ICI has been the largest supplier of fibres in the UK, while in the 1960s Courtaulds entered downstream textiles production to ensure its own fibre sales. By the mid-1970s, the British textile industry, headed by ICI and Courtaulds, was the most concentrated in the world (Shepherd, 1983). Levels of vertical integration have also been high, with the largest firms having textile and clothing manufacturing operations as well as owning retail outlets. The UK clothing industry is itself highly concentrated, with the top ten firms supplying 32% of the national market (Anson, 1991). But along with massive firms such as Coats Viyella, Tootal and Dawson, large numbers of small clothing firms have continued to exist, especially in the East End of London, Nottingham, Leicester and Scotland.

According to Toyne *et al.* (1984, p. 153), the 1970s strategy of Courtaulds and other major groups in the sector was characterized by vertical integration and limited differentiation of products, the aim being to resist competition on price from low-cost Commonwealth producers (who were taking increasing shares of UK markets) by investment in advanced technology, by exploiting economies of scale linked to long runs of standard products and by greater market power. However, reliance on mass produced, standard items did not prove a successful strategy to cope with cheap production from developing countries. The emphasis on large-scale production accorded a lower priority to design, innovation and adaptability. Import penetration continued to grow in the 1970s and the balance of trade in textiles and clothing continued to deteriorate, leaving the UK with one of the worst deficits in Europe.

In the 1980s, British companies recognized the need to diversify their product ranges. However, on the issues of concentration and vertical integration, contradictory developments have taken place. On the one hand, the formation of Coats Viyella in 1986 by the merger of Coats Paton and Vantona Viyella followed hard on the heels of a series of mergers orchestrated by the Viyella group. The new company has become the largest textiles and clothing firm in Europe and the eighth largest in the world (*Fortune*, 1991). Its business activities cover manufacture of threads and handknitting materials, yarns and fabrics, homewares and garments, as well as ownership of clothing retail chains such as Jaeger and Country Casuals. Hence, Coats Viyella has contributed massively to the trend in UK textiles and clothing to high industrial concentration and extensive vertical integration. Indeed, Coats Viyella's interest in acquiring Tootal resulted in a reference to the Monopolies and Mergers Commission.

On the other hand, the trend towards smaller company size that occurred in Italy appears to have influenced the thinking of Courtaulds, which for long was the largest UK firm in textiles and clothing. In 1989 the UK filament weaving business (the original part of the Courtaulds empire) was sold to Japan's largest textiles firm, Toray. In 1990, Courtaulds effectively split into two by demerger. While Courtaulds Textiles has become a separately quoted company on the Stock Exchange, whose activities include spinning, fabric and clothing manufacture, Courtaulds continues to manufacture fibres.

In addition, it is worth noting that ownership structures reflect only part of the equation. Within large companies, changes in internal organization have been implemented in order to foster the speed and flexibility of response associated with small firms. Thus within Courtaulds the parent company has directed strategy and acted as a banker for subsidiary companies who operate as quasi-independent enterprises (Anson, 1991).

Concentration is also marked in the UK distribution system. In Britain 70% of all clothing sales are made by multiple retailers and department stores, a higher proportion than in any other Western economy (Zeitlin and Totterdill, 1989). Elson (1990) noted that in 1986 just four multiples (Burton Group, C & A, Storehouse and Marks and Spencer) accounted for almost 30% of the UK clothing market of £12 billion. The pre-eminence of Marks and Spencer is well known, but what is interesting is that it still sources some 80% of its garments in the UK. Thus although Marks and Spencer is known for its tough negotiations, it underpins the livelihood of a large number of British clothing manufacturers. On the other hand, major retailers such as the Burton Group and Foster Menswear do not give similar preference to UK manufactures. Sourcing from low-cost foreign suppliers has been a key element of their competitive strategy and has contributed to the UK trade deficit in textiles and clothing. Moreover, multiple retailers in Britain tend to rely on 'value-for-money' products rather than style and quality, although in recent years there has been a tendency on their part to increase the design appeal of their goods.

The market power of the major retailers conditions opportunities for small manufacturing firms in specific ways. They have been marginalized by the recourse of most multiples to imported goods. Those chains with whom they do trade have rarely offered the same incentive to innovate in terms of design and fashion as has been the case in Italy. The relationship between small UK textile and clothing firms with the multiples has tended to require process expertise from the producer, while the distributor provides design input, often for 'value-for-money', low fashion goods (segment 6, Table 2.1). Thus many small UK producers have not moved up-market, have not invested heavily and have not been involved in the origination of fashion ideas to the extent of their counterparts in France or Italy. (These key themes will be developed in subsequent chapters in relation to the small firms in our survey.)

Indeed, Britain has not been a fashion leader since the 1960s. Although the top UK designers enjoy an international reputation, commercial success has often eluded them in Britain as markets have generally been less fashion-led than Italian ones: hence there has been proportionately less drive from the market towards innovation and creativity. British shoppers have a reputation for putting low price before design.

At the same time, distributors' margins are high and have been rising. Elson (1990) recorded that the gross margin for clothing retailers was on average 29% in 1961 but had risen to 36% in 1984. In addition, mark-ups of 50% were significantly higher in major chains with over 200 branches than the 35% margins found in one-outlet retailers. It seems reasonable to hypothesize that massive discounting in seasonal sales by multiple retailers has distended the price–quality relationship as perceived by consumers: where higher prices are not a guide to higher quality, the principle of economic rationality would predict that shoppers turn to cheaper goods. These factors limit opportunities for domestic producers seeking to increase non-price competition and stimulate cheap imports from low-wage countries.

Owing to these various factors, trading conditions have been difficult for UK textiles and clothing producers in general, and for small firms in particular. The industry has traversed a difficult period, with 22 000 job losses in 1989 and 11 000 job losses in knitwear and hosiery alone between 1987 and 1990 (Davies, 1990).

2.5.2 Italy

The success of Italian textiles–clothing in national and international terms is indicated by the fact that it is the third largest industry in Italy and by the size of its trade surplus. Italy is the leading exporter of textiles and clothing in the EC, with a positive balance of trade. In 1989 the textiles surplus amounted to 2.7 billion dollars, while in clothing it reached 7.4 billion dollars (GATT, 1989). This is partly because Italy is the leading source in Europe of high value-added products in knitwear and silk. Consistent trade surpluses have made Italy the major success story in recent years of the textile and clothing industries of developed nations.

The Italian textile–clothing industry has a dualistic structure. There are a limited number of large, vertically integrated firms, such as Marzotto and Miraglio-Vestebene, which combine textiles and clothing production, as do state-owned firms such as Lanerossi, Lebole and Fila. Nationalized firms accounted for 10–15% of Italian production in the 1980s, but their performance was poor (Tuloup, 1987, p. 65). Yet the major part of the industry is composed of large numbers of small firms. Indeed the trend in Italy since the 1950s has been towards a disaggregation or 'deintegration' of the structure of textile and clothing industries. This has led to an increase in the number of small firms. Firms of 100 employees or fewer came to dominate the sector. Moreover, the level of inter-trading and interdependence between small firms has been extremely high within localized 'industrial districts', creating high levels of local synergy (a theme to be discussed in depth in Chapter 6).

Both market conditions and legislation help explain the 'deintegration' of industry. Firms with fewer than 15 employees are regulated by a looser legislative framework than larger firms, in which conditions relating to hiring, redundancies and salary levels are more rigidly laid down. Further, small firms proved better able to adapt to changing markets. Italian fashions have an extremely rapid rate of change, requiring considerable flexibility on the part of producers. The ability to cater for demanding local tastes enhanced the development of exports since selling to diverse foreign markets likewise requires considerable flexibility. Indeed the dynamism and adaptability of the small firm sector contribute greatly to the Italian success story in textiles–clothing.

Italian strategy in textiles and clothing has three main components: creativity, modern equipment and exceptionally high levels of specialization. Impressive levels of creativity are prominent not only in the work of world famous designers such as Gucci and Armani, but also exist at the level of small, family-owned firms which through minor but incrementally important innovations contribute to the vitality of Italian textiles–clothing. Secondly, Italian small firms have invested heavily in new equipment. Between 1974 and 1982, Italy was the major purchaser of shutterless looms, buying more than France and Germany combined (Jacomet, 1989, p. 128). High levels of investment have ensured the livelihood of Italian equipment manufacturers such as Rimoldi, Macpi and Necchi. Reciprocally, a healthy engineering sector in the forefront of technical innovation has contributed to the success of the firms to whom it supplies. Thirdly, very high levels of specialization (often in a single stage of a production process) explain the ability to invest in the latest and most efficient equipment for the particular activity that is the firm's forte. An inter-firm division of labour, based on subcontracting by specialism within 'industrial districts', has led to scale economies secured in a quite different way to 'traditional' large firm strategies. Rather than trade on capacity *per se*, small firms exploit both highly specialized skills and low administrative costs, and a capability to respond rapidly to changes in demand.

The effective functioning of the system depends on the existence of an integrated local value-chain, called a *filiera* in Italian. As distinct to vertical integration where a number of successive manufacturing stages are undertaken within a single company, this type of integration occurs in a context of dispersed ownership where producers who are specialized in a single manufacturing activity successively pass products downstream for further processing. Thus there is a high level of interdependence, usually within a limited geographical area or 'industrial district'. Garofoli (1986) listed nineteen such industrial districts in Italy. Major regional concentrations of small-firm textile-clothing activity include Como (silk), Carpi and Prato (wool).

The most famous example of the combination of high volume merchandizing achieved through the co-ordination of small producers and retailers is that of the Benetton empire. In the 1980s, Benetton owned seven factories (five in Italy, one in France and one in Scotland). The rest of its garments were produced by over 200 subcontractors with an average size of 30 employees. Benetton has over 3000 shops in Italy and around the world, of which only a minority are under Benetton ownership: the greatest number are operated on a franchise basis. All Benetton shops, factories and subcontractors are linked by an on-line computer system. Computerization has three major advantages: it speeds transmission of orders; it facilitates management of inventory; and it permits 'real-time' analysis of market trends. Fashion, style and the ability to satisfy diverse and rapidly changing markets have been the major forces propelling the expansion of Benetton (Tuloup, 1987, pp. 76–82). By contrast, Italian department stores, such as Upim and Standa, which sold standardized and generally low-cost clothes, contracted in the 1980s.

Overall, the success of the Italian textile and clothing industries is linked to an extended phase of intense restructuring with high levels of investment. Between 1970 and 1980, there was a tripling of sales per employee (King, 1985, p. 142). But as the industry became more capital intensive, the need for labour declined proportionately. But these trends need to continue, given Italian labour costs which are nearly as high as those in Germany and the USA. In brief, the Italian industry has a strong performance record, and although it is not insulated from the problems faced by competitors in other developed countries, it does retain a significant advantage.

2.5.3 France

The French textile and clothing industries benefit from a number of strong features. These include traditional pre-eminence in *haute couture,* together with a world-wide reputation for French style and elegance. The list of leading French fashion designers is too long to reproduce here, but any list would include Dior and Pierre Cardin. France also has strengths in mid-market segments, exemplified by such internationally successful brands as Lacoste and Nafnaf.

Overall, however, despite strong performance by specific companies, adjustment by the French textile and clothing industries to changing world conditions has been relatively slow and problematic in comparison to Italy. GATT statistics (1990) show that France runs significant deficits in both textiles (1.1 billion dollars in 1989) and clothing (2.7 billion dollars in 1989). Between 1970 and 1979 employment in textiles and clothing fell from 709 000 to 355 000 (INSEE, 1990a, pp. 72–3). A further 15 000 jobs were lost in the first half of 1991, while one of the major firms in the sector, VEV-Prouvost, had made a loss in 1990 leading to what the French press called 'an unprecedented crisis' (*Nouvel Economiste,* 1991).

A number of factors have played a contributory role in explaining this variable performance. Toyne *et al.* (1984, pp. 152–3) pointed to the damaging effects of French state policies. State aids distorted competition and retarded successful adjustment to market conditions. The predilection for protectionism preserved uncompetitive elements of the industry for too long. The availability of undemanding, colonial markets led to a degree of complacency and inertia. Once colonial markets were opened up as a result of the loss of France's empire in the 1950s, and once France itself was exposed to trade liberalization due to the creation of the EEC in 1957 and to successive GATT rounds, the weaknesses of large sections of French textiles and clothing were exposed. French firms found they had to compete in open, international markets and were slow to modernize their structures and methods. Yet, as Jacomet has indicated (1989, p. 168), import controls did not meet with equal approval from all textile and clothing firms. For example, clothing manufacturers saw the importing of fabric from low-cost producers as a means of preserving their own competitiveness.

The structure of the French textiles and clothing industries is characterized by relatively low levels of concentration. In the manufacture of threads, woven fabrics and knitwear, the ten largest firms together accounted for less than 30% of employment or sales within their subsector in 1987. In 1988 total turnover for the French textiles industry was 113 billion francs, with weaving being the largest sector in terms of sales (27.2 billion francs), closely followed by knitwear and hosiery (27.2 billion francs) (Lewis, 1990b, p. 64). In textiles production there were 2443 firms with over ten employees in 1987, employing a total of 208 281 employees, giving an average firm size of 85. In the same year, the ten largest firms in clothing together accounted for around 10% of employment and sales. In clothing, there were 2953 firms in 1987, employing a total of 155 446 employees. Thus the average headcount per firm in clothing was 52 (Ministère de l'Industrie, 1990).

Part of the explanation for the fragmentation of the textile and clothing industries relates to official policies. French governments in the 1960s did not display the same passion for promoting concentration in textiles as they did in other sectors. This was partly due to the difficulty of finding appropriate partners for the state to deal with, and partly due to political reasons, since Gaullists did not want to lose the support of the conservative elements in the industry (Berrier, 1978). Nevertheless, in the 1970s the trend to mergers and takeovers accelerated, sometimes helped by state funds (Mytelka, 1982). DMC, Agache-Willot and Boussac were the sector's biggest firms until 1980, which saw the formation of France's largest textiles–clothing corporation, Prouvost (Delanoë, 1975; Alcouffe *et al.*, 1987).

At the start of the 1990s, France's largest textile and clothing firms included Chargeurs (wool), DMC (cotton), VEV-Prouvost (cotton and knitwear) and Brochier (silk) – the latter now taken over by the Italian firm Ratti. State-owned Rhône-Poulenc is a major producer of man-made fibres. In clothing the major firms included Devanlay, DIM and Bidermann. The largest firms have been characterized by a degree of vertical integration: the activities of VEV-Prouvost extend from trade in untreated wool to manufacture of woollen articles through to retail chains such as Rodier and Pingouin. In general, however, even the largest producers tend to concentrate on their own specialities. Rather than undertake every element of the value-chain in-house, they subcontract and buy in the 'missing links' (Jacomet, 1989, p. 190).

The French distribution system is also highly fragmented. In 1982 there were approx. 83 000 sales points in France, of which 60% were specialist retailers of textiles and clothing (Conseil Economique et Social, 1982). Specialist retailers accounted for 53% of textile–clothing sales in 1977, falling to 50% in 1987. Large chains comparable to Marks and Spencer do not figure as prominently in France as in the UK, but clothing sales in supermarkets have expanded rapidly to take 17% of the market in 1987, whereas their 1977 market share was 10% (Lewis, 1990b, p. 72). However, the fragmentation of the distribution sector entails higher costs for producers and consumers.

On the other hand, regional concentration of producers is high. Three regions – Nord-Pas de Calais in the north, Rhône-Alpes in central France and Alsace-Lorraine in the east – together accounted for some 58% of upstream textiles employment in 1984. The pattern of regional specialization in clothing is different, however, with the major producing regions being (in order of importance) the Loire Valley, Nord-Pas de Calais, the Paris region and central France, and Rhône-Alpes (Ministère de l'Industrie, 1987).

An intriguing example of high local concentration of textile–clothing firms is the Sentier area in the heart of Paris. In the Sentier over 2000 firms have gathered in a small number of narrow streets and specialize in exceptionally fast turn-round times, variously making street fashions or reacting to them as they happen (Montagné-Villette, 1990; Lenglet, 1991). The high division of labour and high degree of interconnection between small firms located in a small geographical area is perhaps the nearest equivalent to an Italian 'industrial district' in France. Similar new concentrations of clothing production have sprung up in inner city areas of Lyon and Marseille (Montagné-Villette, 1990).

In summary, the characteristics of the French textile and clothing industries place them in an intermediate position between the British and the Italian models. As in Britain, large French firms continue to try to exploit advantages of scale, but are handicapped by the fragmentation of consumer demand and of the retail system. As in Italy, France's many small and medium-sized firms trade on their flexibility, seeking to adapt to constantly changing markets but with degrees of success that vary from the outstanding to the mediocre. Unevenness in performance across the various subsectors of the textile and clothing industries has resulted in an overall loss of international competitiveness and allowed increased import penetration from developing countries.

2.6 LOCALITY STRUCTURES AND STRATEGIES

Each of the three major areas to be studied in this book – Leicester, Lyon and Como – have strong traditions of textiles–clothing production. These traditions have resulted in a distinct manufacturing profile in each, creating both opportunities and constraints for local firms. In line with the overall theme of this chapter, the following subsection sets out the industrial characteristics of the three textiles and clothing communities, while discussion of the economic history and social milieu will be held over to Chapter 5.

2.6.1 Leicester

Leicester, a major city in the East Midlands with a population of 280 000, has over the centuries abandoned specialist silk manufacture and concentrated in volume manufacture of knitwear and hosiery, including both underwear and outerwear garments. In the 1980s some 40 000 people were employed in those subsectors.

A sense of industrial community among local textiles–clothing firms emerges from their high degree of spatial concentration. Although some have located outside the city limits, encouraged by easy road transport and lower rents, hundreds remain in central districts. Thus two zones of geographical concentration can be discerned: a regional zone (within a 30 km radius of Leicester city centre), and within this, a localized zone (5 km radius). It appears that operating in Leicester City, or county, still confers (or is perceived to confer) advantages on the many knitwear manufacturers who operate there.

In terms of structures, Leicester knitwear is characterized by the presence of large numbers of small and medium-sized firms. From 1950 to the early 1970s, it looked as though large capital-intensive fibre-producers like Courtaulds would increasingly dominate knitted fabric production and assembly. This has not occurred due to a combination of reasons. Economies of scale in knitwear were not uniquely appropriable by large firms: efficient levels of production could also be achieved by small to medium sized firms. Indeed the potential for large-scale manufacture generally proved more limited than expected. Secondly, investment in such a competitive, import-ridden industry has no longer looked attractive to large firms. Thirdly, given that the technology is relatively stable and the machinery is durable, reliable used equipment has been available at affordable prices, facilitating entry by newcomers with relevant prior experience.

Low barriers to entry in knitwear have meant that from the first comprehensive industry survey of firms in 1930, small firms have dominated numerically. In a 1954 survey by Pool and Llewellyn (Wells, 1972), there were 1419 establishments, 322 with under ten staff. Three-quarters of industry employment and two-thirds of output by value were in establishments with under 500 employees, of which most were independent companies rather than subsidiaries. The use of unskilled homeworkers is also a feature of local textiles production.

Knitwear is an industry in which firms are prone to come and go. Mounfield (1972, p. 377) claimed some 200 new firms were started between 1948 and 1967, with a similar number terminating. This pattern has continued to exist in recent years. However, regional industrial instability has risen as Britain's knitwear industry came under increasing pressure from foreign competitors. UK output peaked in the late 1960s and has been declining from the 1970s, with the exception of hosiery, as is indicated in Tables 2.4 and 2.5.

Table 2.4 UK index of output of hosiery and knitted goods

1975	1976	1977	1978	1979	1980	1981
100	105	106	103	101	93	89

1982	1983	1984	1985	1986	1987	1988
88	88	90	92	92	93	88

Source: Central Statistical Office (1975–88) *Monthly Digest of Statistics*, (Code 436).

Table 2.5 UK output of principal products (millions of units)

	Underwear/ sleepwear		Outerwear		Hosiery (pairs)	
	Units	Index	Units	Index	Units	Index
1975	14.56	100	11.28	100	59.67	100
1980	12.82	88	9.10	81	58.36	98
1985	7.99	55	7.84	70	62.79	105
1988	7.16	49	7.32	65	66.64	112

Source: Central Statistical Office (1975–88) *Monthly Digest of Statistics*, table 11.4.

These national figures indicate some of the difficulties faced by Leicester as a volume producer of knitwear. For years industrialists have been criticized for preferring long order runs and being relatively inflexible. They have been exhorted to move up-market via higher-quality and higher added-value (fashion) products. Although to some extent they have done so, Leicester still competes mainly on inexpensive and 'value-for-money' products for local and national markets (corresponding to segments 5 and 6 in Table 2.1). The better-quality items are sold to the large retail chains, while lower-quality, cheaper products are sold in market stalls and in small, down-market retail shops throughout the country.

The area's tendency to compete on price rather than product differentiation has met increasing difficulties because of cheap imports from developing countries. Producers such as Hong Kong have moved away from 'bargain-basement' goods and also offer 'value-for-money' products, rather than just low prices *per se*. Many textile firms have closed down in the past two years, including a few plants owned by the largest employers, N. Corah and Courtaulds. The UK recession of the early 1990s inevitably deepened the problems, especially as Leicester knitwear firms operate in markets where growth is low and competition is high.

2.6.2 Como

The province and town of Como are situated close to Switzerland in one of the most northerly parts of Italy; the northern mountains and lake shores are underpopulated and relatively non-industrial. The Province of Como has a population of approx. 776 000, with the town of Como having around 96 000 inhabitants. While the neighbouring towns of Lecco and Cantù specialize in metalworking and furniture, Como is the 'headquarters of silk manufacturing' (King, 1985, p. 144). In addition, the Province of Como contains two other textile areas, one specializing in velvet and corduroy and the other in nets and curtains. Although the province accounts for only 6.4% of Italy's textile employees, this figure rises to 40% for silk weaving. The tradition and image of the Como area revolve around its specializations in silk, its reputation for quality and its highly integrated industrial structure.

Indeed silk implies quality. As Anson and Simpson (1988, p. 237) have indicated, 'the industry is the epitome of high value/low volume niches'. By and large, the raw material has been too expensive for low-fashion goods. Como's handkerchiefs, neckerchiefs and ties are usually marketed under the names of the best-known international fashion stylists and sell mainly to middle-market segments, though some go to luxury markets (segments 1 and 2 in Table 2.1). Depending on year, the area exports 50–70% of its production, with the USA as its major market, followed by Germany, France and Japan (Associazione Serica Italiana, 1982–90). In 1985, Como accounted for 10% of Italian textile and clothing exports.

Textiles–clothing production in the Como area is characterized by the presence of a large number of small and medium-sized firms. In line with the national trend in Italy towards greater industrial deintegration, the total number of firms in Como Province increased by 21.3% between 1971 and 1981. Although employment in textiles–clothing declined over the long term from over 50 000 in 1951 to around 30 000 in 1981, the fall was a consequence not of economic recession, but of considerable new investment in machinery, resulting in higher levels of productivity (Biffignandi, 1987). By 1981, there were 1281 firms in the textiles and clothing sectors. They included 616 silk weaving firms employing 11 928 workers, and 248 finishing, printing and dyeing firms with a total of 10 359 employees. The vast majority of silk weaving and finishing firms have fewer than 100 employees, as is illustrated in Table 2.6.

Table 2.6 Textiles employment: Como, 1981 (percentages)

Firm size	1–9		10–99		100–499		500+	
	COs	EMPs	COs	EMPs	COs	EMPs	COs	EMPs
Weaving	64.7	10	32	51	3	25	0.3	14
Finishing	30	2	58	51	12	47	–	–

Key: COs = companies; EMPs = employees.
Source: ISTAT, *VI Censimento generale dell'industria, del commercio e dell'artigianato*, 1985, vol. II, tomo 1, Fasc 13 (Como).

In 1981, 51% of weaving firms and 25% of finishing firms were officially classified in the category of small or 'artisanal' firms, enabling them to enjoy concessions in terms of taxes and 'soft' loans and greater flexibility in employee relations.

Despite appearances of fragmentation due to the existence of large numbers of independently owned firms, industrial integration – in the sense of interdependence between firms in a localized production cycle – has been crucial to Como's success. We shall discuss extensively this key theme in Chapter 6.

Competition within Europe comes mainly from Lyon. Although it was fierce up to the 1960s, Como replaced the French city as the highest-volume producer of silk products in Europe. Competition from the Far East has, however, been on the increase. In the past, Como manufacturers imported raw silk from China and re-exported silk fabrics, including large quantities of the comparatively standard product crêpe de Chine. In recent years, however, China has diversified from raw silk into the production of woven fabrics. There have been concurrent problems concerning the supply of raw silk, as China has linked exports of raw material to purchases of fixed quantities of home-produced silk fabrics.

Como producers reacted by refining their sourcing and production strategies. To safeguard their supplies of raw material they started to produce raw silk locally; production in 1986 amounted to approx. 31 000 tons (Anson and Simpson, 1988, p. 237). They have also encouraged other countries (notably Brazil) to cultivate mulberry leaves and raise cocoons. In addition, local merchants have been importing cheaper woven silk from China and having it finished at Como. These developments directly threatened some Como weaving firms, who chose therefore to abandon the production of crêpe de Chine. Reconversion options for weavers have involved reinforcing their specialisms by working with more sophisticated mixed fibres, as well as increasing the fashion content and design complexity of their fabrics in order to outpace Third World producers. Indeed some local firms are moving downstream to concentrate on design, dyeing, printing and finishing, as well as wholesaling. Most of these activities are highly specialized, requiring sophisticated machinery, skilled labour and considerable technical know-how. These competitive strategies aim to maintain product differentiation in quality terms and thereby preserve Como's lead.

2.6.3 Lyon

Lyon is France's second industrial city after Paris, with a population of 1 106 055 in the 1982 Census (Bonnet, 1987, p. 9). It is situated in the heart of France in the Rhône-Alpes region, and it is the region's major city. Rhône-Alpes today has the second largest regional concentration of textiles in France and the fourth largest in clothing, employing over 50 000 people in textiles–clothing in 1988 (INSEE, 1988). Lyon has been a major European centre for silk production and has a reputation for top-quality fabrics in a range of natural and man-made materials. Moreover, in recent years Lyon producers have marketed a range of high value-added, technical textiles that complement traditional specializations (Meilhaud, 1991). However, the role of textiles production in the Lyon economy has declined, with employment in the sector falling from over 36 000 people in 1966 to 12 000 in 1984 – just 6.6% of local industrial employment (Bonnet, 1987, p. 36).

The structure of the textiles and clothing industries in Rhône-Alpes is extremely fragmented. In 1988 there were some 550 textiles firms, 160 knitwear firms and 300 clothing firms according to official statistics issued by INSEE (1988). The average number of employees per firm was 50, indicating a preponderance of small to medium-sized enterprises. Typically, firms in the region are highly specialized and rarely exercise more than one industrial activity. Although the full range of upstream transformation activities exists in the region (including yarn manufacture, weaving and finishing), the single most important activity is weaving, which alone accounted for 43% of turnover in the Rhône-Alpes textiles and clothing industries in 1987.

It is worth noting that the French balance of trade has been far healthier in upstream textile production than in downstream clothing manufacture (Table 2.2). The higher level of French international competitiveness in textiles is also indicated by regional export figures. In Rhône-Alpes, in 1987, fibre and yarn producers exported 46% of their total output, while weavers exported 37%: this strong exporting record contrasted with weaker performance in knitwear and clothing, which exported 16% and 20% of production respectively (INSEE, 1988).

Thus the relative buoyancy of the textile and clothing industries in Rhône-Alpes, as compared to other textiles–clothing regions in France, such as the Nord-Pas de Calais, is partly explained by strengths in upstream textiles where competitiveness is higher. As Verret (1989) has pointed out, in upstream processes 'traditional' producers have largely closed the gap in manufacturing costs between themselves and 'new' producers. In the case of Rhône-Alpes, the level of turnover is far higher in upstream than downstream firms, as emerges from Table 2.7. This is particularly marked for the weaving firms. Moreover, using turnover per employee as an approximative measure of productivity, it transpires that clothing firms have the lowest levels of productivity in the region while, first, weavers, and secondly, fibre/yarn manufacturers, have the highest. This is not especially surprising as clothing manufacture generally requires a large labour input while upstream textiles production is capital intensive. But labour productivity, taken in conjunction with regional specialization by subsector, helps explain the relative strength of the textile and clothing industries in Rhône-Alpes. With around half of firms specializing in upstream processes characterized by capital intensity and high levels of productivity, and given local traditions of quality, innovation and design, firms in the locality hold competitive advantages over Third World producers competing mainly on low wages. International competitiveness is strong, hence the high levels of exporting already recorded.

In summary, textiles and clothing production in Lyon has not emerged unscathed from the sharpening of international competition. Garment manufacturers have been as hard hit in Lyon as elsewhere in Europe.

Table 2.7 Average numbers of employees and turnover for textile–clothing firms in Rhône-Alpes, 1987

	Average no. employees	*Average turnover (£ million)*	*Turnover per employee*
Fibre/yarn production	32	1.5	£46 900
Weaving	41	3.2	£78 000
Knitwear	61	2.1	£34 400
Finishing	55	1.7	£30 900
Clothing	57	1.5	£26 300

Source: INSEE (1988) Textile-habillement: Rhône-Alpes dans le peloton de tête des régions, *Bref Rhône-Alpes,* **1018** (21 September), p. 3.

However, traditions of quality and specialization – especially in high value-added, upstream activities – have helped the local textiles industry to weather the storm of international competition.

2.7 CONCLUSIONS

The major developments in textiles–clothing manufacture and distribution have been internationalization and the search for increased flexibility. Increased flexibility, in turn, has often required that firms deepen their specialization(s) and find new ways of differentiating themselves from competitors in terms of products, processes or levels of productivity. Economies of scale associated with large factories have tended to become less realizable as production runs have decreased in response to variegated demand. On the other hand, quick, flexible response to changing market conditions is facilitated by decentralized, 'lean' production systems displaying high initiative, creativity and low turn-around times. Thus in the 1980s the highly concentrated textile–clothing production systems of Britain and, to a lesser extent, France, did not always produce hoped-for advantages of scale efficiency. Centralization of decision-making, long production runs and a heritage of work organization that institutionalized long lead times ran counter to the need for quick response. Small and medium-sized companies in the 1980s generally proved more agile and responsive. Consequently, large companies made attempts to reorganize in the direction of greater flexibility in order to emulate small firms.

These developments make comparative studies of regions containing large numbers of small firms all the more relevant. Analysis of the profile of the textile and clothing industries in Leicester, Lyon and Como has highlighted a number of major commonalities, though elements of divergence also exist. All three areas are characterized by a lengthy history in textiles and clothing. In each area myriad small firms collectively account for significant output; but from similar beginnings, each has developed its own, specific character. While industrialization around Como has been closely linked to rural production patterns, Leicester is a fairly typical industrial city in the East Midlands and Lyon has developed into a major industrial conurbation. Each city originally held a strong position in silk products. Leicester lost that position very early; Lyon silk declined in quantity of output over the twentieth century but maintained its predominance in the small, *haute couture* end of the market; while since the 1960s, Como has become the European leader in silk output in volume terms.

Historical trends have led to differences in specialization in textiles–clothing, both at regional and company level. Whereas Como and Lyon have maintained a mid- to up-market profile in a range of woven fabrics, Leicester's specializations have often been inadequately distanced from a model of low-quality, high-volume production, resulting in increased exposure to low-cost imports from developing countries. Hence, whereas all three areas have had to fend off growing international competitive challenges in recent years, Leicester has been worst placed. Yet the difficulties of achieving higher levels of specialization to generate greater added value are not peculiar to Leicester, but indicate the challenge to be faced in the 1990s by all firms in the sector.

3

Small firms in developed economies

3.1 INTRODUCTION

In this chapter we address the characteristics of small firms, while in Chapter 4 we shall focus on the individual proprietor as a complementary unit of analysis. We begin with a review of the salient literature, addressing the significance of small firms in mature, Western economies. This leads into a discussion of the apparent economic and geographic factors underpinning the emergence and development of local small firm communities in the three countries we have chosen to study. We then present some broad, comparative findings about the firms who participated in our own research.

Before the Bolton Report of 1971, there was comparatively little serious and systematic consideration in Britain of the part that entrepreneurial drive and determination might play in arresting what was then a secular decline in small firm activity. Statistics were hard to find; even today reliable and detailed data on the scope and impact of small firms are by no means readily available in an appropriate form. Yet anecdotally, and as a result of many research projects since the era of Bolton, we know that the entrepreneurial instinct is alive and well in Britain, as elsewhere. Indeed, as we shall see, the significance of small firms in the British, French and Italian economies (and societies at large) is really not in doubt, especially in sectors like textiles and clothing which have a long history of contributing to the economic health of European Community countries.

Again, it is only in the past twenty years or so that much attention has been devoted to the proper role of governments and other agencies in encouraging a vibrant small firm sector. A plethora of new initiatives, grounded in ideology and pragmatism according to circumstance, has aimed to stimulate entrepreneurial activity in all three countries. Concurrently, increasing consideration has been given to the issue of what can realistically be expected of small firms in economic terms.

On the evidence of recent years, we see also that being a small firm owner remains a difficult and at times precarious way to earn a living. In particular, the founding of a new enterprise, that is directing tangible resources, knowledge and motivations to perceived market opportunities (regarded by many as the essence of entrepreneurship), is a high-risk activity. Moreover, if the firm is to thrive and develop, it requires specific resources and human qualities which later need to be supplemented – perhaps even supplanted – by still others. The study of small firms and their proprietors continues therefore to be a valid and important focus of economic and business research. Indeed all these facts and circumstances have resulted in an explosion of academic and general interest in small firms.

Publications can be located on a continuum. At one extreme, there are plenty of very readable, practical handbooks for would-be entrepreneurs. Their tone is typically prescriptive, yet despite new research findings, they tend to promulgate old myths about small firms and entrepreneurs (Curran and Stanworth, 1984). At the other extreme, there are academically rigorous works aimed at other researchers, public policy-makers and possibly consultants. This ought to mean that there is now a good deal of knowledge available to proprietors based on systematic firm-level research into 'proactive' entrepreneurship. Yet the lessons from such research have not always proved readily transferable in practice. Happily, though, studies which take the small firm and the entrepreneur as relevant units of analysis, and which are based on fieldwork in which researchers actually encounter small firms and their owners, are increasing in number.

Understandably, though, individual studies have tended to focus on single regions and countries. When international comparisons were the overt *raison d'etre* of a particular initiative, published commentaries have still tended to remain nation-centred, severely limiting the cross-national comparability of findings (e.g. Goffee and Scase, 1987; Levicki, 1984; OECD, 1982; Sengenberger, Loveman and Piore, 1990; Storey, 1983). Admittedly, there are exceptions (e.g. Amin, Johnson and Storey, 1986; Bannock, 1980; Cooke and Imrie, 1989; Oakey, 1984; Peterson and Schulman, 1987); none the less, there are still relatively few studies to have generated cross-national comparative data within a common format as we have presented in this book.

3.2 THE IMPORTANCE OF SMALL FIRMS IN BRITAIN, FRANCE AND ITALY

3.2.1 Small firm status

In theory, the status of small firms can be assessed quantitatively by their number, by the contribution they make to gross domestic product and employment, and qualitatively by their esteem in society at large, most particularly as reflected in the priority which governments, major banks and other interested parties accord their welfare and development. In practice, quantitative assessment is made problematic by definitional difficulties and by the paucity of reliable, comparable time-based data both before and after the landmark Bolton Report (1971) in the UK (Cross, 1983; Curran and Stanworth, 1984). Such difficulties become acute when making international comparisons (Ganguly and Bannock, 1985).

For example, what precisely is a small firm? In the UK, the Bolton Report (1971) distinguished small establishments (which may be owned by large corporations) from small enterprises, or true 'small firms', characterized by having negligible market shares, and by being managed in a personalized way, typically by the owner, who enjoys notional autonomy in terms of managerial responsibility and strategic direction. In practice, it is wise to relate any definition involving the number of staff employed to the particular sector under consideration since across the extractive, manufacturing, distributive and other service-based industries, labour intensity varies widely. Other criteria for defining small firms have been used from time to time, but in our study we accepted the spirit of the Bolton definitions, which in manufacturing proposed a limit of 500 staff, though other sources have variously used 200 or 100 as an upper bound. In the French and Italian contexts, similar headcount-related definitions are applied.

During the 1960s, the French and the British were rather slow to recognize the contribution of small firms in a modern economy. One consequence is that data available from that period to form baseline comparisons are limited and somewhat inaccessible. Up to the early 1970s, the British inclined to accept uncritically the prevailing sentiment of 'big is beautiful'. Thus there was a tendency to look on the demise of the small firm sector as a natural trend (Boswell, 1973), albeit one accelerated by difficulties arising directly from the then prevailing high capital transfer taxes that frustrated offspring from inheriting the family business. Subsequently during the 1980s, partly as a consequence of having a Prime Minister whose roots were in small business, British government interest in 'small firms' revived and was paralleled by French interest in *petites et moyennes entreprises* (PMEs). More specifically, the French have proved willing to entertain policy initiatives which directly or otherwise have encouraged small firm formation (Bucaille and Costa de Beauregard, 1987; Lataste, 1982; Marchesnay, 1984), whereas the British government has generally preferred to encourage, exhort and facilitate informally via the provision of finance, training and expert advice, notably through the clearing banks and other agencies such as the Manpower Services Commission, the universities and poly-technics.

Italy presents a distinctly different case. The precise contribution of the small firm sector to the Italian economy continues to be difficult to assess with any real precision for a variety of reasons, including its sheer scale and scope. Italy is also said to manifest a larger scale of unofficial or 'submerged' economic activity than its EC counterparts. Moreover, the small firm sector is one of manifest paradoxes; advanced manufacturing technologies are not infrequently part-and-parcel of what might otherwise be considered 'cottage industries'. In any event, according to Bamford (1984), 'the importance of small business to the Italian economy as a whole has no equivalent in other western, developed countries'. Most certainly, the Italian economy has benefited directly from its small firm manufacturing sector as evidenced by thriving exports in all manner of goods. These include textiles and clothing, ski equipment, leather and other household goods, furniture and ceramic tiles, to name but a small selection. It is also important to note that many of these sectors have grown to international prominence since the 1950s.

It is a matter of some debate to what degree the Italian small firm sector is significant because of, or despite of, the contribution of central government. The less bureaucratic legal/fiscal regime applicable to firms with under 15 employees has undoubtedly encouraged small firm formation. Equally, it has in some cases tended to discourage growth of integrated units beyond this size. Rather, it seems that growth of the small firm has been achieved by fragmentation into two or more business units which by virtue of family and social ties subsequently retain commercial linkages.

3.2.2 The scale and scope of small firm activity

According to Cross (1983, p. 91) there were about 1.5 million small UK businesses in the early 1980s, employing 6 million people, with a further 2 million self-employed, constituting about a third of the working population and generating a quarter of the GNP. One count of unquoted and unincorporated businesses cited by Cross was approx. 2.3 million in 1980. More recently, Daly and McCann (1992) provided an official estimate of 1.8 million businesses in the UK in 1979 (including the smallest), whereas by 1989 the comparable figure had reached some 3 million. To put these data into context, this implies that a net figure of 500 new businesses per working day were formed in the UK during the decade to 1989, resulting in firms with under 500 staff providing about two-thirds of total private sector employment. Since late 1989, sadly, these gains have been partly reversed by the prevailing economic recession, so there is reason now to doubt whether the net stock of small UK firms will grow during the next few years much beyond the substantial levels achieved in the late 1980s.

In France there were, according to Barreyre (1984), approx. 3.6 million small firms in 1980 including the self-employed. Limiting the definition of small firms to artisanal firms (under 10 employees) and PMEs (10–499) only, official statistics indicate that there were about 1.9 million in total in 1979 vs 2.1 million in 1988. Of the latter figure, approx. 1.25 million were PMEs and

0.85 million were artisanal, with the latter category known to be growing by some 20 000 per annum in the late 1980s (Arnaud, 1990; INSEE, 1990b; Ministère de l'Industrie, 1990); thus during the 1980s new firm formation in France has also been buoyant.

After rapid expansion of the Italian small firm sector in the 1950s, there was a period of comparative stability in this population, followed by renewed expansion in the late 1960s and 1970s, coinciding with the partial decline and fragmentation of the large firm sector. Many analysts attributed these changes to the impact of trade union militancy and rising labour costs, especially after the introduction of the Workers' Statute in 1970. Subcontracting out to small firms was seen as an expediency to circumvent these tough employment regulations from which very small firms were exempt. As in Britain during the 1980s, it can also be argued that social as well as economic factors encouraged the formation of small units. Today it seems safe to conclude that the number of small Italian firms exceeds 3 million. Indeed, according to Bamford (1984), the 'submerged' component of the Italian economy alone encompassed at least 1.5 million people – some 10% of the working population in the early 1980s – and was predominantly centred on small, family-based production units.

Of greater significance than numbers of small firms is the share of employment generated by them in the three countries. Across all employment sectors of the UK economy, firms with under 500 staff provided 66% of employment in 1989 compared to 57% a decade earlier. Corresponding figures for firms with under 200 staff were 55% and 49% respectively. Thus the share of employment in small UK firms has risen as the number of firms has grown, though proportionately not as fast, reflecting the small size of many of the newest. Turning to the manufacturing sector, the proportion of employment in small manufacturing firms with under 200 employees in the early 1960s was 31% in the UK, 51% in France and 66% in Italy (Bolton, 1971, p. 68). In France PMEs with 10 – 499 staff provided 38% of manufacturing employment in 1973 and 48% in 1985 (Bucaille and Costa de Beauregard, 1987), while the equivalent 1988 UK datum was 61%.

Averaging the estimates made by Bamford (1984) and Oakey (1984) for share of employment in manufacturing firms with under 100 employees for the three countries in the early 1980s yields: UK 18%; France 36%; and Italy 62%, suggesting a continuing trend to smaller units in Italy. Ganguly and Bannock (1985, p. 129) have demonstrated that, as one might expect, small manufacturing firms were typically bigger than small service-based firms, hence the former remained significant in their ability to generate employment. However, it should be noted that small firms' share of GNP even in manufacturing does not match their share of employment because undercapitalization restricts the level of productivity they can achieve compared with big firms. International comparisons here are highly problematic, being confounded by within-sector differences in technological sophistication, as well as by differing types and proportions of product output, not to say problems of accurate recording.

Similar conclusions about the importance of small firms emerge when we look at employment by **size of establishment** or productive unit, though the patterns are markedly different among the three countries. For many years small units have been much more important in France and Italy than in the UK. In 1963 approx. 27 000 small UK establishments provided 2.1% of manufacturing employment compared with 186 000 (10.8%) in France and 245 000 (18.5%) in Italy (Hindley, 1984, p. 53). Levels of employment in small units also vary considerably by **sector**, with relatively lowly capitalized industries like shoes and garments manufacturing accounting for a bigger proportion of output in small firms and units.

Although these various data are best treated as indicative, they would seem to suggest that over recent years – certainly up to the close of the 1980s – small firms have held or increased their share of employment in all three countries. Yet this conclusion probably masks a secular decline in manufacturing, for as Storey (1983, p. 4) has noted, 'generally, the small firm sector has provided a reduced proportion of manufacturing jobs over time in most countries'. It is certainly true that many of the new firms formed during the 1980s have been in service activities, notably in Britain, where about a third of small firms are now service-based. However, the argument for linking the decline of manufacturing jobs to the growth of service-based jobs is not clear-cut.

3.3 ECONOMIC AND GEOGRAPHICAL FACTORS IN SMALL FIRM DEVELOPMENT

Several parallel developments help explain rising small firm activity. Most notably, these include economic, geographic and social factors. As the latter will be treated in greater detail later in this book, only brief reference will be made to them here, though in practice all of the factors are interrelated to a significant degree.

One major factor in small firm development has been the secular trend from agricultural employment – surprising perhaps to British readers, this trend gained momentum in Italy and France after the Second World War. Yet by 1979, agriculture accounted for only 14.8% of Italian civilian employment compared with 32.8% in 1960 (Ganguly and Bannock, 1985, p. 17). The corresponding figures for France were 9.0% in 1979 vs 22.4% in 1960. Thus in both countries over this period there was a sizeable pool of labour available for absorption by manufacturing and more recently service-based businesses. In contrast, the corresponding figures for Britain were only 2.6% by 1979 as compared with an already-low 4.1% in 1960.

Though one might suppose that the British experience defines a 'floor' to agricultural employment, ongoing improvements in farming productivity (allied to the EC's policy of 'set-aside' which aims to take additional farmland out of active production in all EC countries) are likely to sustain the trend away from agricultural employment, albeit in smaller numbers than hitherto. A plausible hypothesis is that since many big businesses are still shedding or redeploying labour in the wake of recent automation projects, these people will find employment principally, if at all, in small firms.

In contrast, disenchanted British agricultural workers quit the land in numbers from the early days of the Industrial Revolution right up to the 1930s and beyond. Throughout, the long-standing and largely British phenomenon of primogeniture ensured that land-ownership remained in the hands of the comparatively few. The average farmworker owned neither land nor home, nor had any prospect of so doing. Thus farmworkers sought work and accommodation in big cities. Family connections with the rural areas were brutally severed in less than a generation; likewise in France.

By contrast, fewer than half of all farms in postwar Italy comprised single, consolidated properties – 68 000 of them comprised over 20 components parcelled out to children and grandchildren (Heseltine, 1989). Thus in Italy many more farmworkers had a financial interest in the means of production. A modest income from their smallholdings was sufficient to keep them away from the big cities and, in some cases, underpinned the creation and development of new business activities in the quest for a higher standard of living. The somewhat longer-term perspective afforded by this security of land tenure often legitimated and facilitated the employment of younger family members. These small businesses usually related to the processing of locally available materials in relatively traditional, labour-intensive activities such as shoes, other leather goods, textiles and clothing. By the 1970s, the successful firms that took root in the immediate postwar era were making a significant contribution to the development of the Italian economy – and more recently to exports also – in a wide range of manufactured goods. Indeed they are a prime reason why the Italian economy has remained competitive against formidable opposition from the low-cost countries of the Far East (Porter, 1990).

This pattern contrasts with the UK where the typical small business entrepreneur in the 1950s and 1960s was either a skilled industrial worker who set up a firm acting as a subcontractor to his former employer or someone who set up a service-based business in maintenance and repair work, or in the retailing and allied trades. As noted, the late 1960s and 1970s saw something of a hiatus in small firm formation, followed in the 1980s by a definite revival. However, it must be remembered that many such firms were born out of the adversity of unemployment, and despite support from the banks, have often remained woefully undercapitalized.

In all three countries industrialization has tended to be more extensive in the northern half of each country, save for the London area in Britain and

Lyon and Marseilles in France. In the north and north-central regions of Italy the shift in focus from agriculture to manufacturing gave rise to local centres of industrial concentration and expertise, each generally focused on a single sector of manufacturing. Most are in a geographic triangle of central/northern Italy, sometimes referred to as the 'Third Italy' (Bagnasco, 1977). In the south of Italy the comparative absence of small family farms stymied a parallel development, with emigration from the region as a consequence; nor were governmental 'top-down' attempts at industrialization notably successful.

However, localized industry sector concentration is not a recent phenomenon. Traditional manufacturing localities involving small firms have long existed in all three countries. Taking textiles and clothing as a specific case, the Borders region of Scotland, the counties of Leicestershire, Nottinghamshire and Yorkshire in England; Lyon and the Rhône-Alpes region in France; and Prato and Como provinces in Italy, are good examples. In some instances, the formation of relatively homogeneous immigrant communities has cemented this process by 'importing' a supply of well-established skills in traditional crafts. This has been the case, for example, in the UK in Leicester and in Bradford.

Over the past two decades or so, the rise of small firms has been concurrent, paradoxically, with the growth of the biggest firms, often via merger with or acquisition of smaller companies. By the 1980s, the top 100 British manufacturing firms accounted for about half of total UK manufacturing output compared with around 42% in the mid-1970s and 22% in the late 1940s (Utton, 1984). France and Italy have also emulated the trend to increased scale of the largest firms. This trend was prompted largely by the quest for enhanced profitability, as demonstrated by evidence across Europe that firm size correlates quite well with scale of plant, and that increased scale tends to go in hand with increased labour productivity (Samuels and Morrish, 1984). Medium-sized firms thus tended to decline as a competitive force, and were consequently taken over, closed down or disaggregated into smaller units via management buyouts. But increasing productivity and rationalization within larger, merged units also reduced demand for labour. So the employment gains made by the UK small firm sector in the early 1980s were contemporaneous with – and arguably the obverse side of – a massive labour shakeout from big manufacturing industry. A consequence was that many of the new small firms found work as subcontractors to much larger units, evidently on a marginal, vulnerable basis.

It follows that attributing the evident rise in small firm activity to what one might call 'autonomous entrepreneurship' needs cautious scrutiny. Rather, while it could be argued that the UK experienced a good deal of 'forced entrepreneurship', in Italy the theory of 'economic dualism' gained ground for a time. Put simply, this posited the coexistence of an advanced, innovative and capital-intensive large firm sector alongside a backward, traditional and labour-intensive small firm sector. In large firms a mostly skilled, unionized workforce was guaranteed good conditions of work and pay, while in the small units a non-unionized, often unskilled and/or female labourforce had little choice but to accept low wages and insecure conditions of work. Small firms acted as a buffer, providing large firms with, in effect, a workforce easily expanded or contracted in line with changes in demand – hence flexible, incremental production capacity at low cost (Berger and Piore, 1980; Goldthorpe, 1984; Paci, 1973). Similar arguments can, no doubt, be advanced in many mature economies including France and Japan.

To recapitulate, explanations of the development and current role of the small firm sector have become complex and multifaceted. Causes and effects of change are frequently not clear-cut: autonomous initiatives on the part of entrepreneurs, and economic and other trends including sectoral deintegration, appear to have all played major parts. A notable feature of small firm activity is the comparatively 'long-wave' cyclical nature of new firm formation. The most obvious conclusion is that a variety of contextual factors appear to underpin the formation of new firms, and while there are generalizable aspects to this process, it is ultimately specific to the locality and circumstances of the time. In this respect, the textiles and clothing sector, having developed fully to maturity while maintaining a high proportion of small firms is no exception.

That said, small firms have changed and diversified since the 1970s, defying simplistic analyses seeking to treat them as a homogeneous (and backward) sector. Indeed an issue currently the subject of much discussion and research concerns the demonstrable ability of small Italian firms to innovate and use advanced technologies in what have been thought of as rather traditional, change-averse industry sectors (Gerelli, 1983; Lassini, 1984; Riva, 1983). Some would also argue that small firms have become more innovative and indispensable when they have become more specialized (Favaretto, 1986; Lassini, 1986). In any event, it is probable that the implementation of advanced technologies and innovative work practices in small firms enhances their credibility as perceived by their large firm clients, enabling better mutual accommodation over their respective spheres of competence and economic contribution. Such adjustments can, for example, encompass partnerships and other forms of collaboration.

Yet despite the recent buoyancy of small firm activity in all three countries, it would be unwise to suppose that the trend is necessarily sustainable in all sectors over the medium to long term. In textiles and clothing the fierce competitive pressures from newly industrializing countries, noted in Chapter 2, evidently pose major challenges. Given their undoubted vulnerability, especially in times of recession, small enterprises arguably need to secure a range of technological and managerial competences to gain competitive advantage and bargaining power *vis-à-vis* larger companies if they are to survive and prosper in their chosen sector.

3.4 SMALL FIRMS IN THIS STUDY

This, then, is the small firm background to our three-country study. We have sought to suggest that small firms remain a significant contributor to economic development in Western countries, although their precise importance varies from industry sector to sector, and over time.

Yet the aggregate economic analysis of small firms sheds little light on why they are more significant in some sectors than others, and offers few real clues as to their future prospects in particular sectors. This is one reason for a study like this to concentrate on a particular sector and to consider similarities and differences across local contexts. Thus, having reached the decision to study textiles and clothing, our next step was to focus on particular localities with a long history of operations. In Leicester, Lyon and Como, we chose three such localities manifesting readily definable specializations allied to geographic localization.

Not surprisingly, a good deal of what follows in this and subsequent chapters emphasizes the small firm contribution to the three local economies. In so doing, it is not our intention of course to deny the contribution of large firms, though our findings confirm the phenomenon of fragmentation in Italian industrial structures already noted by others. We continue in this chapter by presenting some background details about the small firms which contributed to our research.

3.4.1 Characteristics and backgrounds of the firms

Our intention was to target independent (autonomous), family-owned firms, and in this we have largely succeeded (Table 3.1). Three-quarters or more of firms in each sample were effectively controlled by the proprietor and immediate family and, in a majority of cases, the family had virtually outright ownership. In cases where the controlling interest was held by outsiders, it was generally in the hands of non-family partners in Como, whereas in the other localities it was more likely to be a corporate owner.

Table 3.1 Ownership of firms

	Lyon	*Como*	*Leicester*
Family owns 90%+ of shares	68	53	62
Family owns 50–90% of shares	9	21	24
50%+ non-family owned	23	26	14
Totals	100	100	100

Virtually all the proprietors claimed to be actively involved in their firms and, for most, it appeared to be their sole business activity.

The available forms of legal status of firms vary somewhat from country to country, making precise comparisons difficult. The combination of sole tradership and partnership (including in Como special small firm status) accounted for only 4% in Lyon and 12% in Leicester, but 36% of the firms in Como. In Leicester 84% of firms were private limited companies compared with 32% in Como and only 12% in Lyon. Although it follows that 84% of the French firms were public limited companies (compared with 32% of Italian firms and only 4% in the Leicester sample), this is not unusual in the French context since the *société anonyme* (SA) is not necessarily a quoted company and is often preferred by family firms.

Table 3.2 Age profile of firms

	Lyon	Como	Leicester
% of firms founded:			
pre-1900	21	0	10
1900–44	35	14	18
1945–59	23	9	5
1960–9	5	39	5
1970–9	9	23	32
1980–9	7	15	30
Total	100	100	100
Median age (yr)	52	25	15

Given the dominance of family ownership in all samples, one would expect differences in legal status to be linked to other factors, such as age and size of firms, and this is broadly true. The French firms emerged as older (Table 3.2) and larger (Table 3.3) than the others. In fact on three measures of size presented in Table 3.3, namely sales turnover, productive assets and employee numbers, the French sample contained the biggest firms, the UK sample the smallest. The only exception to this general pattern is that the median number of full time employees in Leicester was 50 staff per firm compared with only 20 in Como, but 84 in Lyon.

Given these substantial between-sample differences, it is worth discussing whether they have arisen from real differences in population characteristics, notably the nature of the value-adding tasks undertaken in the three localities or from sampling quirks. The specialities of the firms sampled are fabrics (notably silk) manufacture in Como, hosiery, knitted fabrics and garments in Leicester and woven fabrics and garments in Lyon. Thus we see

Table 3.3 Size of firms

	Lyon	Como	Leicester
(i) by Sales turnover (£ x 1000)			
% of firms with sales:			
Under 100	0	9	4
100–499	7	19	24
500–999	5	19	17
1000–1999	5	6	22
2000–4999	35	28	24
5000+	48	19	9
Total	100	100	100
Median sales (£ x 1000)	4800	1600	1000
(ii) by Productive assets: machines/equipment (£ x 1000)			
% of firms with assets:			
Under 100	15	28	36
100–499	6	17	35
500–999	24	17	17
1000–1999	22	25	10
2000–4999	18	13	2
5 000+	15	0	0
Total	100	100	100
Median assets (£ x 1000)	1250	860	250
(iii) by Number of full-time employees			
% of firms with:			
1–9 staff	14	41	22
10–49	19	32	28
50–99	42	15	20
100–199	16	9	26
200–499	9	3	4
Total	100	100	100
Median staff headcount	84	20	50

asymmetry, both in terms of technologies and product emphasis. The Leicester firms were principally knitwear manufacturers. Garments other than hosiery are made almost entirely via cut-and-sew processes, often from fabrics knitted by the same firms. In contrast, the manufacture and application of woven fabrics dominated in the other two localities. Of the two localities, garment manufacturing was more important for our Lyon firms than for our Como firms. None the less, as can be seen from Table 3.4 (which provides more detail of the **value-adding chain** of each locality, expressed in terms of principal activities), fabrics and garment makers exist in all three samples. This is corroborated by the observations made in Chapter 2 on the characteristics of the textiles and clothing industries in the three localities, and suggests that while the samples may be considered reasonably representative of firms in the respective localities, care must naturally be exercised in drawing broad conclusions from the bald comparative statistics on size, age and value-chain specialisms.

Table 3.4 Value-chain profile of the three samples

	Lyon	Como	Leicester
% of firms having as their principal activity:			
Fabrics manufacturing	42	34	2
Garments manufacturing	27	11	69
Non-garment product manufacturing	9	23	7
Services/distribution *	6	23	15
Vertical firms [†]	16	9	7
Totals	100	100	100

* Wholesaling, specialist services, excluding retailing.
[†] Making fabrics, garments and wholesaling, etc.

By 'vertical firms' we mean manufacturers who are engaged in several stages in the value chain. In some cases, their activities apparently include the distribution of finished products. They tend to be the larger, integrated firms. In Como a sizeable proportion of the sample were specialist wholesale distributors of fabrics and garments, and there were also producers of accessories as well as fabric processing specialities such as dyeing and finishing. In all three countries retailers were excluded from the research. It is clear that Como and Lyon manifest a wide range of firms with specialist local skills and activities, while Leicester firms, in contrast, appear relatively generalist in their focus.

As noted in Chapter 1, we are confident that our sampling frames were representative of the localities, but we cannot wholly discount the possibility that questionnaires returned from all three localities have somewhat over-represented the proportion of longer-established firms. It is possible that proprietors of larger, well-established firms were more likely to have time for and be interested in research like this, particularly in view of its international orientation and our promise to feed back aggregated findings. Conversely, proprietors of smaller, more marginal firms may simply be suspicious of and reluctant (for whatever reason) to participate in what they may perceive as 'official' surveys. For similar reasons, the data from completed questionnaires almost certainly under-represent minority elements in each community, especially in Leicester where a sizeable proportion of small firm proprietors of Asian ethnic extraction came to Britain predominantly after 1972.

We make these observations because it is prudent to recognize the limitations of any study, but aside from these caveats, we do not believe that any other response biases occurred differentially among the three communities. It follows that while we may, for example, be led to overstate the median age of the generality of small firms in each locality, the observed differences among the observed age profiles within this sector are, in our view, reliable. In particular, the evidence in Table 3.2 points to an active rate of new firm formation in Leicester during the past two decades.

Turning specifically to size differences among the three groups, these may have arisen from value-chain considerations, such as greater capital intensity in woven fabrics manufacture than in knitting. We might also expect greater capital intensity in upstream processes (fabrics) than in garment making where capital requirements are offset by higher labour intensity. It is true that in all three countries garment-related activities have historically been favoured points of entry for entrepreneurs because technology has been relatively well understood and stable, and labour available and cheap. The entry of new players over time was facilitated by the availability of pre-used, but still productive, equipment made available by longer-established operators as they upgraded, or in times of recession closed down.

This explanation is plausible and consistent with the observation that while family-owned firms in Lyon penetrated the relatively capital-intensive weaving sector in the past, now that modern equipment has become highly sophisticated, productive and extremely expensive, recent entrants have effectively been deterred. Certainly, the lack of young French firms sampled would support this view. But it should be noted that the Como firms (whose median age is only half that of the Lyon firms) have achieved a median level of productive capitalization already two-thirds that of their French counterparts. Thus the fact that capital investment is a very effective entry barrier has not deterred the Como firms to the extent that one might have predicted, given the Lyon data. The principal reason for this, we would argue, relates to process specialization, a phenomenon we will consider more fully later.

The straightforward hypothesis that observed size differences are largely age-related cannot be ignored. However, we have some doubts over the degree of impact that age has had on firm growth and size. A detailed examination of the data certainly indicated that the link is far from deterministic. Further, we suggest that the observed size differences among the three samples are by no means inconsistent with the unfolding economic and social conditions already described, namely that new firm formation and growth is a function of factors somewhat or largely specific to each country, region and industry sector. Thus in Lyon the small firm sector had largely reached maturity by the time of the Second World War and evolved incrementally thereafter. Family firms have survived and (as will be seen) passed on to second or third generations. New firms have emerged in small numbers, discouraged by the high cost of entry and the presence of strong competitors. In Como the agrarian drift began later and persisted longer; this was coupled with a tendency of proprietors to stay loyal to traditional industry sectors. Subsequently, local circumstances have not encouraged the merger of small business units which, on the whole, have therefore remained comparatively small and local.

In Leicester the industry was largely established by the turn of the century, and having reached a mid-century peak, experienced secular decline with the ascendancy of the 'big is beautiful' industrial philosophy of the 1960s and the emergence of low-cost overseas competitors. The stock of small firms was rapidly eroded as founders retired or died in the 1960s and early 1970s (Boswell, 1973). Thereafter, revival was signalled by the seminal Bolton Report of 1971, and materially aided and accelerated by a variety of factors, notably the later emergence of the 'enterprise culture'.

3.4.2 The trading profiles of the firms

By **trading profile** we mean, specifically, details about the customer base enjoyed by the firms and the nature of their trading relationships. From

Table 3.5 Number of customers served by firms

	Lyon	*Como*	*Leicester*
% of firms with:			
Under 10 customers	9	9	29
11–20	2	9	17
21–30	2	16	9
31–50	4	21	9
51–100	20	5	10
100+	63	40	26
Total	100	100	100

Table 3.5, we see that the French firms predominantly had a large customer base: 83% had over 50 customers. The other samples are more polarized, with about half of the Italian firms and a third of the UK firms having over 50 customers. In the Leicester sample around half of the firms had less than 20 customers. To some degree, this reflects their comparative youth, but even so, it is clear that the Como firms (with a not-so-dissimilar age profile) have spread their trading net more broadly.

This conclusion is corroborated both in terms of dependence on their single biggest customer (Table 3.6) and geographic spread of sales (Table 3.7). Thus, for example, almost eight in ten of the Lyon firms sold under 20% of their output to their single biggest customer, compared with six in ten in Como, but only three in ten in Leicester. At the other end of the scale, a substantial minority of Leicester firms (22%) sold more than half their output to one customer, suggesting a higher level of dependency than elsewhere.

Table 3.6 Sales to single biggest customer

	Lyon	*Como*	*Leicester*
% of firms with:			
0-9% of sales to the biggest	50	30	15
10-19%	29	30	16
20-29%	17	14	27
30-39%	0	13	15
40-49%	2	5	5
50%+	2	8	22
Total	100	100	100

Table 3.7 Geographic scope of customer base

	Lyon	*Como*	*Leicester*
% of firms who are:			
Mainly local/regional *	11	12	16
National [†]	54	37	75
Export oriented [‡]	15	27	7
Internationally oriented [§]	20	24	2
Totals	100	100	100

* More than 50% of sales done locally/regionally.
[†] Less than 50% of sales done locally/regionally.
[‡] Nationally oriented firms exporting 26-49% of sales.
[§] Firms which exported more than 50% of sales.

From Table 3.7, we see that Leicester firms were substantially more parochial in terms of where they do business. Less than one in ten of them claimed to secure a quarter or more of their sales outside the UK, whereas almost a third of Lyon firms and almost half of Como firms claimed to achieve this level of exports. Again, in both the French and Italian samples around one in four/five firms claimed to export more than half their output, which we define here as an international orientation.

According to these measures, then, it seems fair to state that the Como firms in particular were less vulnerable to the whims of a few customers, more widely based in terms of market geography and in particular more export-oriented than were the Leicester firms. A probable reason for the national as opposed to international profile of the Leicester firms is the prominence of national multiple clothing retailers in the UK, not paralleled to anything like the same degree in France or Italy. These retailers have been very important customers of the Leicester firms and perhaps, as a consequence, the latter have not been encouraged to look further afield. As regards the Lyon firms, there was also a strong bias towards a non-local, if still predominantly French clientele, which could point to a lack of international competitiveness, an issue to which we return in Chapter 8.

Business relationships also have implications for the **types of contract** the supplier firms can negotiate. Table 3.8 shows a marked pattern of one-off contracting on the part of the Como firms (as opposed to ongoing, regular contracts) which was not matched elsewhere. Leicester firms claimed the highest proportion of regular contracts (approx. two-thirds of the sample). While regular contracts have their benefits, promoting continuity and perhaps signifying trust in relationships, they can also come to signify a lack of innovation – in design, for example – and possibly an unwillingness on the part of other firms to contest the status quo.

Table 3.8 Type of orders enjoyed by firms

	Lyon	*Como*	*Leicester*
% of firms having:			
One-off contracts	39	48	24
Mixed	11	12	11
Regular contracts	50	40	65
Totals	100	100	100

In any event, the data in Table 3.9 certainly demonstrate the seemingly short-term and opportunistic outlook of trading relationships in Como. For the Italians a tendency to one-off contracts was evidently linked to a short-term outlook and a perception of opportunism dominating mutual **trust** in these relationships. In marked contrast, trust and a long-term outlook were more likely to be perceived by the French in their dealings. As regards the Leicester firms, despite their high proportion of regular business, they were closer to the Como firms than the Lyon firms in their perceptions of opportunism and short-termism, suggesting that the bargaining position of Leicester firms *vis-à-vis* customers may actually be less secure than one might initially suppose.

Table 3.9 Perspective on trading relations

	Lyon	Como	Leicester
(i) Short-term vs long-term			
% of firms reporting:			
Short-termism	21	19	34
Long-termism	26	5	17
(ii) Opportunism vs mutual trust			
% of firms reporting:			
Opportunism	12	49	24
Mutual trust	37	30	22

Note: Not all firms replied to these questions, hence replies do not total 100%

We were also interested to know about business relationships in terms of possible subcontracting arrangements and activity co-ordination among local firms. Subcontractor status is one key indicator of the role a firm fulfils in the value adding chain. Here we distinguish three potentially significant categories of firm: (i) **non-contractors**, which neither contracted work out to other firms nor claimed to work on a subcontract basis for others; (ii) **prime contractors**, namely firms which contracted out to others, but did not contract in, and (iii) **subcontractors**, which principally contracted for others, though of course some of them, in turn, contracted work out to yet other

Table 3.10 Contractor status of firms

	Lyon	Como	Leicester
% of firms who are:			
Non contractors *	7	9	30
Prime contractors *	51	44	32
Subcontractors *	42	47	38
Total	100	100	100

* See text for definition of term.

firms. These data are shown in Table 3.10, demonstrating marked differences among our sample. We see that only a small proportion of the Lyon and Como firms were autonomous, non-contractors as defined above, whereas fully 30% of the UK firms claimed to be. The major proportion of Lyon firms in the sample (51%) classified themselves as prime contractors, the firms on which others rely (vs 44% in Como and 32% in Leicester). The proportions of subcontractors were similar in each sample (range 38–47%), but a significant difference was that in Como more than half of these did not contract out further, that is they were literally at the end of the contracting line.

These differences suggest structural variations in the make-up of the three localities, with Como showing the most evidence of small-firm subcontracting behaviour, consistent with disaggregation and specialism in the value-adding chain. In Leicester the reverse appears true: a substantial proportion of firms claimed to produce finished products without external contracting support. The status of the prime contractors in Lyon was corroborated by the high proportion of French firms which perceived **co-ordination of efforts** among them and their immediate trading partners. The proportions of the Como and Leicester samples perceiving activity co-ordination were lower. For the proprietor, perceived co-ordination among firms is, not surprisingly, associated more with trust than with opportunistic behaviour, and with a longer- as opposed to shorter-term perspective, exemplified in the French sample. That said, we think it is also linked in all three areas with perceptions of **control**. In other words, from the respondent's viewpoint co-ordination is more likely to be perceived as something a prime contractor does, solely or in consultation with the subcontractor(s) (we shall have more to say on this issue in Chapters 6 and 7).

Where subcontractors are used, they are predominantly other moderate-sized firms. Almost half of the Como firms which subcontracted out also used skilled (self-employed) craftworkers, about double the proportion in Leicester and Lyon. In contrast, half of the Leicester firms which subcontracted out used homeworkers, that is people with few specialized skills. As regards the nature of the workforce employed within the firm, skilled staff formed the majority in about two thirds of the (generally smaller) firms in Leicester and Como, compared with under half of the Lyon firms. Thus there is an association between high capitalization and greater use of unskilled staff in Lyon firms which is not observed in Como to the same extent (the implications of which we address in Chapter 4). Moreover, the patterns of contracting in the three localities are evidently related to other aspects of industrial structuring and specialization, to which we return later.

3.5 REVIEW OF INITIAL FINDINGS

Direct comparisons among the three local industrial communities must be made cautiously. Each community has a distinctive heritage and historical path of development up to the present time, evidenced in terms of skills, products and industrial processes.

Of the three localities, Lyon is home to the longest-established and generally the largest of the small firms we surveyed. An evident consequence of greater age is that comparatively few of the Lyon firms are still managed by their founders. Most are now in the hands of second- or even third generation family members. Though still privately owned, they are being run as organized, mature businesses. Many of the Lyon firms in our research appeared to be responsible for co-ordinating the work of other firms in the value chain (or *filière*), as well as enjoying a broad spread of customers, nationally and internationally. Although comparatively small in absolute terms (the median sales value of the sample was £4.8 million equivalent, median staff level of 84 people), they can be described as having secured entrenched, quality-driven positions, based on established reputations and a purview extending well beyond the Rhône-Alpes region.

The Como firms in our sample present a different case. While there is a long tradition of local silk manufacture, four in five firms in our sample were formed since 1960; thus they demonstrate clearly the postwar industrialization of the region, corroborating similar findings by other researchers. Our sense is of a vibrant and generally self-confident local industrial economy. We noted high capital investment in productive equipment relative to the size of the firm, whether size is measured by sales or employee headcount. In other words, the typical Como firm has become extremely productive. The family has also remained an important influence on the proprietor, but this has not led to large and potentially unwieldy organizations. Moreover, despite what we believe to be a well-developed sense of local community, Como firms in our study were not parochial. On the contrary, almost half of them claimed to export at least a quarter of their output, the highest proportion of the three localities.

In line with Porter (1990), who attributed much success of Italian small firm communities to cut-throat internal competition, our findings show that Como proprietors on balance were more likely to adopt short-term and opportunist competitive postures than their counterparts elsewhere. Thus despite (or because of) the success of Como firms in recent years, the community of firms in and around Como is not immune from competitive pressures. Yet, as we shall argue in more detail in Chapters 6 and 7, the locality can also be supportive of divisions of labour into specialisms which, in turn, have spawned a wide number of subcontractor firms. As regards external threats, there is currently much debate in the local community as to the optimum future responses that firms should make, individually or collectively.

Turning to Leicester, we observed another quite different set of circumstances. Leicester has a proportion of long-established small firms, as does Lyon; but like Como, it has spawned a great number of new firms in the post-1960 era. Two-thirds of the firms in our Leicester sample are in this category, with almost half of these formed after 1980. None the less, over the past decade or so Leicester has not been a thriving textiles and clothing community and, in some respects, it is surprising that so many new firms were formed. Many of the newer firms appeared to be run by people who may reasonably be termed 'forced entrepreneurs', following a new career after working in bigger firms. Many of their firms were small, even by the standards of the sector (median sales turnover of the sample was £1 million, median headcount 50 staff). The phenomenon of 'phoenixism', discussed in Chapter 6, may also be partly responsible for the small size of some firms.

Another difference is that Leicester firms were markedly less likely to export, below 10% exporting a quarter or more of their output. On the plus side, it could be argued that this is the result of concentrating their efforts on meeting the needs of important UK customers, and indeed Leicester firms were also the most likely to report regular contracts from domestic clients. But it is self-evident that a strategy which creates dependence on a limited number of customers with strong bargaining power could be detrimental to the development of constructive relationships with others. This is demonstrated by the fact that over four in ten Leicester firms derived more than 30% of their sales revenue from their single biggest customer.

Some 30% of Leicester firms claimed not to engage in any form of subcontracting – inwards or outwards – with other firms in the locality. The strategy of non-contracting is seen to be associated with other forms of autonomy. On the positive side, this included selling products under their own house name. On the less positive side, arguably, it included minimal dependence on help from the proprietor's family. The non-contractor firms appeared to be quite successful, so we observe only that a strategy of high autonomy implies that operating the firm in Leicester is probably perceived by the proprietor largely as a matter of convenience, not as an opportunity to exploit the skills and resources of other local firms. Of more cogent concern was the generally low level of capitalization of Leicester firms in our sample. By the standards of the typical Como firm, the typical Leicester firm was exceedingly marginal in terms of capital support for the business, even after making due allowance for differences in the technologies applied. For the simple fact is that Como firms of a similar age have invested heavily, and in so doing appear to have made productivity enhancement a valuable source of competitive advantage.

3.6 CONCLUSIONS

In this chapter we have explored some characteristics of small firms. We began with a brief description of the way that small firms have been viewed in developed Western economies in recent decades, in particular in the three countries chosen for our study. We concluded that, albeit for differing reasons, small firms have been a significant factor in each of these economies and, as far as one can presently judge, they will as a category hold or even possibly increase their share of some sectors, notably services, in the foreseeable future. However, in relatively traditional and possibly declining manufacturing sectors of a developed economy, even if small firms hold or somewhat increase share, they could still experience declining absolute output and levels of employment, which must be a source of concern. The textiles and clothing sectors are unquestionably under threat from low-cost imports from NICs and other emerging nations.

Turning to the subjects of our study, our initial findings make it clear that we are dealing with three distinct localities of small firms whose individual characteristics deserve, and will receive, further elaboration. All three localities have a variety of successful small firms – and these small firms and their proprietors presumably have quite a lot in common, as theory and extant research would suggest. Yet beyond the recipes for the success of individual firms, we must also consider the effects of the context(s) in which they operate on their individual and collective development.

All in all, we think it is a plausible hypothesis that, given an appropriate operating context, small firms have the potential to fulfil a crucial role in the future survival of mature sectors in developed countries. How (or indeed whether) they can continue to do so will form recurrent themes in subsequent chapters.

4

Entrepreneurship
in the firm

4.1 INTRODUCTION

In this chapter we address the nature of **entrepreneurship** in small firms and implications for the management of small firm development. We focus specifically on aspects of entrepreneurship within the firm, including proprietors' characteristics, behaviour (style of managing) and outlook. We use ideas from past research to help make sense of our own findings. Then in Chapter 5 we consider the proposition that entrepreneurship is in fact a social process, broadening the discussion to take account of the effects on proprietors and their firms of operating in a specific context defined by the particular characteristics of the locality, the industry sector and the milieu in which it operates.

4.2 THE SHAPING OF ENTREPRENEURIAL BEHAVIOUR

4.2.1 Entrepreneurship: some conceptual issues

Individual entrepreneurial behaviour has been hypothesized to be shaped by the joint effects of personal traits and environmental conditioning. Several key points emerge from various studies of entrepreneurial characteristics. Traits of personality have an important bearing on entrepreneurial outlook and motivations (Morse, 1977; Chell, 1985, 1986). For example, the classic portrayal of entrepreneurs suggests that typically they have a high 'need for achievement', they are innovative, oriented to action and change, and above all, they value autonomy and independence. However, the latter traits are themselves to some degree culturally bound. As Stanworth and Curran (1976) have commented of the British and US contexts, 'there is a strong cultural bias favouring individualism, and this finds expression in many ways. Economic individualism... founding and operating a business of one's own, is one of the most legitimate of all culturally prescribed forms of individualism.'

A significant driving force presumed to lie behind the formation of many new firms is the fact that founders become frustrated by inertia and bureaucracy in large firm environments – real or perceived – causing them to pursue their own paths. Yet although new firm formation may be thought to define classic entrepreneurship, the latter implies more than founding and running a successful small firm. It also requires continuing innovating and championing behaviour, often involving novel and risky ventures.

Such behaviour is important, of course, in big firms too. Indeed, Norburn (1989) argued that the entrepreneurial qualities of chief executives in large British firms are what sets these leaders apart from their senior subordinates. In fact theories of entrepreneurship dovetail with theories of leadership, particularly in relation to managing small groups (Schein, 1983; Vroom and Yetton, 1973; Zaleznik, 1977). The phenomenon of **intrapreneurship** (explicit entrepreneurial behaviour in big firms: Burgelman, 1983) is now widely thought to be worth encouraging. If this trend continues, it may affect the long-run supply of independent entrepreneurs. For if people find an outlet for their entrepreneurial instincts within employment, they will presumably be less motivated to start their own firms.

But in any event, it would be wrong to suppose that the classic 'thrusting entrepreneur' model is universally applicable or accepted. Even where it might be thought clearly to apply, for instance, to the famous entrepreneurial 'founding fathers' of the Industrial Revolution, such entrepreneurs were generally motivated by more than a desire for personal gratification. More generally, as Hofstede (1980) has shown, national cultures and outlooks vary in broadly systematic ways, so it would seem plausible to suppose that such variations will affect the nature of entrepreneurial behaviour in different localities. A similar conclusion was reached by Swords-Isherwood (1980) when he looked at differences between UK and European managers.

Stanworth and Curran (1976) argued that many entrepreneurs are, in a sense, social misfits or as they expressed it, 'socially **marginalized**'. Research shows that many hail from a minority or otherwise disadvantaged community, have only modest educational achievements and often retain feelings of being socially disadvantaged in one way or other. In this respect, their frustration with the 'establishment' may reflect not so much unfulfilled talents as an inability (or lack of opportunity) to 'play the system' to their own advantage.

Historically, most business entrepreneurs have been male, though this is slowly changing: Carland and Carland (1991), for example, reported on a recent US study of 457 small business proprietors, 30% of whom were women. Welsch and Young (1984) and the Carlands suggested that although it makes sense to talk of an 'entrepreneurial personality', by-and-large gender is not a significant factor determining entrepreneurial behaviour *per se*. On the other hand, gender may, via life conditioning experiences, differentially affect the propensity of the sexes to become entrepreneurs (Cromie, 1987; Watkins and Watkins, 1984). Moreover, in attempting a 'start-up' women still face considerable problems of discrimination, according to Clutterbuck and Devine (1985). Thus for the present the question of whether entrepreneurship has significant gender-based antecedents remains unresolved.

What has become generally accepted, however, is that irrespective of gender, the entrepreneurial situation has its less attractive aspects. Anecdote and research suggest that small firm entrepreneurs are highly involved and stressed (Williams, 1985). Ideally they should be tolerant of risk and ambiguity. In practice, family relationships often suffer because the entrepreneur commits much time and personal energy to the business (Gibb and Scott, 1986; Milne and Thompson, 1986; Ponson, 1985; Scase and Goffee, 1980). It can also be lonely: the archetypal or classic Anglo-American entrepreneur appears to enjoy relatively few sources of advice and help, the reverse side of the trait of self-reliance. Where professional advice is to hand, the entrepreneur may be innately suspicious of it, or take the view that it is beyond the financial means of the firm.

As already hinted, a consistent European finding is that, contrary to the classic model (or perhaps myth), financial rewards and business growth ambitions are rarely such important motivators as personal fulfilment (Cromie and Ayling, 1989). Indeed, where direct comparisons of entrepreneurial behaviour of people with differing geographic, sociocultural and economic backgrounds have been made (e.g. Hitchens and O'Farrell, 1987; Ward, Randall and Kremar, 1986; Wilson and Stanworth, 1987), it has been found that many factors impinge on the development of entrepreneurial behaviour.

With this comment in mind, we may now present findings about the backgrounds and characteristics of the proprietors in our study, before considering more systematically the emergence of patterns in entrepreneurial behaviour relating to the management of small firms.

4.2.2 Personal backgrounds of the proprietors in this study

Our study was directed at the proprietor or chief executive of the small firm, and with only a few exceptions it was that person who responded to our request for information. The following analysis, in which we report on various characteristics of our respondents including their background, out-look and role in the firm, is therefore based on proprietors' own responses.

Almost all the proprietors were male: though textiles and clothing hold considerable interest for many women, only three in each of our Leicester and Como samples, and none in the Lyon sample, had professionally extended that interest. It is possible, however, that the partners of many proprietors actively participate in the firms.

All respondents were host country nationals, though 12% of the Leicester sample were born outside the UK. Whereas 87% of the French sample and 93% of the Italians hailed from their regions (Rhône-Alpes and Lombardy respectively), only 57% of the British proprietors recorded Leicester (city or county) as place of birth; most of the others merely stated 'UK', rather than naming a place. These data could suggest that geographic mobility is lower for the Lyon and Como proprietors than for their Leicester counterparts. Equally, it is possible that many Leicester respondents hail from the Midlands region, if this is defined geographically as being of a size comparable with the aforementioned French and Italian administrative regions. Moreover, there is a strongly implied personal or pragmatic affinity with each locality, given that: (i) nine out of ten proprietors in each sample had lived in their respective locality for at least ten years, and (ii) few said they would willingly relocate their firms outside the area.

Table 4.1 Age profile of proprietors

	Lyon	Como	Leicester
% of proprietors aged:			
Under 30 years	0	0	4
30–39	22	14	15
40–49	20	25	28
50–59	41	39	37
60+	17	22	16
Total	100	100	100

Of Lyon proprietors, 60% had some form of post-school higher education (i.e. a university degree or professional qualification), compared with 46% of Leicester proprietors and only 26% of those in Como. Overall, under a quarter of respondents were less than 40 years of age. The age distributions of respondents are shown in Table 4.1. In each sample the median age was between 50 and 59 years, the UK sample being rather younger than the others, in line with the relative youth of the UK firms. However, given that a much bigger proportion of the Leicester firms were formed after 1970 than elsewhere, it is perhaps surprising that their proprietors are not significantly younger than we actually observed.

It turns out that each of the three groups presents a substantially different personal profile. Based on those proprietors for whom we have the data (ranging from 89% to 94%, according to sample), only 20% of the Lyon proprietors had been directly involved in founding their firm, compared with 68% and 78% respectively in Como and Leicester (see Table 4.2). Most non-founders in each sample had inherited the business. From replies to other questions it transpired that many of the French executives joined the family firm soon after completing their education. In fact only 19% of them claimed to have had work experience in other small firms beforehand and even less, i.e. 7%, had previously worked elsewhere in the industry. These figures contrast sharply with the Italian and British groups, where over six in ten were founders of the firm. Moreover, 30% of the Italian and 40% of the British groups had gained prior work experience in other small firms. Around half the proprietors from Como and two-thirds from Leicester had previously worked in the textiles and clothing industry.

Table 4.2 Status of proprietors

	Lyon	Como	Leicester
% of proprietors who are:			
Founder	20	68	78
Inheritor	65	27	17
Purchaser	15	5	5
Total	100	100	100

Note: Excludes 'no replies' (under 12% in each sample).

It is also instructive to consider the founder proprietors in Como and Leicester as a separate subset. The median age of the founder when the firm was started was 31 years in Como compared with 35 years in Leicester. This has several implications: because the typical Como founder proprietor had received fewer years' schooling and higher education than his Leicester counterpart, both groups of founders had had a similar number of years' work experience (a norm of approx. 14–16 years) prior to setting up their firms. Thus the typical Como founder was (when compared age for age with his Leicester counterpart) the proprietor of a longer-established and more valuable business. Self-evidently, because he started younger he had also gained somewhat more managerial experience of running his own firm than his typical Leicester counterpart.

The typical Como proprietor had gained experience in similar small firms before branching out on his own. We speculate that setting up his own firm has generally been perceived as a logical career move predicated on local role models, whereas in Leicester the evidence is consistent with the typical entrepreneur founding his own firm in early middle life, as an opportunistic response either to the frustrations of organizational life in big firms or to redundancy. In contrast, the typical Lyon proprietor in our sample – being a second or later generation descendant of the founder – had moved deliberately into the family firm at an early stage in his career. This conclusion is evidently consistent with the greater age of the French firms.

4.2.3 The influence of family context

More than three in every four of all the proprietors in each sample were in control of the firm by virtue of having a dominant equity stake, albeit sometimes shared with other family members. Thus we may note the continuing influence of the family, even though some firms are now sizeable businesses. Influences beyond the immediate family were also detected – directly in terms of personal assistance and financial help from relatives, and indirectly in terms of shared value systems and role models.

We attempted to assess the involvement of the 'extended family', for example, whether relatives contributed to the firm or ran other small firms of their own, and whether proprietors preferred to employ other family members where possible (Table 4.3). Our interpretation is that in Lyon firms the immediate family appears to be influential by maintaining a tradition of support for the privately owned small business. In a sense, these families have created 'business dynasties'.

Table 4.3 Family support for entrepreneurship

	Lyon	Como	Leicester
% of proprietors saying:			
Relatives provide practical help in my business	12	45	14
Relatives run their own firms	23	25	16
I prefer to employ family members (a little/a lot)	39	36	17

Yet while these French families have had an important role in transmitting capital down the generations, relatives in the immediate family do not appear to be specially active in helping to run the business, though they may run other firms of their own. Of course, in Lyon (and Leicester) firms' practical, day-to-day involvement of family members may simply go unnoticed for much of the time. In Como, by contrast, there appears to exist a local entrepreneurial culture within which it is taken for granted that the laterally extended family of relatives will offer a proprietor technical and administrative help 'on the shopfloor', as needed. Yet it seems that relatives of the proprietor are no less likely to run their own firms, and indeed may be encouraged to do so. Conversely, the family connection appears to be least significant in offering help and support to Leicester proprietors.

Equally, because of the limited financial strength of many of their firms, proprietors may feel that they have little scope to offer permanent employment to family members.

Certainly the Leicester proprietors were markedly less concerned to employ family members than were the others. That said, loyalty to the family by way of providing employment has also to be tempered with a realistic assessment of the expertise offered by family members. When hiring new staff, a large majority of all proprietors claimed to respect formal qualifications: four out of five from Leicester, and nine out of ten elsewhere, claimed to take at least some account of qualifications. Indeed, 73% of the French and 66% of Italians, though only 46% of British, claimed that qualifications were a very important factor in hiring decisions. Logically this suggests that the Latin cohorts have no problem in employing relatives, provided that they are appropriately qualified, whereas the British are possibly more inclined to value relevant prior experience over either family membership or formal training. So it seems fair to conclude that the Leicester proprietors, enjoying less family support than elsewhere, are necessarily more independent and self-reliant in their approach to business than are their Lyon and Como counterparts.

This leads us back to the more general issue of role identities assumed by small firm proprietors.

4.3   PATTERNS IN SMALL FIRM ENTREPRENEURSHIP

4.3.1   Commonly observed role identities

It has long been argued that patterns exist in the background and experience of entrepreneurs. On the evidence of much research, including the seminal work of Smith (1967), Stanworth and Curran (1976, 1986) have argued that 'three...latent identities occur with some frequency in relation to the role of the small firm entrepreneur'. We present these three identities below, together with a more recent identity proposed by Lafuente and Salas (1989); they are:

(i)   the artisan identity;
(ii) the classic entrepreneur identity;
(iii) the professional manager identity;
(iv) the family-oriented entrepreneur identity.

The **artisanal entrepreneur** is likely to have craft-based skills and lack formal education, business-related or otherwise. He tends to be product and production orientated, rather than market or growth oriented, and his business will be competence-driven. This identity emphasizes intrinsic satisfactions, notably personal autonomy, freedom to select one's colleagues and to determine the nature and quality of one's products and services.

Income, *per se*, is secondary to other forms of gratification. Perhaps because the artisan is not unduly concerned with growth and financial affairs, business survival is frequently problematic. As already noted, the artisan may perceive himself to be socially marginalized and the *raison d'être* of the firm may contain intrinsic contradictions from the proprietor's perspective. Thus, for example, Stanworth and Curran (1986) argued that the artisan may come to perceive sustained growth not as a solution to this perceived social marginality, but a factor likely to reinforce it. For growth usually creates the need for more formality and structure in the firm, to the point where proprietors were 'beginning to feel like employees in their own firm'.

The **artisan** is similar to Smith's (1967) craftsman-entrepreneur, who tended to have a working class background and a limited, technically orientated education, and to be something of a 'loner'. He too was likely to believe that product quality should override mere profit considerations, and be rather autocratic and paternalistic towards staff. His desire for autonomy made him equally suspicious of trade unions and outside sources of capital. The firm's success tended to be based on excellent quality and delivery, and to be strongly associated with the personal contribution and credibility of the craftsman in the eyes of his customers. Finally, he tended to adopt a short term outlook and have little regard for planning.

In today's technologically advanced societies the artisan category presumably includes highly skilled people without commercial experience or acumen who nevertheless found their own science-based firms, often with commercial support from an outside organization such as a bank or the management team in charge of a science and technology park. Despite their qualifications and support structures, the evidence is that a lack of commercial awareness allied to unrealistic ambitions is a recipe for major difficulties for small firm proprietors operating in high technology sectors, as elsewhere.

The **classic entrepreneur** archetype resembles the classical economists' view of entrepreneurship. He is not necessarily better qualified than the artisan in a formal sense, but he has an overtly commercial outlook which means he is market- and opportunity-driven. He tends to be less directly involved in the firm's value-adding processes, and more willing to hire and to delegate to other staff with relevant competences. His own contribution is largely that of instigating and co-ordinating. The firm is likely to grow faster and go further than that of the artisan because increasing its size and earning potential are significant motivators for such an individual. He is also likely to be outward looking and innovative, either technically or commercially (Carland, Hoy, Boulton and Carland *et al.*, 1984).

Unlike the artisanal small-firm owner, the **classic entrepreneur** is impatient to break free from the constraints imposed by small firm status, if necessary seeking external finance, even though this dilutes his personal control to a significant extent. Smith's (1967) 'opportunist-entrepreneur' shared many of the above characteristics, was relatively well-educated and socially integrated. Entrepreneurial status was quite likely to be part of a deliberate career plan.

Stanworth and Curran (1986) posited a third type, the **professional manager entrepreneur**, a second- or third-generation small firm owner who construes his major business challenge as being to identify and promote new initiatives if the firm is to grow beyond its founding possibilities. This entrepreneur is also likely to be well-educated and conscious of the custodian aspects of his role; and being an effective administrator is likely to be a high priority. He is especially concerned to acquire managerial status, meaning notably that his capabilities are recognized by colleagues and peers in the business community.

These three types have been generally well supported by the literature. However, one should be mindful that these identity types are based principally on what one might term an Anglo-Saxon cultural and business heritage. In a study of Spanish entrepreneurs, Lafuente and Salas (1989) identified four types, three of which conformed broadly to those outlined above. However, they proposed a fourth type, which has some immediate relevance to our own study, namely the **family-oriented entrepreneur**. This type is intermediate in identity between the artisan/craftsman and the classic (risk-taking) entrepreneur. He is characterized by modest educational achievements and a strong concern for family welfare. It is, for example, very likely that family priorities are taken into account in the formation and subsequent development of business activities. Though it is not made entirely clear from the reference, it seems probable that the family-oriented entrepreneur will take heed of advice from and actively involve other family members in the firm.

Contrary to previous findings, Lafuente and Salas' study did not provide strong support for the view that the type of entrepreneurial identity has a substantial effect on the size of the resulting firm. Though the family-oriented entrepreneur identity has so far found less corroboration in the English-language journals than others, we suggest that it should nevertheless be considered as a significant type, not simply as a hybrid form. An 'identity' of this type may well prove useful in describing and explaining much entrepreneurial behaviour in Italy, perhaps in France too. For convenience, some of the major characteristics of the four types are summarized in Figure 4.1.

That said, all of the above are ideal or archetypal characterizations. Most small firm proprietors probably have hybrid identities. It can be argued that underpinning their various true identities are a number of dualistic **tensions** having considerable potential for characterizing individuals. These dualities would for example include: (i) inwardness as opposed to out-wardness of outlook; (ii) bias towards growth (and concomitant tolerance of risk taking) vs a preference for stability and the status quo; (iii) preference for intrinsic fulfilment vs material rewards; (iv) independence of thought

Table 4.4 Indicators of entrepreneurial role identity

| Characteristic | Identity type: | | | |
	Type I (artisan)	Type II (classic e/p)	Type III manager	Type IV (family e/p)
Educational achievements	Modest	Good	Fair/good	Modest
Qualifications	Craft	Craft or commercial	Commercial/ professional	Craft
Prior work experience	Similar/ craft - based	No pattern/ none	Little or none	As Type I/ supervisory
Reason for proprietorial status*	Desire to do better/loss of job	Exploit a perceived opportunity	Inheritance/ professional training	Security/ desire to do better
Basic values	Skill/quality integrity	Growth/ opportunism	Professionalism	Family well-being/quality
Attitude to growth/risk innovation	Conservative	Tolerant of change/risk	Positive, but conscious of custodianship	Conservative
Principal reward sought	Intrinsic (quality)	Material	Peer-group esteem	Security for family
Outlook beyond the firm	Limited to valued trade contracts	Extensive trade network	Extensive trade and professional	Trade contracts. Other: limited, beyond family
Independence vs interdependence	Self-reliant	Reliant on self/others	Reliant on self/others	Reliant on the extended family
Involvement in operations	High	Moderate	Low	Moderate/high
Delegation/ to staff	Limited	To trusted subordinates	To hired specialists	To family members
Attitude to staff	Autocratic or paternalistic	Trusting but 'hard-nosed'	Manager to subordinates	Paternalistic
Time horizon	Short-term/ but patient	Short-term impatient	Medium-term/ impatient	Medium/long term/patient
Typical style of planning	*Ad hoc/* limited	Informal/ adaptive	Formal/ systematic	Informal/ family-focused

Sources: Various; adapted principally from Stanworth and Curran, 1976, 1986, and Lafuente and Sales, 1989.
*Exploiting a perceived opportunity is to some degree obviously a motivating factor for all types.

and action (meaning, in practice, a tendency to self-reliance or even isolation) vs interdependence (networking or relationship-forming behaviour); (v) personal involvement in day-to-day activities, as opposed to delegating and coordinating and (vi) a planning bias (implying a medium-to long-term outlook) vs an opportunistic bias (implying a reactive, short-term outlook). Such factors presumably relate to implicit human values (normative beliefs) about appropriate behaviour in context, deriving from personal traits, predispositions and life conditioning, (re)interpreted in the small firm situation in which they locate themselves.

A relevant question is to ask to what extent these entrepreneurial identities are stable over time. Do individuals progress from one identity to another? Mintzberg (1973) offered a set of managerial process types which mirror the entrepreneur types. In his terms these were: (i) entrepreneurial ('great man' theory: entrepreneurship-as-heroic-feats); (ii) adaptive (drawing on the heuristic models of Cyert and March, 1963, and Lindblom, 1959; and (iii) planning (after Ackoff's, 1970, 'planning-as-anticipatory-decision-making'). Mintzberg's argument was that as firms grow there is a tendency for them to professionalize and to move from an opportunistic or adaptive style to a planned style. Yet he did not suggest that such a move was inevitable, and he affirmed a belief in mixed or hybrid processes.

> Stanworth and Curran (1976) claimed that: a small firm which survives the formative (i.e. artisanal) period and enters a period of sustained profitability constitutes a context conducive to the adoption of a classical entrepreneur identity. The goals associated with the artisan identity will have been at least partially realised and the new... situation of the firm is favourable to the possible emergence of a new self-definition for the entrepreneur.

Yet they remained sceptical whether the transition occurred frequently, because it required the artisan to reject so many of the assumptions underpinning the firm's foundation and growth, as well as his own role. While identity changes cannot be wholly discounted as entrepreneurs learn and mature, it seems more plausible that personal qualities will tend to promote continuity in adult behaviour. The major practical implication for this study is that we should accept the likelihood that observed entrepreneur types in each locality will be comparatively stable rather than transient.

To recapitulate, much prior research suggests that the behaviour patterns of small firm entrepreneurs are the outcome of personal traits and choices, yet influenced by whatever general or particular conditioning effects they have experienced in the social and economic contexts where they have grown up and later founded their firms. These influences include social and cultural milieu, including the family. Other effects include the individual's education and training experiences which have led to a particular set of skills and the professional 'identity' associated with them.

Despite a seemingly infinite variety of potential traits and influences, their description in terms of a limited number of role identities has seemed useful to many researchers when exploring entrepreneurial behaviour in small firms. We are no exception; thus we now consider the nature of entrepreneurship among the small firm proprietors in our three localities in these same terms.

4.3.2 Role identities of proprietors in this study

The following commentary (based on both questionnaire responses and personal contacts with proprietors) is offered in order to suggest that although some examples of all the named entrepreneurial role identities are probably to be found in each locality, broadly systematic differences exist among the three samples. In other words, the typical entrepreneur tends to view his firm and manage it somewhat differently, according to locality. In saying this there is clearly a risk of overemphasizing differences: for instance, it goes almost without saying that the boss of a small firm is necessarily much involved in everything to do with it. On this score, the proprietors in our study have much in common: two-thirds or so in each sample claimed direct involvement in the firm's production or other value-creating activities, for example. Most had a strong commitment to the firm as evidenced by their spending a lot of personal time on the firm's interests outside normal working hours (81% of Lyon proprietors, 86% in Como and 71% in Leicester). Yet when we consider the organizational roles they adopt, we do see differences.

Referring again to the entrepreneurial role identities in Table 4.4, our contention is that relatively few of the respondents in any of the localities are classic entrepreneur types. One basis for this conclusion relates to the growth ambitions and achievements of these proprietors. In response to the statement 'I have no desire to make the firm a lot bigger than it is now', 48% of Leicester proprietors and 58% of Como proprietors agreed with it. In contrast only 14% of the Lyon sample agreed. Moreover, in answer to the

Table 4.5 Reported growth profile of the firms

	Lyon	Como	Leicester
% of proprietors reporting:			
Rapid growth	24	35	11
Moderate growth	47	44	53
Relative stability	22	16	12
Relative decline	7	5	24
Totals	100	100	100

question 'Which best describes the firm's progress over recent times?', only a third of Como proprietors and a quarter of Lyon proprietors reported achieving rapid growth, less still in the Leicester firms, despite their comparative youth (Table 4.5). On balance, the Leicester proprietors were almost as likely to report stability or relative decline as growth. So the motivation and ability to grow is by no means universal among these proprietors.

None the less, size can be construed in a variety of ways, and as we recorded in the previous chapter (see Table 3.3), some of the Lyon and Como firms have achieved a substantial size, particularly as measured by sales turnover and investment in productive assets. The measure of growth on which Leicester proprietors have apparently performed best is employee headcount, though this achievement must be interpreted cautiously, given that knitted garment production is labour intensive.

It is clear that for most of these firms growth has been steady, rather than explosive and that while some proprietors remain growth orientated, many have more modest ambitions. For the most part, growth has been built on current and well understood opportunities, not by pioneering new markets or 'breakthrough' technologies, for instance. Thus, on the growth criterion we conclude that although many entrepreneurs in Leicester and Como founded their own firms, the evidence that they are market and opportunity orientated founders in the 'classic' North American mould (or myth) is slight.

Though the same conclusion applies to the French proprietors, they clearly constitute a different kind of group again. As indicated, most were second or later generation proprietors. A majority had received formal higher education and training and entered the firm more or less directly upon completion of their education. In a number of respects, they were evidently more 'executive-minded' than their counterparts elsewhere and were more likely to claim to identify with a professional co-ordinating role.

One measure of this was their willingness to delegate to functional specialist managers employed in marketing, finance, production, and so on. More than two-thirds of Lyon respondents employed at least three such specialists (Table 4.6), in marked contrast to the other localities. They were also markedly more likely to use outside market research (36% of firms vs about 20% in Como and Leicester). Thus we are happy to conclude that the best description of the identity of the typical French proprietor in our sample is indeed professional manager. This is corroborated by other facts. First, that 88% of them belong to at least one business-related association. Secondly, that only in Lyon did more proprietors perceive a long term and trusting business atmosphere in the locality, and by inference a planning as opposed to a purely opportunistic orientation on the part of local executives generally.

Table 4.6   Use of specialist managers

	Lyon	Como	Leicester
% of proprietors who employ:			
No specialists	9	34	41
1 – 2 specialists	22	41	24
3+ specialists	69	25	35
Total	100	100	100
% of proprietors who employ *specialists in:*			
Production	80	53	38
Selling/marketing	71	53	45
Design	78	43	40
Exporting	56	30	19
Technical	38	43	22
All other	13	0	10

Turning again to the Leicester proprietors, many of these had worked in the industry for some considerable time before going solo, so that they had accumulated a good deal of technical knowledge relevant to the running of a successful clothing business. They were also likely to apply that knowledge by participating directly in the firm's operations, as evidenced by the substantial proportion (41%) who employed no specialist managers in the firm (Table 4.6). Where they did use a specialist, it was often in selling (45% of cases), suggesting that many proprietors prefer to concentrate their efforts inside the firm.

However, we know from other questions that external trade contacts were important to all three groups, with over 80% claiming to meet customers and suppliers regularly in person. Given also a tendency for Leicester proprietors towards self reliance and comparative independence (i.e. little desire to collaborate systematically with other local firms), coupled with perceptions of short-termism, it seems fair to conclude that many of them have outlooks consistent with the artisan identity. We speculate that many had drifted or evolved into small firm ownership rather than realizing a burning, long-run ambition to head their own 'empire' and become wealthy entrepreneurs in the 'classic' fashion. For those Leicester proprietors who did not conform to the artisan identity, the best description appears to be that of 'professional manager', though as we have noted, few were second-generation managers, as in Lyon.

In a number of respects, similar comments apply to many of the Como proprietors who had typically been engaged in the industry all their working lives. They appeared to know its ways and activities inside-out. They were likely to be actively engaged in the production and design processes; three-quarters of them employed no more than two specialist managers, and indeed a third employed none. Bearing in mind the tendency for the Italian firms to specialize more intensively, coupled with their comparatively small number of employees, our conclusion is that the Como proprietors often personally contributed the critical knowledge resources and competences on which the firm depended and thrived. If so, there would seem a clear artisanal component to the identities of many of these proprietors. Yet the decision to found a new firm was generally implemented after years of work experience in the locality. So it can be argued that new firm formation in Como has often been a matter of identifying and filling particular niches, based on technical and other kinds of competence.

Finally, there was the issue of (extended) family. Referring back to Table 3.1, ownership of these (virtually all) private firms was principally shared among family members. In the one-in-four cases where it extended beyond the immediate family, our inquiries suggest it remained in the hands of people well known to the family. Consistent with this observation, Table 4.3 also reminds us that Como proprietors (like those in Lyon) frequently have relatives who are also proprietors of their own small firms. Thus the immediate and extended family within the locality feature significantly in the thinking of the typical Como proprietor. For these reasons, we argue that most of them are well characterized either as artisans or family entrepreneurs. On the other hand, as in Lyon and Leicester, some undoubtedly conform more closely to the professional manager identity.

Having said that, one respect in which the theoretical archetypes may be wanting is in regard to innovation. The classic entrepreneur is often portrayed as innovative and adaptive. Such types are supposedly able to recognize and exploit the commercial potential of innovations, whether their own or from others. The professional manager identity manifests and requires less personal innovativeness, though the use of specialist subordinates may still enable institutionalized innovation. As for the artisan, his personal values are orientated more to craft-related concerns of continuity, integrity and security, quite possibly implying less regard for innovation.

The evidence from the small firms in this book is that when an innovation involving the firm has occurred, it is fairly likely to be stimulated by the firm itself (and in many instances, given the modest size of the firms, to involve the proprietor himself). Table 4.7 shows the extent of recent autonomous innovation claimed by proprietors in respect of product designs and technical process innovations. Of the three groups Como firms were most likely to have innovated autonomously in product designs and Lyon firms in technical innovations. But in each of the three cases, a third to a half of all proprietors felt able to claim that their firms had innovated recently.

Table 4.7 Sources of autonomous innovation by the firm

	Lyon	Como	Leicester
% of proprietors claiming a recent autonomous innovation in the area of:			
Product design	36	54	30
Technical (process) innovation	53	44	38

When one asked about the nature of changes that proprietors have made to enhance the viability and competitiveness of their firms, a broad spread emerged. Table 4.8 documents the most significant of these, the percentages expressing the balance of affirmative responses over negative ones. Thus it can be seen that clear majorities of proprietors claim to have improved product quality and variety, equipment standards and flexibility to customers' needs. In Como and Lyon there has also been a pattern of increasing the number of regular customers.

Table 4.8 Changes affecting competitiveness of firms in recent years

	Lyon	Como	Leicester
% of firms with:*			
Improved standard of equipment	73	71	64
Improved quality of output	68	64	66
Increased product variety	59	68	82
Improved flexibility to customers	62	47	73
More regular customers	35	36	21
Faster delivery times	50	45	55

* The percentages express the excess of affirmative responses over negative ones.

Of course, innovation by the firm depends on the presence in the firm of innovators. It is plausible that the presence of specialists is linked with internal innovation, especially in design and production. Around eight in ten of the Lyon firms have design and production specialists (Table 4.6). In the Como firms the percentages are lower (between four and five in ten), which may reflect the more direct contribution of Como proprietors to the process. The Leicester proprietors made quite limited use of specialists in design and production, around four cases in every ten.

All in all, from the evidence of these firms we feel that there is reasonable justification for concluding that the conceptual typology of entrepreneurs understates the priority that small firm proprietors attach, in general, to the need for innovating. Indeed, as we shall argue in Chapter 7, the ability and willingness of a small firm proprietor to innovate must be considered in terms that go beyond the individual business unit.

4.4 MANAGING SMALL FIRM DEVELOPMENT

We now move from a consideration of the entrepreneurial identity of individuals to a discussion of the processes of managing the development of small firms. In particular, we touch on the problems of managing growth and the various stages of transition as the firm expands and matures. We then offer findings germane to these issues as they affect proprietors in this study.

4.4.1 Practical problems of managing small firm growth

One can liken the post-formative period of the small firm's development to a journey. Drawing on Boswell (1973), Fourcade (1984–5) and Stanworth and Curran (1986), the early stages might be termed embarcation and setting a realistic and purposeful direction. Barber, Metcalfe and Porteous (1989), Cromie (1991) and Binks and Coyne (1983) reviewed the many problems of managing young, small firms, especially for growth. Four kinds of managerial difficulty hindered the successful long-run development of firms:

1. Lack of specialist skills and know-how.
2. Continuing inability to access finance and other key resources.
3. Difficulties in understanding, much less controlling, the external environment of the firm, especially its trading links.
4. Internal organization, notably the need to marry an innovative outlook with formal managerial skills.

The entrepreneur needs to develop many skills, or at least recognize personal limitations, thus compensate by seeking external advice and help, and/or recruit specialists as the firm grows. In theory, there are plenty of external sources of support; in practice, small firm proprietors may not know where that help can be found, be too suspicious to ask and unwilling to expend time and effort, or simply be unaware of the need until it is too late. Many are unwilling to share information about the performance of the firm or its future intentions with employees, independent directors or outsiders. They naturally prefer fellow directors to be family members or trusted friends rather than dispassionate professional advisers. This can be an excellent thing: families may provide a supportive and committed environment. But a negative consequence is that proprietors faced with a variety of conflicting value-driven pressures then find it hard to form and implement objective strategies and plans (Bamberger, 1983; Robinson *et al.*, 1984), and to get professional financial advice (Hutchinson and Ray, 1986).

Skills and resources in small firms generally continue in short supply, particularly when the firm is growing fast. The major gaps typically include technological and commercial know-how, facilities, labour and finance. A shortage of cash may preclude hiring or otherwise acquiring specialist skills and investing in capital equipment to increase output and productivity. On the other hand, Rothwell and Zegweld (1982) noted how some small firms can establish themselves as technological innovators. The implication is that shortcomings in commercial strengths and acumen may be mitigated by a firm's technical strengths, provided that it is seen genuinely to specialize (Oakey, 1984).

Cash shortages are one of the most central problems for many small firm proprietors. Despite the many potential sources of finance, it is exceedingly difficult for under-capitalized European entrepreneurs to raise new equity or loan capital on terms they find acceptable (Hall, 1989). Many still feel, rightly or not, that banks invariably prefer to commit funds to low-risk ventures, and often to firms not currently in need of funds. Patently, without adequate capital, all other resources will be undersupplied too.

Self-funding clearly limits achievable rates of growth. Yet we found that reinvesting profits was generally the main source of funds for expansion in all three localities. Virtually all of the Lyon and Leicester proprietors, and three-quarters of those in Como, claimed that this process was somewhat or very important. More specifically, around three-quarters of the former samples and over half of the latter said that reinvesting profits had been very important in achieving growth. Accepting 'soft' loans from family and friends or other sources is an acceptable and comparatively widespread practice in France and Italy, apparently less so in Britain. Many big firms are also sources of working capital for their small trading partners, though others ruthlessly exploit small and weak suppliers.

Continuing to meet a market need usually holds out the prospect of long-run survival. The small firm must try to remain well-matched to the needs of its chosen market. Environmental changes, be they social, economic, technical or regulatory, influence market needs, posing opportunities and threats to which the entrepreneur may (or may not) be sensitive. Business failure could be the result of not changing when change is indicated, or of changing responsively but inappropriately. Further, since many small firms subcontract for big ones, their markets are subject to unilateral policy changes by their customers. These factors suggest the need for small firms to monitor their environments carefully for signs of future threats and opportunities, although McGee (1989) concluded that a lack of resources to face market challenges remained ultimately a more significant challenge to small firm viability than external factors *per se*.

The trading network also forms a significant moderator on the survival prospects of the individual firm. Apart from the trading network, other links to the external environment can variously include banks, consultants, trade unions, universities, technical and trade associations, local and national government agencies, regional associations and industrial development agencies. Managing external links should therefore be a key task. However, it is entirely possible that proprietors with an extremely independent outlook may ignore legitimate opportunities for fruitful collaboration.

4.4.2 Managing organizational transitions

Another relevant kind of analogy with a journey is that of negotiating difficult passages and, more specifically, coping with problematic transitional episodes in the organization of the small firm and its competences, and ultimately in respect of leadership succession.

Founding skills alone are most unlikely to ensure the long-run viability of the emerging firm, even if it remains responsive to external opportunities (Bosworth and Jacobs, 1989). The managerial skills for effective long-run development change significantly in nature and ideally a founder should develop accordingly, but at the same time come to terms with the need to delegate to others and introduce new specialist skills into the firm.

Truly problematic episodes often become construed as crises. In part, this is because their resolution makes demands on entrepreneurs for which they may be temperamentally or practically unprepared (Greiner, 1972; Pitt, 1989, 1990). Not all small firm proprietors will experience such crises, though many do. Some resolve the dilemma when their firms reach a stable plateau, after which they are not motivated to continue the 'journey'. More generally, we can say that transitional phases require appropriate advice, resources, leadership skills and managerial styles. Growth beyond small firm status generally takes at least a decade – probably two – if indeed the firm ever ceases to be small; many in Europe do not. Throughout the process of maturation the status of the small firm remains inextricably linked to the life history of the founder, sometimes even ceasing to trade when he retires or dies. More typically, firms grow via a series of episodes best characterized as relatively incremental development, punctuated by periodic crises or discontinuities (Mintzberg, 1979). The courage of the proprietor to acknowledge and catalyse such 'disturbance events' and then to have the resilience to ride out these storms is a crucial test (Perry, 1986; Pitt, 1989).

The more traumatic transitions evidently include: (i) terminating the proprietor's direct involvement in the value-adding processes of the firm; (ii) delegating responsibilities to specialist managers, who often have to be recruited externally; (iii) implementing a comparatively formal managerial hierarchy; (iv) managing the succession of the founder by a second-generation family member; and/or (v) the admittance of non-family shareholder directors to secure expansion capital, and/or the shift to non-family, professional managers. Each transition is often accompanied by a change in the culture of the firm from a less structured and familial style to one that is more formal and disciplined. Even if the founder remains associated with the firm during several of these transitions, he may come to feel increasingly peripheral to the emerging needs of the organization, accelerating his decision to retire or dispose of his controlling interest.

Managerial succession frequently has an adverse impact on the risk-taking and innovation postures of the firm and hence its development potential. If the management of any transition – but especially succession – is poorly handled, it becomes a significant barrier to future viability and growth (Boswell, 1973), even a factor resulting in organizational demise. Conversely, the ability of a proprietor or his successors to remain responsive to uncertain, but potentially rewarding market possibilities, is an important human factor in enabling continued development. Paradoxically, the more successful the firm is, the sooner and more acutely the proprietor will experience the management difficulties referred to.

4.4.3 Managerial issues in the firms in this study

Salient comparative features of the organizational status of the firms are presented for convenience in Table 4.9. The Lyon firms present the most straightforward picture. Since many of the Lyon proprietors had entered their firms soon after completing their education, and since their median age at the time of the study was in the middle fifties, it seems fair to conclude that in most cases their accession took place quite a long time ago and that problems in its wake have, for the most part, been resolved without traumatic shifts in firms' directions.

In any event, growth continued to be regarded as a necessary and legitimate aim of many firms. In more than nine out of ten cases, they now employed specialist managers, so that a more formal management structure was in place. A further proprietorial succession phase would appear likely in many of these firms within a decade or so, but there seems no overriding reason to suppose that the established organization pattern will be unduly disrupted by this event.

In Como and Leicester the firms were predominantly still run by their founders, who will also face problems of succession within a decade, or two at most. Direct contacts with a number of Leicester proprietors led us to believe that their firms will be more likely to remain private than go public. The successor could be a family member, where an obvious candidate exists. However, we noted considerable pessimism on the part of some Leicester proprietors in respect of future expectations and objectives, and we would expect that some, possibly even a majority of the firms contacted, will ultimately be wound up or sold. Since four in ten Leicester firms were still without specialist managers, the problem of succession will coincide in a significant minority of cases with the need to implement a more formal approach to organizing. In the absence of an established structure, the risks of transition are greater and the net worth of the firm to an outsider much lower. Thus in Leicester there is much work to be done by some of the proprietors if their firms are to secure a viable future that is no longer largely or wholly dependent on the current founder-proprietor.

The Como firms present a different picture again. Specifically, there was a comparatively high incidence of specialist subcontractor firms with proprietors who evidently preferred a 'hands-on' role, also associated with relatively few specialist managers. For if (as in three-quarters of cases) there are only one or two such specialists in an otherwise established firm, the proprietor must still have been personally responsible for at least one major business function. Moreover, these firms are characterized by high assets per employee, but small headcounts.

One consequence of proprietors being actively involved in the business is that there was less possibility for them to adopt a reflective, co-ordinating or professional manager role. Another consequence, we would argue, is that these circumstances ought to act as a real constraint on the capacity of the proprietor to cope with increasing staff numbers in the quest for growth. Failure to delegate means he must personally spend more time on matters of operational, not strategic, importance: time spent doing, not thinking about future developments.

There would appear to be a paradox here. The typical Como firm is successful commercially, yet its proprietor has apparently not yet accepted the role change to a professional manager as has occurred in Lyon. There is no question that measured in terms of sales, assets, age, etc., many of these firms are big enough for this change to have taken place, yet many are persisting, in conjunction with a relatively small headcount, in an artisanal or family entrepreneur role. Arguably, the Como firms could be on the point of transition, since the proprietor can probably still manage 20–25 staff in a personalized way that would simply not be feasible with 80. But has the managerial transition been postponed at the cost of constraining headcount and therefore healthy growth in organization structure and style?

One explanation could be that Como founders have found readjustment too problematic and have not tried; in these cases, the transition will coincide with their retirement in ten years or so. An alternative explanation is that the Como firms have remained small in terms of headcount because their proprietors have a positive determination to retain a hands-on, involved style of managing. Such a choice, conscious or not, will certainly tend to preclude headcount growth, and as we have noted in Chapter 3, in this respect they are actually encouraged by regulations favouring units of under 15 staff. But the corollary is that to increase the level of business activity without growing, the size of the organizational unit has logically required the Como proprietor to opt for greatly increased mechanization or external subcontracting, both of which we actually observed, and which will be considered in more depth in Chapter 6.

Entrepreneurship in the firm

Our earlier finding that 58% of Como respondents said they did not wish to grow their firms significantly becomes understandable if we equate the firm with the organizational **unit** – and more specifically with staff headcount – rather than with the level of business **activity** generated by the firm. On this basis, the circumstantial evidence is strong enough for us to say that the outlook of the typical Como proprietor differs markedly from his counterparts in the other localities (see also Pitt, Bull and Szarka, 1991).

Table 4.9 Proprietor role, firms' age and size

	Lyon	*Como*	*Leicester*
Median age of firms (yr)	52	25	15
% of family-controlled firms	77	74	86
Median number of staff	84	20	50
% with 'professional managers' *	63	29	42
% with 3+ specialist functional managers	69	25	35
% with no specialist managers	9	34	41
% seeing trust over opportunism [†]	25	-19	-2

*   Proprietors with a 'professional manager' identity (see text for explanation of term).
[†]   Excess of responses affirming trust perceptions over opportunism, expressed in percentage terms.

To summarize, the three groups of proprietors in our study presented distinct combinations of personal traits and organizational strategies. In part, the differences map the relative ages and maturity of firms; however, closer inspection of Table 4.9 indicates that this is not the complete answer. In the terms discussed, the professionalizing of managerial approach may sometimes begin in relatively young firms, just as it can sometimes be postponed in relatively older ones. While we hesitate to attribute all these differences directly to proprietorial attitudes and behaviour, we believe the evidence points to their influence being significant in this respect. Moreover, given our earlier comments about the shaping of entrepreneurial behaviour itself, we attribute these organizational differences indirectly to the distinct cultural and business contexts in which the three groups are located.

4.5 SUMMARY AND CONCLUSIONS

In this chapter we have considered the nature of entrepreneurship in the firm. We began by discussing some of the influences on individual entrepreneurial behaviour. We noted the widely accepted view that entrepreneurship in small firms is partly the product of personal traits and of environmental conditioning. Drawing on the literature, we then elaborated four role identities which we used to interpret the outlooks and approaches of typical proprietors in each locality.

Though a proportion of entrepreneurs are doubtless motivated by the prospect of personal aggrandizement, the classic entrepreneur characterization much beloved of US authors and business mythology is actually an extreme type, certainly in the European context. Our own work supports that of others in suggesting that typical small firm proprietors in a mature sector of European industry are unlikely to conform to this stereotype. In fact we concluded that in Lyon the dominant type was the professional manager; and in Como it was a mix of artisans and family entrepreneurs, with a fewer number of professional **managers**; while in Leicester it was a mix of artisans and professional managers.

We then considered briefly the problems of managing small firm development, including the need to establish a mature organization structure, to clarify the evolving contribution of the proprietor within that structure; and we examined the issues of managing transitions in general, and succession in particular.

On the basis of these various arguments, we concluded that the three sets of proprietors in Lyon, Como and Leicester tend towards distinct characteristics by virtue both of their differing personal situations and the stage of development of their firms within the local industry context. This is not to imply that each locality has only one approach to entrepreneurship; rather, the proposition is that despite variations among firms within each locality, one or two broadly convergent approaches to managing small firms have emerged over time within each group of proprietors we sampled. Whether these approaches will remain convergent is, of course, another matter.

This also raises the question of why such convergence, if any, is associated with the nature of the locality and the operating environment it creates for proprietors. Most certainly, we would argue, at least some of the managerial issues we have touched on clearly go beyond the bounds of the firm, for example, strategic choices about specialisms in the value-adding chain, environmental monitoring and assessment, access to scarce human and other resources and, above all, sources of trusted advice. The proposition we explore further in the following chapters is that locality characteristics and structures are actually very important influences shaping the nature of entrepreneurship and the development of the small firms in that locality.

5

Entrepreneurial development of industrial communities

5.1 INTRODUCTION

As promised in Chapter 1, we have now discussed the textiles and clothing industries by adopting a number of perspectives, including entrepreneurship and the small firm. From considering entrepreneurship as a wealth-creating activity in the **firm**, we now move to treat entrepreneurship as a more broadly based activity anchored in the **local industrial community**. By this, we mean that individuals are enculturated within the community and the prevailing sociocultural milieu. Small firm proprietors, their families and colleagues are part of, and contribute to, the business climate in which particular work practices and relationships have emerged and thrived. Thus, in general, entrepreneurial behaviour draws on the prevailing norms, assumptions and expectations about the nature of successful practices in the local industry; Spender (1983, 1989) has termed this the 'recipe'. Although the norms or rules-of-thumb contained in the recipe are naturally evolving over time, in the shorter term they become largely taken-for-granted. Indeed the underlying assumptions may prove to be quite long-lived and resistant to change, even extending from generation to generation.

The implications are, first, that entrepreneurial development is likely to be quite specific to a locality and, in some respects, idiosyncratic – at least, as viewed by outsiders with differing backgrounds and assumptions. Secondly, it may be very hard to make sense of their present assumptions unless one appreciates something of the evolution of the community. Thus we argue that it is both necessary and productive to adopt a longitudinal (historical) perspective to understand why entrepreneurs in an industrial community think and act as they do. This perspective not only helps to disembed the social processes involved, but also hints at the likely future directions in which entrepreneurial activity will develop in that community.

Accordingly, this chapter contains a brief account of the history and socio-cultural characteristics of the regions and localities of the small firms in our study, as well as observations about entrepreneurial behaviour that go beyond the individual firm.

5.2 ENTREPRENEURSHIP AS A SYSTEMIC, EVOLUTIONARY PROCESS

A good deal of the English speaking literature treats entrepreneurs and their firms as **atomistic entities**, almost as if divorced from wider social and economic structures. A recent strand of thought, however, portrays entrepreneurship as a **social process** (Goffee and Scase, 1987; Smilor and Gill, 1986). The clear implication is that entrepreneurial activity is located within a context or social system. Small firms and their proprietors are part of a broader social milieu, being immersed in a typically well-delineated industrial community. The needs and problems of such proprietors must therefore be addressed in contextual terms. Arguably, this premiss has characterized the French and more particularly the Italian literatures for a considerable time.

A long-established local industrial community has been subjected to a wide variety of conditioning factors – external as well as internal, and social and cultural as well as economic. Historical conditions have shaped the attitudes of – and opportunities for – today's entrepreneurs. This effect is most accentuated when a geograhical locale is characterized by a strong culture, for as Goffee and Scase (1987) have shown, societal, regulatory and economic contexts vary so greatly that entrepreneurial behaviour and prescriptions for success will be country- and usually locality-specific. A full picture of an industrial community must therefore take account of its social and cultural as well as economic milieu, and its particular attitudes as well as specific skills and know-how.

The significance of the milieu is not the rich (and fascinating) detail, *per se*; rather, it is that in conditioning and shaping the business decisions of individual entrepreneurs over the long run, it engenders a community-specific and particularized collective path of entrepreneurial development. By 'collective', we do not imply, for example, a bias to collaborative rather than competitive mechanisms; we seek merely to emphasize the aggregate role of many small firm proprietors subscribing to a largely shared set of assumptions, leading to a significant degree of convergence towards a common recipe involving mutual accommodations among the individuals and the contributions made by their firms to the output of the business community.

This community development path is separate from, though necessarily linked to, the emergence, growth and possible decline of individual firms over time. As such, it is clearly an evolutionary phenomenon and evokes various implicit biological analogies. Just as the individual proprietor has a natural life-cycle, so there is an analogy between the individual firm and a living organism with a natural cycle of birth, development, maturation and decline (Greiner, 1972; Kroeger, 1974). d'Amboise and Muldowney (1988) have reviewed no less than eleven biological analogies or models of the growth of the individual firm, including the life-cycle or maturation model itself, cell division and specialization and metamorphosis.

Although the maturation model has been questioned (e.g. Stanworth and Curran, 1986), it remains a powerful intellectual influence. For example, when examining the development of knitwear firms in and around Leicester between 1945 and the early 1970s, Boswell (1973) appeared to accept the model as not only relevant, but virtually inevitable, doubtless because of the link between the development of a small firm and the human life-cycle of its proprietor. Firms could be expected to thrive for a while, but would ultimately wither away or grow into (or be subsumed by) a larger publicly owned corporation for which (by inference) different survival rules would apply. In short, a small firm could expect only a limited independent life-span. Indeed we know that small firms are most vulnerable when small and young (Gallagher and Stewart, 1985; Shailor, 1989; Storey *et al.*, 1987). In one study of 'post-natal mortality', 40% of new UK firms failed within four years (Harrison and Mason, 1987). The problems of small French firms are not dissimilar (Bertolini and Tudway, 1982; Eme and Laplume, 1981). Evidence of this kind may help explain why the 'atomistic view' of small firms has held sway.

In marked contrast, the Italian literature has emphasized the supportive effects of a local industrial community on individual entrepreneurs, hence on their firms' survival prospects and independence (Paci, 1980; Trigilia, 1986). One might draw a second, simplistic analogy between the set of proprietors whose firms comprise a local industrial community and a herd population of wild animals. This collective perspective on small firms has been developed formally as the so-called **population ecology model** (Hannan and Freeman, 1977). What distinguishes it from other perspectives on small firms is its fundamental lack of interest in or concern for the fortunes of any particular firm or entrepreneur. Purposive firm-level strategic choices made by individual proprietors – for example, to serve one market (an 'ecological niche') rather than another – are held to be essentially natural variations within the reference population in response to prevailing environmental circumstances.

But when an entrepreneur makes a fortuitous choice, the success his firm thereby derives will generally lead either to emulation or accommodation by others. This is a typical herd reaction to events and, in essence, is the mechanism of natural selection or economic 'survival of the fittest' within that population. To the extent that there is some variety in the 'strategic' decisions of individual proprietors – not to say differing abilities in the implementation of the chosen strategies – we would expect marked variations in the performance of firms within a population. Proprietors will, quite reasonably, try to learn from the performance of peers in their quest for security and growth. Knowledge therefore accumulates and disseminates within the community about how best to survive and prosper in the prevailing environment. Members who ignore the opportunities to learn via this social process or who merely fail to act on such knowledge tend not to survive.

This being so, know-how germane to the firms' broadly shared aim of adding value for the benefit of a particular external clientele is cumulative and intrinsically valuable. Over time, this know-how becomes increasingly sophisticated and locality-**specific** or idiosyncratic. Accordingly, we may expect that it will be jealously guarded and become distributed in more-or-less systematic ways among the actors comprising the community on a 'need to know' or 'who-may-benefit' basis. To suggest just one example, a proprietor whose firm subcontracts work to a handful of trusted suppliers is offering the latter considerable support through their developing relationship reinforced with ongoing *de facto* communication of relevant know-how. Contractors may reciprocate by offering other salient knowledge in return. The sum of all such particularized know-how can be considered as the essential 'glue' that binds firms to the local industrial community and confers a distinct pattern of style, purpose (direction) and competences upon it.

Maturation and ecological analogies are by no means beyond criticism. The individual firm is a social system which evolves without necessarily maturing in a biological sense. Individual proprietors and hence their firms have, in principle, the ability to anticipate and to plan for the longer rather than shorter term. This quality clearly differentiates a firm from an organism. On the other hand, the fact remains that the development of the small firm is closely linked to its proprietor, who undoubtedly *is* an organism, albeit a sophisticated one. Moreover, as Hedberg (1981) has noted, whereas individuals learn, organizations have an extraordinary capacity for failing to act intelligently on the results of past experience.

To summarize the argument, the process of development via natural selection within the entrepreneurial community, albeit moderated by the sophisticated nature and behaviour of human actors, is very likely to orientate the population or community of firms towards specific, apparently successful, directions. An observed orientation (for example, a shared preference for producing high-quality goods) encourages and builds on particular and possibly distinctive assumptions, characteristics and know-how. This points, in turn, to the emergence of a path of evolutionary entrepreneurial development that is specific to the local community of firms. An important characteristic of a thriving community is that it will tend to sustain momentum in its learning and innovating, underpinning the continuing process of accumulating and enhancing its relevant commercial and technical assets and expertise (Nelson and Winter, 1982; Pavitt, 1989). Other things being equal, it should therefore enjoy above-average survival and growth prospects.

The overlay of an homogeneous sociocultural and economic milieu on a confined geographic space further enhances this process. However, Spender (1989) offered a cautionary observation. Within a well-established industrial sector, this convergence of recipe – widely shared assumptions about best **practice** in respect of markets, technologies and operating procedures, etc. – invariably contains the seeds of possible threat to innovating momentum, manifest even as outright complacency when the sector or community is comparatively isolated from external influences. Thus one can see a local community of successful small firms being subject to opposing tensions. On one hand, there are pressures for radical change ('continue innovating to keep ahead of the game'); On the other hand, there are tendencies to incremental change ('build on what has worked well in the past'). Since the legacy of past successes is not lightly discarded, one might reasonably anticipate much continuity in the overall evolutionary path of a given community.

This is not to say, however, that the paths of apparently similar communities will necessarily be convergent in respect either of their pace or directions of development. We develop this important point in Chapter 9; for the moment, we continue to examine ideas relating to the notion of community development path.

5.3   OBSERVED PATTERNS OF ENTREPRENEURIAL DEVELOPMENT WITHIN AN INDUSTRIAL COMMUNITY

Small firm proprietors cannot escape conditioning by the macro and micro environments to which they are exposed, including the availability (or lack of) skills, resources, finance and opportunities deriving from local attitudes and trends of industrial development. The collective development of the actors comprising an industrial community depends on a wide range of factors, some, in principle, common to all, others unique to a locality and its combination of skills, technologies and, above all, entrepreneurial characteristics. Central to the successful development of an entrepreneurial community, however, are the means it establishes for supporting the contribution of its individual entrepreneurs.

The most practical aspect of a small firm community is arguably its capacity to help entrepreneurs ameliorate their shortcomings in skills, know-how, resources and bargaining power. This points to the need to understand the nature of both co-operative and collaborative relationships whereby this process may occur. In the past, a widely practised collaborative mechanism was the cooperative, still a significant economic phenomenon in some areas and cultures (Chaplin, 1982; Cornforth, 1986; Hunt and

McVey, 1984). More recently, inter-firm alliances (usually underpinned by interpersonal networks) have become significant and widely recognized (Nueno and Oosterveld, 1988; Oakey, Rothwell and Cooper, 1988). In the English-speaking business world franchising (Hough, 1982; Stanworth, Curran and Hough, 1984) is an example of a formal alliance benefiting many small and subordinate small firms. Like technology transfer (Lowe, 1986; Rothwell and Beesley, 1989; Watkins and Horley, 1986), the knowledge transfer is typically from a larger leading firm to smaller ones. Somewhat unusually in the small firm context, however, franchising is non-local in its economic impact.

Franchising and cooperatives appear to constitute opposing poles of a continuum defined by the degree of entrepreneurial co-ordination from the 'centre of gravity' of the set of co-operating firms. In the former case, all major decisions about products, markets and technologies are taken by the franchisor and mandated (as definitive know-how) to franchisees who are clearly subordinate in the process. The franchisor retains the initiative for strategic development of the overall network of firms, whereas in marked contrast important decisions in true cooperatives are the province of individual members, usually negotiated democratically as circumstances dictate.

The science and technology park (Gibb, 1985; Oakey, 1984, p. 152) is a further example of co-ordination, specifically as a means of providing appropriate conditions for innovative small firms to incubate and to stimulate technology transfer from the science laboratory to a broader public. The more successful parks appear to be those which have transcended the status of being merely a cluster of high technology firms and have become a truly **synergistic community** of entrepreneurial and technical skills. But as Oakey (1984, pp. 151–2) has noted, though centres of innovation like 'Silicon Valley', in northern California, provide empirical evidence of the spontaneous emergence and continuous development of an effective community, we should not expect others easily to emulate this success elsewhere merely by local entrepreneurial initiatives or government policies, however well-intentioned. 'Silicon Valley' also provides evidence of intense competition among firms in the community, some of which have prospered and become major corporations, while others have long since demised and been forgotten.

Still, it is hard to deny that a concentration of dynamic and flexible small firms, both geographically and technologically, appears in principle to have an excellent chance of stimulating the entrepreneurial motivations of many capable individuals and thus the continuing formation and growth of enterprising local firms. The crucial factor may actually be the promotion of a supportive micro-environment (rather than a technologically advanced one, *per se*), with a strong sense of belonging and a high degree of common purpose. A shared culture accustomed to combating adversity is often a common thread to this evolution. Ethnic minority communities can be cited as an example. However, while it is true that ethnic localities based on traditional sectors of industry such as knitwear in Leicester (following the sudden influx of East Africans of Asian extraction in the early 1970s (e.g. Ward and Jenkins, 1984) have succeeded, Jones and McEvoy (1986) sounded a cautionary note against invoking ethnicity as a major factor in economic success.

More generally, the evidence from many areas of the world suggests that entrepreneurial activity manifests a contextually specific, surging, almost wavelike pattern of development, arising from a variety of pressures and tensions. The most severe of these include social, cultural and economic dislocations or discontinuities, sometimes resulting in (or being the product of) emigration or other physical relocation, broad irreversible patterns of major socioeconomic change (e.g. the shift from agriculture to manufacturing industry), technological discontinuities (e.g. the shift from labour-intensive to mechanized production methods) and even, on occasion, the outcome of governmental regulation. These arguments underline the fact that entrepreneurship is not an atomistic process occurring evenly across time and space. Rather, development is determined by evolving social and other factors. Thus an entrepreneurial path of development centred on a given community is located in time and space and is quite particular to that community.

On the other hand, there is empirical evidence to suggest that patterns in the development process can still be discerned. Amin, Johnson and Storey (1986), for instance, have posited three distinct models of sectoral development, which they argued have quite broad incidence. In the first, the so-called **Birmingham (UK) model**, entrepreneurial self-employment and consequent small firm growth is associated with corporate restructuring whereby a big firm sheds peripheral activities, which it then tries to buy-in as needed from the external market. The preferred supplier is often a former employee. This form of 'deindustrialization' produces small firm proprietors who are in a sense victims of 'forced entrepreneurship'. This is essentially a model of entrepreneurial activity that is low-technology and big firm dependent. Amin, Johnson and Storey argued that because it is generally the result of industrial decline, it is unlikely to be a motor of new economic activity, a conclusion corroborated by Shutt and Whittington (1987).

In contrast, in the **Boston (USA) model** new jobs are technologically advanced and economic buoyancy has been boosted by: (i) proximity to centres of technological and other academic excellence (Harvard and MIT); (ii) US defence spending; and (iii) ready access to venture capital. Small young firms founded by highly qualified, technologically literate entrepreneurs have grown fast, creating considerable wealth which has then had a local multiplier-effect on GDP and jobs, boosting the low-technology manufacturing and service economies. While this model is conceptually attractive as a motor of economic development, as we have already noted it depends on the convergence of various factors which may not exist or be feasible in other locations.

Amin, Johnson and Storey's **Bologna (Italy) model** was held by the authors to be, in many ways, the best archetype of local economic effectiveness involving small firms. It featured entrepreneurs working in local clusters of small, flexibly specialized firms, generally in relatively traditional manufacturing sectors like ceramics, knitwear and furniture, but using up-to-date methods and competing on efficiency and quality rather than low price as such. Typically, chains of subcontractors are co-ordinated by trading firms, usually merchants with external market contacts. The comparatively convergent social and work-related (artisanal) backgrounds of the entrepreneurs has facilitated not only the emergence of specific districts, but also the observed forms of intra-community structuring of firms. However, Amin, Johnson and Storey also argued that the uniqueness of the industrial district model lies in the notion of **critical size**, whereby the cluster creates economic synergy on the back of social cohesion in a way that unquestionably transcends the success of an individual proprietor or the survival of a particular firm. We shall discuss these phenomena in more detail in Chapter 6.

Because the persistence of a localized zone of effective entrepreneurial activity is a function of a wide range of technological, fiscal and sociological circumstances, one cannot easily transport any particular model of behaviour to a different context. Oakey (1984, p. 2), for example, warned that 'merely renaming dilapidated industrial estates as science parks' in the UK would not emulate American successes in the absence of thoroughgoing, thoughtful polices. Subsequent events have demonstrated the justification for his pessimism. Even in Cambridge many of the advanced firms founded in the early 1980s with the benefit of proximity to a pre-eminent scientific university have struggled to survive.

None the less, the essence of 'enterprise culture' may well be captured in both the US and Italian models. One can certainly argue that the sociocultural attributes of the locality and the attributes of the entrepreneurs are demonstrably as important as the economic context. Achieving a critical mass of expertise patently depends in part on sociocultural factors: to emulate the Boston model elsewhere would require the presence of an adequate number of intelligent, well-trained people with a love of technical puzzle-solving allied to an unshakeable belief in their personal ability to succeed. These people act as magnets to others of similar outlook, forming a centre of social, economic, technical and intellectual cohesion. In contrast, the Italian model appears to owe much more to the promulgation of geographically localized communities with close-knit, familial ties.

But if one is to avoid the risk of advocating obsolescent models, it must be recognized that any model of entrepreneurship is evolving and changing

over time. The American and Italian examples illustrate that over a twenty-
to thirty-year period major advances can and are made. Thus one might
expect ethnocentric tendencies within local UK communities to diminish
over time as ambitious entrepreneurs start to exploit opportunities beyond
the confines of the locality by trading with partners who do not share the
same implicit assumptions about business behaviour and best practice
(Ward, 1987). Applying this logic to other local industrial clusters, one is
entitled to ask how, and how fast, such evolution will occur.

To recap, a variety of theoretical and empirical sources point to intra-
industry patterns of small firm entrepreneurial behaviour which appear to
influence the nature and direction of industry development in particular
and persistent ways. Local clusters of small firms engaged in similar and
often interdependent economic activities are an obvious manifestation of
this proposition. Indeed the work by Amin and his colleagues suggests a
few archetypal patterns of community-based development based on actual
localities which may help explicate particular cases elsewhere. More
generally, there seems little doubt that the development of small firm
communities requires a consideration of the sociocultural, structural and
other characteristics that particularize entrepreneurial behaviour therein
by conferring special benefits (and problems) on local small firm proprietors.
This, then, is the justification for first considering the evolving background
of our three communities of small firms as the precursor to a discussion of
characteristic patterns of entrepreneurial behaviour in each.

5.4 THE HISTORICAL DEVELOPMENT OF THE THREE COMMUNITIES

Lyon, Como and Leicester all have a centuries-old involvement in textiles–
clothing but in each a distinctive combination of social, cultural and
economic factors have conferred a particular character on the development
of the industry in the area. This character can only be appreciated by review
of salient features of local history.

5.4.1 The regional and industrial history of Lyon

Lyon (France's second biggest industrial city after Paris) has followed a
classic development path based on extensive and diverse industrialization
within an urban context. Already in Roman times it lay at the centre of a
number of international trading routes. In the Middle Ages it become a
centre for commerce and finance. Today its most famous national and
international bank is the Crédit Lyonnais. Lyon also has the second largest
stock market in France (after Paris).

The city's industrial development began in textiles. Skills in silk
manufacture were imported to the city by fifteenth-century *émigrés* from
Venice, Florence and Genoa (Plessy and Challet, 1987). The eighteenth

century saw the rise of the silk industry in Lyon, and by the nineteenth century its international hegemony in silk production was assured. The Jacquard loom was invented and developed there, reinforcing the reputation of local producers for high-quality output, creativity and productivity.

The traditional feature of Lyon textiles production was the system known as the *fabrique lyonnaise*: this system developed its own commercial customs and traditions, of which some – notably, a dense network of subcontractors – still exist today. In this system merchants and wholesalers were based in Lyon but developed commercial connections in Paris and with the rest of the world. Production, however, was centred on Lyon. Merchants had materials made up to their specifications by subcontractors, or *façonniers*. Batches tended to be small and highly customized; quality was at a premium and the subcontract producers were generally small and highly specialized. In the early days of the industry manufacturers were individual or family-based artisans located in the city – initially at its centre, but later for reasons of space, light and hygiene they moved onto the steep hill known as the Croix-Rousse.

The craftsmen who worked the high looms were known as *canuts*. Inasmuch as they relied on the *fabricants* for materials and designs, they were not independent artisans, but their high skill distinguished them from the emergent industrial proletariat. They had a marked sense of social identity and developed a strong political consciousness, being extensively involved in the worker insurrections of 1831 and 1834. Political unrest and the availability of more docile labour outside the city, coupled with the trend to mechanization, extended the 'putting-out' system into the outlying small towns and the countryside. Factories sprang up in and around Lyon and industrialization spread to other textiles centres including Saint-Etienne and Roanne, whose origins can be traced directly to the 'putting-out system' of the *fabrique lyonnaise*.

Depending on the nature of the material and the quality level required, work was subcontracted either to factories or to skilled artisans. As silk production was the most demanding in terms of skills, reliance on skilled artisans remained high. However, continuing demands for higher wages and better conditions by the *canuts* and other workers led textile merchants to respond by diversifying away from total reliance on silk. By the end of the nineteenth century, the dispersal of textiles output to Lyon's environs had resulted in the decline of the industry in the city itself. Cayez (1980) estimated that whereas textiles accounted for two thirds of all economic activity in Lyon in 1868, by 1891 it had diminished to only a third.

During the twentieth century, a number of distinguishing features of textiles–clothing production in Lyon have changed or even disappeared. The role of the *fabrique lyonnaise* in channelling goods to outside markets gradually broke down as competition between merchants and producers developed. The manufacturers learned how to market their own goods, cutting out the middle-man. Competition from Como then challenged and overturned the dominance of Lyon in silk manufacture.

Sectoral diversification was another factor behind this trend. The industrial base of the region extended dramatically during the late-nineteenth and early-twentieth centuries to make Lyon one of the major industrial cities of Europe. Expertise in dye-making for textiles finishing led to the development of chemical companies having a wider client base than just textiles. The advent of synthetic fibres in the 1930s and the subsequent growth of the industrial giant Rhône-Poulenc gave a further twist to the interweaving of the textiles and chemical industries. It also led to a concentration in synthetic fibres production that created a near-monopoly for Rhône-Poulenc by the 1960s. In recent years, Rhône-Poulenc has become a major French multinational and has been in state ownership since 1981.

The end of French colonialism in the post 1945 period marked a change in markets. French textiles and clothing manufacturers were ill-prepared to compete in open, world markets. Company closures, rather than start-ups, became the order of the day. An era in Lyon textiles was over (Laferrère, 1960; Cayez, 1980). The fast-growing engineering industry became the largest employer – with the chemicals and textile industries in second and third place respectively (Labasse and Laferrère, 1966; Bonnet, 1987). While textiles and clothing remain economically significant to Lyon, it is important to realize that the industrial conurbation is no longer in any sense economically dependent on this sector.

Though the 'golden age' of small firm start-ups in France from 1946 to 1960 (Bucaille and Costa de Beauregard, 1987) had a marked effect on the French small firm population, it was by no means as significant for the Lyon textiles and clothing sector as earlier generations had been. Yet owing to their powers of adaptation (Robert-Diard, 1987), specialized and highly competitive components of the industry have survived and prospered. Even today, significant 'pockets' of small firm producers exist and thrive within the region. These firms, numbering something over a thousand, are engaged in activities across the spectrum, including fibre production, weaving, knitting, finishing and garment construction.

The historic dispersal of the *fabrique lyonnaise* combined with more recent industrial and market trends have resulted in an extremely 'porous' industrial structure. Regional and local linkages in textiles and clothing have diminished as firms have pursued national and international opportunities. Banville and Chavent (1980) noted that 'suppliers and customers are in totally non-regional networks'. Even semi-rural production, such as in the Ardèche and Drôme areas, has largely disintegrated (Roux and Banville, 1979). Within Lyon itself, the textiles and clothing industries are dispersed into a number of geographic areas and technical specialisms. This has produced an unusual milieu with both traditional and innovative qualities.

On one hand, the quality traditions of the *fabrique lyonnaise* have imprinted on the entire textiles–clothing system. Despite the limited economic importance of silk today, it continues to be a reference point, as the upmarket design attitudes characteristic of silk goods continue to influence thinking. As time has gone by, more and more local firms have opted for a commercial strategy emphasizing high-quality products and added-value processes. This accords well with long-held local perceptions of craftsmanship and pursuit of excellence, allied today with modern methods.

On the other hand, the *esprit lyonnais* was based on a high level of specialization and artisanal skills (Laferrère, 1960) which has facilitated considerable innovation in fibre and fabric manufacture throughout the twentieth century. Small and medium sized firms are still the norm. Specialist local producers have pursued excellence by producing innovative composite materials; examples include parachute fabrics, skiwear and high-technology materials incorporating glass and carbon fibres for the electronics and aeronautical industries. These developments have been accomplished by firms once considered to be silk specialists (Labasse and Laferrère, 1966; Bonnet, 1987; Mcilhaud, 1991).

Laferrère reported that up to and including the postwar period, Lyon textile entrepreneurs were generally self-made, with 'spin-off' companies common. Today there are few signs of this kind of dynamism. Yet the locality continues to be successful, the result in no small measure of the national and international reputation built up by local firms over many decades. Thus there is a curious blend of internationalist outlook allied to strong local identity and pride. A number of small and medium sized firms claim family involvement going back to the middle of the seventeenth century. Local dynasties have formed, of which the Gillet family is probably the most famous; some of the latter's assets were acquired by Rhône-Poulenc. It is no surprise therefore that such dynasties have a respected place in the local 'scheme of things'. One consequence of the many generations associated with these successful family businesses is that today's owners tend to be part of the well-educated middle class.

Despite the comparatively low level of regional intertrading arising from the dispersion of specialisms, local entrepreneurs are frequently acquainted with one another. This social-cum-industrial milieu, combining innovation with tradition and familiarity with distance, gives the Lyon textiles community a distinctive identity. The present-day outlook of Lyon small firm proprietors is technocratic and professional, being directed beyond the region and rarely parochial. While local connections remain important, the typical proprietor thinks beyond local issues and services national, and indeed often international, markets.

5.4.2 The regional and industrial history of Como

The silk industry centred on the town of Como began in the sixteenth century, but only in the eighteenth and nineteenth centuries did it develop strongly. The hills between Milan and Como became an important area for the production of mulberry leaves and cocoons. Como specialized in silk reeling, throwing and weaving. Milan became the commercial centre where local silk was marketed. From 1815 till 1914 silk represented the single most important manufacturing industry in the newly unified Italian peninsula in terms of exports and employment, contributing roughly a third of exports by value and employing over half the industrial workforce. While much production was based in relatively large mills (averaging 100 workers per mill), some 10 000 artisan weavers worked at home, many on their own hand-looms.

In response to competition from Lyon, the Como silk industry was successfully restructured in the first half of the nineteenth century. The factory system replaced the traditional cottage industry and silk weaving was mechanized between 1880 and 1900. The new machinery meant that fewer skilled workers were needed. Female and child labour increased and industrial wages fell. Industrial relations in the town broke down; there were six major strikes during this period, largely unsuccessful because the workforce was only minimally unionized and divided between a skilled male minority and an unskilled female majority.

As silk weaving based in the countryside around Como became more standardized and partially deskilled, another skilled activity, dyeing, developed in Como itself (Caizzi, 1952). Previously most weavers had subcontracted yarn and cloth dyeing to the important European centres of expertise in Crefeld, Zurich, Basle and Lyon. In the 1900s the number of dyeing firms increased in Como and dyeing, printing and other finishing processes became important local specializations, ultimately acquiring an international reputation. This diversification also encouraged the development of design expertise. Talented local designers produced sophisticated and fashionable patterns, adding to the desirability and prestige of fabrics from Como.

However, during the twentieth century the 'roller-coaster' of the economic cycle successively favoured and ravaged the textile–clothing industry in Como. Only in the early 1960s did a combination of supply-side developments and new market opportunities allow Como silk entrepreneurs to again initiate an expansionary phase. Meanwhile, a silent revolution had taken place in the Como countryside. Farming families set up their own artisanal workshops, often attached to their farm. Many of these were in the building trade, others in metalworking, woodworking and textiles. Domestic looms reappeared and worked day and night. Self-exploitation of the entire family provided a new supply of abundant and relatively cheap labour and was motivated by a desire for economic independence and upward mobility.

This phase of Como's industrialization has less in common with the conurbations of north-western Italy, but more with the formerly rural regions of the centre and north-east whose industrialization occurred in the 1960s and 1970s. The urban centres of north-western Italy (e.g. Genoa, Milan and Turin) industrialized in the late-nineteenth and early-twentieth centuries via large and integrated firms; these developments were aided by foreign capital inputs and by protectionist interventions by central government. In contrast, the north-east and central regions industrialized after 1945, based on small-scale, small firm communities, family capital and local government support. The later mode has been identified with a territorial model of development known variously as 'diffused industrialization', 'localized industries', 'industrial districts' or more simply the 'Third Italy' approach, contrasting with both the industrial north-west and the non-industrial, underdeveloped south or Mezzogiorno (Bagnasco, 1977).

Although there does not seem to be a common explanation for such diffused entrepreneurship, a few critical factors have emerged and given rise to heated debate. These are: (i) rural origins; (ii) the family; (iii) a local culture or subculture; and (iv) local political institutions. Bagnasco (1977), and especially Paci (1980), have identified the 'Third Italy' with a common rural origin, based on share-cropping and extended peasant families used to heavy working routines and division of labour within the immediate family and its branches. Such families functioned virtually as self-sufficient, entrepreneurial units. When the share-cropping system disintegrated in the 1950s and 1960s, they found it easier to move into industrial production as independent artisans and small-scale entrepreneurs than as wage-earners. The significance of the family is clear in this process. Indeed it has been suggested that the persistence of this family form of entrepreneurial activity – well beyond the disappearance of the agricultural system with which it was associated – is a crucial factor in explaining the emergence of diffused industrialization (Bull and Corner, 1992).

However, other Italian researchers have pointed out that many new entrepreneurs in the 'Third Italy' were of urban, rather than rural origins, and in most cases had acquired their experience by previously working as employees in local factories (Forni, 1987; Barbagli, Capecchi and Cobalti, 1988). It is possible that for many families the evolution from share-cropping to entrepreneurship occurred in two stages, with the share-cropper gaining some experience as a wage-earner before setting up on his own. Brusco (1986, p. 196) claimed that the process is complex and 'passes through a sedimentation of managerial competence within the whole social texture'. Bagnasco (1988) has also pointed out with reference to Tuscany that, in the 1950s, 70% of the population were employed in agriculture, while the corresponding figure for the 1980s was 10%. Since immigration to the region during that period has been limited, it must be concluded that today's social groups originate principally from the rural 'reservoir'.

Bagnasco and Trigilia (1985) stressed the role of local cultures, and more specifically political 'subcultures', and institutions in sustaining the formation of close-knit industrial communities. In the former context, Trigilia (1986) saw little difference in enculturation effects between those regions with a predominantly Catholic subculture and those with a predominantly communist one. Whatever the political credo of a region, the fact that the local community subscribed to common ideological/religious beliefs led to solidarity and co-operation within it and to a common identity *vis-à-vis* the world outside. Most important, common traditions and a tight-knit social structure created an atmosphere of trust that was conducive to free market transactions (Bagnasco, 1988).

Bagnasco, in particular, claimed that locally based political institutions sustained the growth of the market by introducing social and welfare measures. The resulting social environment promoted various forms of co-operation and collaboration between firms and between firms and political associations, including trade unions. Trigilia (1986), however, considered that communist local government institutions were more active than Catholic ones in support of economic development. This he attributed in part to historically high levels of political participation in communist regions. Brusco (1986) also maintained that local communist authorities in Emilia-Romagna were more efficient than those in Catholic Veneto. Nanetti (1988, p. 102) has hypothesized that the success of small firms in Italy was due in no small part to the active involvement of local political institutions, especially after the establishment in 1970 of the regions as autonomous administrative entities. Since then they have played an important role as providers of 'services to industry to contain the costs of innovation and restructuring of productive capacity and to secure new markets'.

In short, a range of social, cultural and political factors underpin the **diffused entrepreneurship** phenomenon which is evident in Como, as elsewhere in Italy. Two broad explanations stand out: the first links the development process to market-conducive networks of interpersonal ties and cultures; and the second sees institutionalized, political relations as having a major impact on economic development. The different interpretations are directly relevant to the question of whether **diffused industrialization** is feasible in different environments or even sustainable in its existing ones. The more weight is attributed to sociocultural factors, as opposed to politico-institutional ones, the less likely it seems that this type of industrialization can be exported to other milieux.

As for Como, both mechanisms seem to apply. Up to the 1930s, northern Lombardy (including the province of Como) was a share-cropping area with a strong Catholic subculture. As agriculture declined in importance it was replaced by small-scale industrialization, due largely to the efforts of local families aspiring to self-employment. Local government also played a part: locally based credit institutions, Catholic grass-roots associations, local councils and trade unions combined to provide a supportive legal, financial and political framework for the development of entrepreneurs and small firms.

5.4.3 The regional and industrial history of Leicester

Like the other locations, Leicester has a long industrial history. English hand-knitting emerged in the fifteenth century, as evidenced by the price regulation of knitted caps by Act of Parliament. Knitted silk hose were seen in the Court of Henry VIII around 1545 and were worn by Queen Elizabeth I. By 1600, hand-knitted garments were widely available from many centres in England and Scotland. Leicester was already a noted wool-merchanting centre, but it was only from about 1670 after the introduction of the mechanical knitting-frame, that its prosperity derived substantially from hosiery manufacture.

The trade was incorporated by Royal Charter in 1664. At this time, the main centres of production were London with 500 frames, Nottinghamshire with 100 and Leicestershire with 50, with 100 more scattered variously in the south and in Scotland. (Frames were introduced at Hawick as late as 1771, though this town later became pre-eminent for Scottish knitwear.) Incorporation not only conferred status on the fledgling industry, but at the same time enabled considerable control of acceptable work practices and standards, most notably by limiting entry to the trade and through the training of craftsmen via the apprentice system. This model of industrial structuring and its associated craft culture and elitist mentality was long established in Britain in a great many trades, though often deeply resented by outsiders. A violent trade dispute over these restrictive practices in 1710 led many of the London hosiery masters to relocate to the provinces. Thereafter frame knitting was effectively deregulated; by 1750, Leicester had some 1000 frames vs 3000 in Nottingham, with comparable numbers in use elsewhere in the rural areas of the two counties.

Most British output in this era was of silk garments, though Nottingham concentrated increasingly on wool, using plentiful high-quality regional supplies. Silk production also gradually declined in Leicester between 1720 and 1750 as nearby Derby assumed the mass production of silk thread, given the advantage of its local water power. The Derbyshire cotton hose trade grew rapidly after Strutt's invention of the double-bed frame for ribbed stitching in 1759 and the arrival of mechanically spun cotton thread from Lancashire in 1768. Meanwhile, in a *de facto* division of specialisms, Leicester concentrated on wool worsted. Innovations in cotton spinning were successfully applied to wool fibres around 1788 but mob violence, as in Lancashire, prevented its local development.

According to May (1987), 80–90% of British knitting-frames in the late-eighteenth century (60% of the world-wide stock) were scattered in 253 villages across the Midlands, producing cheap unfashioned hose. Leicestershire itself prospered as a knitwear centre. Merchant manufacturers bought yarns and promoted a system of subcontracting via intermediate agents who diverted the actual work to the stockingers. The agents' position was secure and carried little risk. Poor families working rented frames at home were grossly exploited. By 1812 Leicestershire had over 11 000 (mainly domestic) frames compared with 9000 in Nottinghamshire and under 5000 in Derbyshire. So, in some respects, the local industrial structures at this time may be seen to share similar features attributed to the Italian context, albeit predating it by almost two centuries.

By the early 1800s, rudimentary knitting factories in the town had been set up, albeit little more than collections of hand-frames; yet they more than hinted at the direction of future entrepreneurial progress and were widely feared and disliked. Between 1811 and 1816, they attracted the attentions of the Luddites (after Ludd of Anstey): working people destroyed many local knitting-frames in protest at the adverse effects on employment (real and feared) of even this limited scale of mechanization. But their efforts at pre-emption of change were largely futile; in 1814, Leicester was connected to the national canal network, which proved the catalyst for the industrialist Nathanial Corah quickly to establish warehouses throughout Britain for the merchanting of knitted goods made in Leicester. As his Leicester factories expanded the town's status as a knitwear centre grew rapidly.

The repeal of the Combination Act in 1824 allowed the formation of trade unions, though they were still denied the right to withdraw labour. As late as 1845, a Royal Commission documented the pathetic state of many workers. The almost universal adoption of the mechanized and later increasingly humane factory system came only during the second half of the nineteenth century in the context of a more liberal political environment and widespread revulsion at the gross exploitation of factory labour and the insanitary living conditions of working-class families in the industrial towns of the north and Midlands.

In hosiery change was also prompted by a series of major innovations. Circular knitting-machines from France were introduced at Loughborough, Leicestershire. Steam power became feasible in 1839 and was used first by Pagets on circular frames and by Cotton (linear warp-knit). Barton of Nottingham began shaping garments on fully fashioned circular frames, while Townsend of Leicester developed the latch needle. The coming of rail transport in 1848 also accelerated local economic development. The Corah family opened the St Margaret hosiery works in Leicester, in 1866, a model of true factory production. Engineering firms formed and grew in response to the need to make and repair equipment for these factories.

But technical innovation and the factory system soon threatened the security of the merchant-manufacturers and their agents. After the factory system was commonplace, the agent became superfluous. Small firms could compete with the big ones only by taking the full risk of stockholding, capital investment and bad debts. Thus the successful entrepreneurial recipe was increasingly seen as the factory system and the exploitation of scale economies. In many industries ownership of the means of production was limited to a comparatively few well-known entrepreneurs such as Corah, who became very wealthy, but who were prepared to reinvest heavily in new factories and processes. None the less, such was the demand for inexpensive knitwear and hosiery products that many new local entrepreneurs entered the market after 1870. During this era of rising prosperity, the trade unions were increasingly influential in support of workers' welfare and the Leicester City Fathers realized the concept of municipal service, creating a wide range of public services, parks and other amenities recognizable today.

A similar pattern of industrial development obtained in Saxony, where by 1892 they had successfully emulated British progress in mechanization. Thereafter, international trade in knitted cotton goods became cut-throat, though British exports of woollen knitwear continued to grow rapidly up to 1914; and the First World War created great demand for army clothing. By 1924, total employment in hosiery was almost 100 000, 50% higher than in 1912. By 1930, there were 1100 knitwear firms in the UK, with 300 employing under ten staff and half of all these in Leicestershire. Technical improvements after 1920 included finer-gauge fabrics for women's hosiery, interlock stitching for more stable fabrics, and more productive machinery. But cheap imports and declining UK exports led to protectionism and the imposition of 50% import duties in 1931. In this protected environment, the industry responded well; Leicester became the biggest world centre of footwear and garment making, according to Mee (1937, p. 82): 'its people are as prosperous as any community in the British Empire, busy at a thousand trades. There is not an article of clothing from head to foot which is not made in Leicester'.

In the late 1930s new developments in machinery and man-made fibres further enhanced the industry. Improved warp-knitting enabled knitted fabrics increasingly to substitute for woven cloths. Paradoxically, despite the dominance of the factory system, outworking continued to be a significant feature of the trade up to and during the 1930s, primarily in comparatively low-skilled assembly work. The first comprehensive industry survey in 1930 showed the numerical dominance of small firms, though the use of outworkers subsequently declined (Mounfield, 1972), faster in fact than in footwear which retained a significant element of craft-based domestic production throughout the 1920s and 1930s. During the Second World War, industry employment fell to 53 000, though Leicester suffered less widespread war damage than nearby Coventry and Northampton.

Subsequently the industry recovered well in peacetime. The local economy benefited from a diversified engineering and industrial base, as well as from agriculture – dairy produce including the world famous Stilton cheese is a local speciality. Small knitwear firms remained important to the prosperity of the community. The proximity of many firms in the city created a healthy local economy, boosted industrial earnings and kept unemployment below the national average, reaching an all-time low of 0.5% in the mid-1960s. Thus, Leicester acted as a magnet for entrepreneurs and others seeking work from elsewhere, exemplified in the assimilation in 1972 of thousands of refugees of Indian extraction expelled from Uganda. Many of these were already experienced traders who settled quickly and were soon contributing much to the city's prosperity, not least in reviving the practice of outworking.

From 1670 when knitting-frames were introduced to the present day, Leicester's population has risen from 5000 to about 280 000, with a further 560 000 elsewhere in the county. Population expansion followed industry development in waves, extending the city outward in all directions, but mainly to the south. Mass production was the dominant, well-entrenched recipe by the early-twentieth century, notably in the hands of eminent entrepreneurs like Corah. Although many small firms always made a significant contribution to the industrial milieu, core values have increasingly emphasized mass production, stability and continuity. Characteristically, labour relations have generally been good, in part because the 'work ethic' has been deeply ingrained in local working people aligned historically with a rich vein of nonconformist Protestantism. In recent times, new ethnic and religious outlooks have been seen, but despite the influx of newcomers, the typical Leicester entrepreneur is still thought to be naturally pragmatic, relatively conservative, unadventurous but tolerant in outlook and to have strong commitment to his family. A useful insight into the popularity of small firm entrepreneurship in Leicester emerges from a comment by Newman (1968), a local writer, to the effect that 'it is quite common to meet directors of companies who have worked their way up from the shop floor... most of [their workers] would like to become bosses themselves'.

But during the 1960s and 1970s, the 'British disease' of rising wages and stagnant productivity, particularly among the largest, unionized employers, contributed to declining international competitiveness of the industry. Though productivity again increased substantially from the late 1970s onwards, fewer jobs have remained in the trade, and even the emergence of many new small firms from the mid-1970s has not been able to reverse this trend. Employment in the knitwear industry in Leicester and district declined to approx. 40 000 in the late 1980s and during the recession after 1989 some 5000 further job losses resulted as many small firms either closed factory units or ceased to trade altogether.

To summarize, Leicester has a long and unbroken association with the knitwear and allied trades. It seems indisputable that local knitwear producers have good reason to perceive that operating in Leicester confers advantages on their activities, in terms of infrastructure and in other ways. Education, for example, has been progressive; for most of the twentieth century modern schools have produced large numbers of young people well trained and enculturated into the local industrial milieu. A university and a polytechnic in the city now complement the technological university at Loughborough, all inaugurated in the 1960s and offering courses relevant to local needs. However, the local industry in recent years has not grown, indeed it has been in decline, which raises the question of just how great these seeming advantages have really been in modern times.

5.5 ENTREPRENEURIAL PATTERNS IN THE THREE COMMUNITIES

The preceding discussion has demonstrated singular elements in each community's development to the present, traced over centuries rather than decades. In part, their profiles derive from differing technical choices leading to distinctive value-chain profiles. But the observed differences cannot, we argue, be explained solely by techno-economic models of development. From apparently similar kinds of beginning, each region and locality has developed a specific, sociocultural as well as technological character.

British industrialization was sufficiently advanced by the end of the nineteenth century that social and work organization (including industrial relations) structures in the textiles and clothing industries were largely entrenched by the start of the First World War. The effects of war and subsequent recession encouraged a continuing shift from agricultural employment to all forms of industry during the 1920s and 1930s. In contrast, the trend from agriculture to industrial employment gained momentum in rural Italy and France only after the Second World War. As noted, industrialization around Como was less intensive and more closely associated with a rural pattern of production than in Leicester, a typical provincial city of the English Midlands. Lyon, in great contrast, has developed into a major European industrial conurbation.

The three industrial communities we have studied share a common feature, namely a plethora of textiles and clothing entrepreneurs whose (mostly small) firms account for a significant proportion of total output. Nevertheless, with such differing stages on which to perform, it is hardly surprising that the profiles of the entrepreneurs in the three communities in our study differ markedly.

In the mature Western markets served by these entrepreneurs, demand has shifted to casual, more fashionable and better-quality fabrics and garments. Seasonal cycles and fashion trends create further unpredictability and turbulence. Arguably, all small firm proprietors should have recognized that sales must be stimulated through design and fashion rather than utility.

As a matter of record, the trends are ones that Italian producers have exploited admirably. As a locality, Lyon has fared less well, though its respected quality positioning has been a good defence against external, low-cost threats. In contrast, the reliance of the typical Leicester entrepreneur on the supply of low-fashion, 'classic' products to the national multiple retail chains has discouraged a search for export opportunities and has left the locality vulnerable to the volatile fashion trends of the past decade or so.

5.5.1   The social dimensions of entrepreneurial behaviour

The small firm proprietor in any community has necessarily to work within its particular opportunities and constraints. Since the small firm proprietor, by definition, cannot exploit a dominant market position, inter-firm contacts and co-ordination may assume particular strategic importance. Realistically, trading and non-trading relationships may be the only means for small firms to overcome comparative deficiencies in resources, skills and knowledge. Thus the extent of shared backgrounds and attitudes of proprietors to their community and its collaborative potential is of interest.

The Como proprietors we studied are typically skilled, self-made entrepreneurs in charge of small and comparatively young family firms. Their immediate origins appear to lie mainly in Italy's skilled working class, and many are only one or two generations away from an agricultural life style. Patterns of land-ownership have had a major impact on the emergence and nature of local entrepreneurship in Como. Families have usually played a major role in setting up firms, providing advice and encouragement, financial support and, of course, willing labour. A good example is provided by one proprietor in our study who said that the firm belongs to himself and his two brothers: one is the administrator, another is in marketing and selling and the third handles production (being a good 'inventor'). Their wives also worked in the firm and so did one daughter of working age with a diploma in textiles. None took a salary, but they all shared in the profits after putting aside what was needed for new investment. The internal organization required to keep this form of extended family together generally stems, we think, from long-standing social practice. The Como model differs from (yet has more similarities with) the Bologna model than it does with the others outlined by Amin, Johnson and Storey (1986).

Over time, there has been an element of cross- fertilization of skills and ideas among local Como proprietors, even though many are in direct competition. To build on personal skills and mitigate excessive competition it was natural for individuals to specialize. If a new activity or process was contemplated, it also seemed natural to set up a separate firm to cope with it, albeit linked to existing activities via family contacts. To a greater degree than in Lyon or Leicester, however, traditions of collectivism in Como have influenced the outlook of working people. There is an inherent identification with the locality that one could easily label as parochial, were it not for the innovative dynamism today of the business community and the outwardness of those firms involved in the export of products to other parts of Italy and far beyond.

Given Lyon's long standing as a cosmopolitan trading centre, its industrial structures are also well established. Small firm proprietors have an understood 'place in the scheme of things' often going back generations. The dynastic aspect of successful small firms makes custodianship a significant responsibility for the current generation of bourgeois proprietors. While it would be wrong to imply that history burdens these individuals, one can appreciate how the firm has a significance not paralleled in other communities. Though the firm may remain intimately connected with the family, not all family members participate in running it: the firm and the family are not synonymous in this sense. In addition, Lyon proprietors are by and large professional managers, accustomed to dealing regularly with other professionals – locally, nationally and in many cases, internationally. They seek and enjoy high status in these contacts. For all of the above reasons, it is natural that they tend to adopt a long-term perspective on the firm in its local context.

Leicester proprietors are mainly ex-employees of larger firms, skilled workers and supervisors, with origins mainly in the lower-middle and blue-collar working classes. Family involvement has certainly played a less significant or systematic part in the formation and development of the firms. There seems little doubt that many of the younger firms emerged as a process of 'forced entrepreneurship' – i.e. 'the Birmingham model'. Though a majority of proprietors are natives of the locality (Chapter 3), there appears to be less collective identification with it than is true of counterparts in Como. Neither, evidently, is there typically the same historical continuity as in Lyon, albeit some firms have a heritage dating back a century or more. The periodic influx of new people with differing cultural assumptions has tended to weaken, rather than cement, social coherence. To be fair, this tendency has not given rise to undue inter-group or inter-ethnic tensions, though neither has it created a cosmopolitan city like Lyon nor as many extra-community links, or for that matter, the kind of cross-fertilization of ideas as in Como. Instead the Leicester firms in our study tended to be run by independent-minded proprietors, and in consequence they prefer self-sufficiency to mutual dependency.

Given that post-school educational attainment tends to correlate positively with middle- and upper-class origins, the educational attainments of the three groups broadly support our comments about class origins. Another clue as to social backgrounds comes from attitudes towards growth ambitions. The high proportion of Como proprietors who claimed not to want to grow their firms significantly may relate to class origins, because in Italy the small family firm has been said to constitute for its owner an instrument for social **success** in the local community where he is firmly rooted. This central figure, assisted by relatives, manages the firm in a paternalistic and autocratic way, and according to Rizzoni (1991, p. 33), 'the management of the firm is almost totally subordinated to the satisfaction of the owner's need for status and autonomy'.

In both Lyon and Como, the prevailing assumption among small firm owners appears to be that they will hand over the business to the next generation. It is an interesting question whether the Como firms whose ownership has changed by inheritance (or is soon to do so) will converge on the pattern of the Lyon firms. In Leicester we found that proprietors often do not expect the firm to remain within the family. The main reasons appear to be the greater independence of Leicester proprietors' sons and daughters and a perception that the purpose of building up the firm is to create an asset for ultimate resale (probably to another middle-aged entrepreneur) to ensure a comfortable retirement, rather than a good start for the next generation. This may help to explain why many of the Leicester firms have invested only modestly and think short term, whereas Lyon and Como owners' expectations require them to anticipate the development of their business on a long-term basis, justifying innovation and capital investment. That said, all three groups claimed to have reinvested profits during recent years in order to develop the business. Only the absolute levels of investment have evidently differed.

Our findings support the view that entrepreneurial attitudes vary according to locality, though they do not support the contention that Italians develop inter-firm or interpersonal relationships which are qualitatively unique. We can confirm that a proprietor generally attaches importance to the fact that his firm operates in its particular industrial community. Asked whether they would relocate their firms outside the community, 58% of the French, 62% of the British and 73% of the Italians said they would not. Responses to other questions indicating generally positive attitudes to the respective locality are shown in Table 5.1. From these responses it is fair to conclude that local exemplars influenced the setting up of a sizeable minority of the newer firms and that contacts in the locality are perceived as quite important, socially as well as professionally. Thus economic and social factors including the weight of industrial tradition, the strength of family history and personal ties appear to mesh closely to explain choice of company location. In contrast, less than 10% of proprietors in any locality considered that organized, local government initiatives had been of any notable help in developing the business in recent years, somewhat at odds with comments in the literature about supportive Italian local government institutions.

When we look at business practices concerned with building local relationships, we can distinguish trading from non-trading contacts. Membership of at least one local or national business association was the

Table 5.1 The value of operating in the locality

	Lyon	Como	Leicester
% of proprietors agreeing that:			
'In the past I gained valuable experience in firms like mine'	19	30	40
'When I set up the firm, I saw others doing similar things and I thought, why not me, too?'	11	25	19
'The firm is a "spin-off" from another local firm'	0	15	17
'The reputation of the locality attracts customers from afar'	42	48	55
'Local contacts are a reliable source of information about business trends'	19	32	24
'There is usually another firm here who can help solve problems'	40	18	38
'To succeed in business I need to keep wide social contacts'	66	40	12
'Having a lot of similar local firms is a threat to us all'	2	23	12
'Local government help is important for small firm development'	9	5	5

norm, though in Leicester the main knitting industry association was by no means universally supported. In all three areas there was some scepticism, even among trade association members, of the benefits of membership. On balance, however, membership of a trade/business association was seen to have some significance for the firm. In contrast, membership of non-business associations (political, religious, etc.) was relatively uncommon and rarely acknowledged to have any bearing on business affairs (Table 5.2).

Predictably, proprietors in all three communities directed their most frequent efforts to trading contacts. Over 80% in each locality had periodic or frequent business and social contacts with both customers and suppliers. As is indicated in Table 5.3, a clear majority did so frequently, except in Como. In Lyon and Leicester a majority also met at least periodically with competitors, but only a third in Como did so. This is consistent with a known tendency in the past for French proprietors to form *ententes* and for the Italians to be innately suspicious of – even aggressive towards – those they regard as competitors. On the other hand, there was a fair measure of agreement that meeting customers and suppliers socially was relevant to cementing business relations. There was a marked difference over the value of keeping a wide set of social contacts, with the French very positive about this, the Italians moderately so and the British negative (Table 5.3).

Table 5.2 Membership of business and non-business associations

	Lyon	Como	Leicester
% of proprietors who:			
Are members of business association	88	76	81
Regard such membership as important for business	55	39	54
Are members of non-business association of any kind	12	12	26

Table 5.3 Patterns of business and social contacts

	Lyon	Como	Leicester
% of proprietors who:			
Meet customers frequently	53	66	65
Meet suppliers frequently	40	42	58
Link business success to meeting customers/suppliers socially	44	40	41
Link business success to a wide set of social contacts	66	40	12

Apart from their bankers whom a majority of proprietors met regularly or periodically, no other category of organization merited personal contact by more than a bare majority of proprietors even periodically (e.g. professional associations, employers' associations), while many organizations including trade unions, local government agencies, university/ technical institutes and business consultants were not even periodic sources of contact for more than a third of executives, usually far fewer. Thus the picture emerges of proprietors who are outward-looking in business-directed ways, but who have relatively little time or enthusiasm for other external contacts. The French were evidently somewhat more orientated to building external networks of personal contacts, and the British least so, but the between-group differences were not substantial.

These issues are not just about sociability. They connect with broader outlooks and behaviour – for instance, the propensity to share information systematically with other firms and to co-operate actively with them. Since we are discussing small firm proprietors, behaviour patterns of the firm with respect to sharing and collaborating largely reflect the proprietor's personal outlook. Based on various questions about the sharing of information and co-operating in various aspects of business, we conclude that proprietors of these small firms were not notably willing to share information, and a significant minority in each sample never shared. This raises the question of secrecy and commercial confidentiality, the extent to which proprietors perceive no benefit in communicating. Of the Lyon group, 33% agreed with the statement that 'there is a lot of secrecy among local firms', compared with 40% of Leicester proprietors and 50% in Como. Secrecy may relate, for example, to the desire to avoid giving away technical secrets. When asked whether they thought local rivalry was healthy, two-thirds of French executives agreed, compared with only half of the British and a quarter of the Italians. Predictably, propensity to avoid sharing information is linked to a reluctance to co-operate or actively collaborate. We asked about a range of specific areas of possible co-operation; clear majorities of firms claimed never to collaborate with others. The most obvious conclusion is that all three sets of proprietors are most unlikely to share information or work collaboratively with others in any situation in which proprietory and commercially confidential knowledge is perceived to be at risk.

Yet it would be wrong to infer undue parochiality among proprietors. Only minorities in each group believed that their business relationships were so well established that they were unlikely to change in the future (i.e. a third in Leicester, under a quarter elsewhere). Likewise, only a minority restricted contacts mostly to firms of a similar size, notably in Como (just over a third compared with under a quarter elsewhere). Very few anywhere said they preferred not to deal with outsiders. Thus proprietors appear well aware of the possibilities for sharing information or co-operating with other firms, but they do so cautiously and only when their commercial or technical status is not likely to be compromised. This is very reasonable, though it begs the question whether small firm proprietors would generally stand to gain more by mutual collaboration than they stand to lose either as a result of such exchanges or by vigorous intra-locality competition.

5.5.2 Community-specific entrepreneurial patterns

As we have already noted, historical circumstances in these three communities have produced local specializations within textiles and clothing. Como and Lyon have opted for woven fabrics and garments, with a rising quality profile. Leicester has specialized in knitwear, staying rather closely allied to high-volume production of average-quality garments. The latter are arguably the kind that producers in developing countries can replicate, given pliant, low-cost labour. Hence, Leicester has suffered more from growing international competitive challenges than have the other communities in recent years. A consequence has been a considerable loss of morale among individual proprietors and individual soul-searching. Only in very recent times has local government – to its credit – recognised the severity of the situation and made appropriate requests for help directly to the European Commission.

One form of analysis we employed to explicate the nature of local recipes adopted by entrepreneurs was statistical factor analysis. This analysis tended to corroborate a range of observations we have already made. Nine composite factors accounted for 95% of the observed variance among the three entrepreneurial profiles, the most significant five accounting for 75% of the variance:

1. Degree of reliance on functional specialists in the firm.
2. Patterns of knowledge-sharing and co-operating with other firms.
3. Size of firm.
4. Achievement of bargaining power (measured by spread of customers and degree of dependence on the biggest).
5. Measures of dynamism (rapid growth, recent improvements in equipment and output quality – often though not always associated with the younger firms).

Other factors included propensity to export, choice of contractor status (e.g. prime contractor vs subcontractor), and putative status as a leading firm in the locality.

On the evidence of this analysis, we conclude that the three localities manifest differing entrepreneurial paths. Como proprietors commonly adopt subcontractor status, forming extensive, vertical trading links. They have chosen to specialize by task or process and few of their firms produce finished products. Many of their firms are characterized by comparative youth and small headcounts. They hire skilled permanent staff and use outside craftworkers as appropriate. Many proprietors personally adopt an artisanal role. Proprietors have chosen (or been obliged) to make big investments in productive assets per employee, so typically they have levered up the productivity of their firms by reinvesting profits in machinery. Allied to their preference for high-quality production, there is often evidence of substantial internal design competence.

Proprietors accept the need to respond rapidly to market and innovation opportunities and to maintain a broad (export-oriented) customer base. They appear to adopt an aggressively competitive approach to equivalent firms in the locality, and behaviour is short term in outlook. By these means, the Italian proprietors have generally been able to manage buoyant and fast-growing firms which have become formidable competitors for their counterparts in other EC nations. Significantly, there is also evidence of *de facto* co-ordination of processes and outputs of the firms in the community in broadly systematic patterns, as we shall see in Chapter 7.

In Lyon proprietors manage well-established firms of a respectable size in a mature and well-structured textile sector, both in consumer and industrial goods. In both they emphasize and have respect for high quality output, with a moderate to high fashion content in consumer markets. Designs are often done jointly with customers. Technical innovations originate mostly in-house or with customers' help. International markets are perceived as important and export sales are substantial. Proprietors are professionally minded, enjoy comparatively high social contact, trust and esteem within their peer-group. Few entrepreneurs appear to have entered the sector recently, evidencing stability and substantial entry barriers. The recipes divide clearly into those favouring prime contracting and subcontracting. Proprietors' roles typically permit delegation of specific responsibilities to specialist functional managers, which is not always the case in Como. Because proprietors have tended to pursue successful well-proven recipes over long periods, it is possible that their outlook towards innovation and change is more conservative than is true of proprietors in Como. But as in Como, they are very export orientated and many of them have extensive contacts outside the locality.

In Leicester there appear to be elements of both Como and Lyon proprietorial outlooks, but in terms of outcomes the impact would seem less coherent. For example, the median headcount of firms is larger than in Como, yet many proprietors have not adopted a professional manager role, with its associated delegation and use of specialists. The typical business is smaller than in the other localities, measured by sales turnover, and is under-capitalized, comparatively and absolutely. But this fact, as we have already noted, is thought not to be merely the consequence of the youthfulness of individual firms. In any event, proprietors evidently compensate by running labour intensive operations, with generally skilled staff in-house and moderately skilled outworkers.

Though there is some evidence of a positive outlook towards co-operating with other local firms, in reality this behaviour is generally informal, not appearing to be well-developed or generally systematic. Subcontractors often expand capacity, rather than provide special expertise. Most chose to produce complete garments. If the recipe of Leicester entrepreneurs does encompass specialization, they typically prefer it to be a focus on a particular market segment (e.g. childrens'-wear), rather than a manifestation of technological prowess.

Despite the youthfulness of many firms, there was little evidence of seeking (much less achieving) buoyant growth as in Como, nor readiness to exploit export markets. Leicester proprietors would appear to undervalue the importance of innovation compared to counterparts elsewhere, and they appear to rely on retail chains and on suppliers (e.g. machine-makers) for new ideas. Products are generally low fashion and of average quality, even though many proprietors claimed to be improving quality by increased mechanization. With some notable recent exceptions, comparatively few of them seem interested in developing and exploiting a fashion position.

A feature virtually unique to the Leicester firms in our study was the incidence of 'non-contracting' firms, meaning those whose proprietors identify success with self-sufficiency, having in-house control of all salient value- adding activities and better-than-average quality of output. This posture appears to be a conscious choice. They tend to be among the bigger local firms, being more formally organized, and more likely to originate their own designs. These particular firms are generally run by proprietors with a 'professional manager' outlook.

Yet despite some evidently successful examples of this approach, the net population of firms has declined in the wake of the recession of the early 1990s. The *Leicester Mercury* (3 April 1992) has reported a net loss of 4500 jobs in local knitwear firms over the period 1989–91, roughly a third of total UK losses in the sector over this period. So it seems fair to conclude that the recipes of Leicester proprietors have conferred only moderate advantage. Not surprisingly, then, many of them are markedly pessimistic about the future. Moreover, the problem for any local proprietor who wishes to respond constructively (but differently from local norms) to market trends is that a strategy for profitable survival must be identified and implemented within the evident constraints imposed by the extant local attitudes strategies and resources.

5.6 SUMMARY AND CONCLUSIONS

In this chapter, we have enlarged the definition of entrepreneurial behaviour from a firm based to an entrepreneur-in-community based concept; analogies with biological maturation and population ecology underlined the idiosyncratic and evolutionary nature of skills and know-how particular to the locality and the entrepreneurs therein. The conjunction of sociocultural and economic characteristics generate rich, particularized (locality-specific) patterns of entrepreneurial recipes. Moreover, some aspects of theses recipes can be interpreted as drawing at least indirectly on ages-old industrial traditions and social attitudes. Thus the history and socio-cultural circumstances of each locality has been reviewed as a way of illuminating the nature of the industrial milieu in each case.

Yet despite the distinctiveness of each community, we think that generic patterns may be discernible in entrepreneurial outlooks and behaviours. Whether or not they can be adequately described using the archetypes proposed by Amin, Johnson and Storey (1986) is a question that we explore in the following chapters. Of much greater significance, we feel, is the overall hypothesis that the local industrial milieu has a systematic influence on its resident small firm entrepreneurs, who are likely to recognize and conform to perceived norms of small firm behaviour and 'tune into' local success recipes. The process is, of course, essentially cyclical, in that past entrepreneurial choices have inevitably shaped the evolving form of the community which, in turn, conditions the scope of present (and future) choices perceived and implemented by the present generation of entrepreneurs. Although these recipes are likely to evolve, the process will tend towards incremental change and manifest considerable inbuilt inertia even rigidity in thinking. Over the short to medium term, then, a community development path is, we suggest, particular to the community in which it is found. For this reason alone, there must be considerable doubt that a path would be easily transferable to another locality.

In the case of Como and Lyon, the evolutionary entrepreneurial cycle would appear to have been largely virtuous, albeit for differing reasons. While the same could be said to be true for Leicester up to the 1960s, during the past two decades the cycle has been vicious rather than virtuous. In the context of evolving national and international market trends (admittedly in hindsight), local recipes can be seen as having been inappropriate. The industrial community is now suffering as a result.

The broader question therefore is whether some entrepreneurial outlooks and recipes within a community are predictable economic cul-de-sacs, while others will prove to make good sense in the future. This is a crucial issue since a given development path is not only particular to a locality, it also contains a good deal of economic and psychological momentum by virtue of the cumulative inheritance of strategies, work practices and customs with which local entrepreneurs have grown up. Thus major change in the local entrepreneurial recipe can only occur through a combination of strong internal and/or external influences operating over the long term.

6

Industrial districts: a model of interpretation for small firms communities

6.1 INTRODUCTION

In Chapters 3 and 4 we discussed the characteristics of small firms and entrepreneurs independently of their geographical location, whilst in Chapter 5 we argued that a rapidly growing body of literature, particularly in Italy and France, has for some time now maintained that the needs and problems of entrepreneurs in tight-knit regional agglomerations must be recognized as distinct and therefore be addressed differently from those faced by entrepreneurs situated outside areas of geographic sectoral concentration. We contend that the two perspectives are largely complementary, and that to adopt one to the exclusion of the other would seriously impair our understanding of industrial communities.

By and large, the mainstream British literature on small firms treats them as individual, autonomous units and does not consider their interrelations within wider industrial structures. There are, of course, a number of works which take a regional perspective (Storey, 1985; Hitchens and O'Farrell, 1987), or look at processes of fragmentation of large firms, leading to small firm opportunities (Shutt and Whittington, 1987). Not even these, however, look into the possibility that small firms in local or regional agglomerations may form integrated **industrial systems**. By contrast, the Italian literature sees small firms predominantly from a regional-cum-structural perspective.

Both strands of interpretation originate, at least in part, from the different pattern of economic development that each country has experienced since 1945. In the UK and France, in the 1950s and 1960s, the small business sector was considered destined to fade and disappear. Many small firms did in fact disappear, though others have subsequently emerged. More salient here is the fact that entire regional agglomerations of small firms either went into irreversible decline or gave way to large corporations: Sabel and Zeitlin (1985) instance metalworking in Birmingham, silk manufacturing in Lyon and the cutlery industry in Sheffield. In Italy, on the other hand, small firms never ceased to account for a substantial proportion of industrial output and employment. Indeed in the past 20 years this sector has experienced renewed growth and vitality, particularly in certain regions and localities (Bagnasco, 1977; Becattini, 1987).

Italian small firms are heavily concentrated geographically, thus forming what scholars have termed 'areas of localized production', 'system-areas' or, following Alfred Marshall (1919, 1966), 'industrial districts'. Furthermore, the efficacy of local industrial agglomerations (or firm clusters) in the creation of economic wealth and the stimulation of innovation has been noted more widely in the developed countries (Porter, 1990).

Despite the fact that the UK and France have fewer examples of 'system-areas' than Italy (Garofoli, 1983a), they do nevertheless exist and in many localities provide, arguably, an irreplaceable source of wealth and employment to the community. Leicester can be considered one such area. Yet neither in the UK nor in France do these areas of localized production generally show the vigour and dynamism of their Italian counterparts. This may explain why they have not attracted the attention of researchers interested in fostering and managing innovation as opposed to damage limitation in conditions of decline. By studying them in cross-comparative perspective, though, it may be possible to detect their specific weaknesses and strengths in order to suggest ways in which their growth can be sustained or their decline reversed.

6.2 COUNTRY-SPECIFIC PRIORITIES TO SMALL FIRMS RESEARCH

The British research on small firms largely focuses on three issues:

1. The contribution made by small firms to the economy and to the level of industrial employment.
2. Their growth potential.
3. Their ability to innovate and to compete effectively.

A recurring, if generally implicit, assumption in the British literature is that a majority of small firms are destined not to remain small, rather they provide a seedbed from which some firms will grow into large ones while others quickly demise. Consequently, small firms which have succeeded in growing are studied to discover what characteristics and what styles of management they possess; similarly, failure factors are identified. Small firms are therefore encouraged to imitate the success factors and avoid the failures (Barber, Metcalfe and Porteous, 1989; Gibb and Scott, 1986; Lewis, Stanworth and Gibb, 1984; O'Neill *et al.* 1987; Scott *et al.*, 1986). Recent attention has focused largely on a posited 'enterprise culture' associated with new small firms, new industrial sectors, expansion and dynamism. By contrast, older small firms have often been ignored, on the assumption that typically they operate in traditional, low-technology sectors, are in decline, and depend too heavily on family support and not enough on an efficient style of management.

In the past, many British studies were also concerned with government policies and intervention in support of small business development. One of the aims of the identification of success and failure factors was precisely to help policy-making bodies target resources towards the healthier and more dynamic small firms, avoiding blanket intervention (picking 'winners'). Some argued that it was possible to predict which firms were likely to succeed and which would fail, and that government policy-making towards small firms should therefore be highly selective (e.g. Storey *et al.*, 1987). The question of the contribution made by the small firms sector to employment creation has also been addressed, particularly in connection with revitalizing the recently deindustrialized areas of the UK (Storey, 1985).

There are therefore a few common strands to this line of interpretation: (i) the emphasis on small young firms; (ii) the belief that small firms are desirable in so far as a few will eventually become large firms; (iii) conversely, acceptance that many others will fail; and (iv) the focus on individual firms' strategies, not (apart from a few exceptions) on the positioning of groups and/or geographical concentrations of small firms.

Turning now to small firm development in France, attitudes and research approaches to the role of small firms in local economic development have evolved considerably, from being fairly negative in the immediate postwar period to being far more positive since the economic crisis of the 1970s (a change of attitudes which also characterized the UK). Between the 1940s and the 1960s, a widespread view held small firms to be 'backward' and inefficient while large firms were considered as progressive and capable of higher levels of productivity (Bucaille and Costa de Beauregard, 1987). Certainly, it has been true that many firms were unable to survive and a number of researchers have charted ensuing regional decline (Beteille, 1978; Chassagne, 1981; Houssel, 1971, 1980; Silly, 1961; Vant, 1974).

Further, 'growth pole' theory as devised and elaborated by the French economist Perroux (1950, 1955) contributed to perpetuating the emphasis on large firms. Perroux's concept of self-sustaining economic development through these growth poles, namely an industry or company which propels economic development, proved to be seminal both in France and beyond. It was taken up by, for example, Boudeville (1968) and by French regional economic planners (Durand, 1972). It was perhaps unfortunate that in the 1960s regional planning informed by growth poles theory tended to equate 'propulsive' industry with large firms.

However, as Darwent (1969) showed, one of the major problems of Perroux's concept was that the growth pole was not primarily conceived in 'geographical space', but in what Perroux (1950) had defined as **economic space**, an abstract realm of economic exchange without reference to concrete localization. In practice, however, planners tended to treat 'growth poles' as being situated in geographic space.

Perhaps the most notorious example of this approach to regional development in France was the huge iron and steel agglomeration at Fos, near Marseille, whose envisaged advantages have proved difficult to realize. In Italy the 'growth pole' theory greatly influenced the (failed) attempt to industrialize the south in the 1960s and early 1970s. These disappointing outcomes were partially responsible for the abandonment of local development induced by exogenous means.

The economic crisis of the 1970s contributed to a revision of attitudes in other ways too. On the one hand, at a time of rising competition and lay-offs, large firms could no longer afford the cost of decentralizing their operations to satisfy planners seeking to smooth out regional imbalances. As new industrial patterns emerged, the economic crisis led to a crisis in the theory of local economic development (Aydalot, 1983, 1984). On the other hand, it gradually transpired – in France and elsewhere – that small firms were faring relatively better than large firms in such priority areas as output and employment (Amar, 1987; Devilliers, 1987).

More recently, elements of a new consensus have appeared. Its principal feature is a far more positive attitude to the value of small firms. Increased importance has been placed on local entrepreneurial culture, inter-firm linkages and the creation of local synergies. These directions can be traced in the works of Bonnetin (1987), Courlet (1986), Dyvrande (1980), Ganne (1983) and Perrin (1984) who each analyse economic and social development within a defined locality.

The overlap with Italian 'industrial districts' theory constituted by these analyses is perhaps even more apparent in the work of researchers such as Ganne *et al.* (1988), Pecqueur (1987), Creusat and Richard (1987), Saglio *et al.* (1983) and Raveyre and Saglio (1984) who treat local economies as 'integrated industrial systems'. However, while there are elements of convergence with Italian approaches, by and large French researchers seem less optimistic about the regenerative potential of local industrial synergies and indeed more sceptical about the ability of local communities to find their salvation alone (May, 1986; Pecqueur, 1987). Hence they stress the importance of the external environment and of extra-regional linkages.

Compared to British and French work, the Italian literature on the industrial organization of small firms is more highly developed. Empirical observation of the small business sector in Italy has had great influence on theory. Bagnasco (1977) showed how entire regions of Italy were able to industrialize, following the creation of myriad new small and family-run firms in traditional manufacturing sectors, particularly textiles and clothing, shoes and other leather goods, woodworking and furniture-making, as well as light engineering. Explanations of a social as well as an economic nature were sought for this phenomenon, and a shift from an agricultural to an industrial society in the 1960s was considered a crucial factor (Paci, 1980). It was also pointed out that the move towards deintegration and the increasing reliance on the work of subcontractors on the part of the large firms in the 1970s had contributed to the expansion of the small firm sector (Frey, 1974; Graziani, 1975; Paci, 1975). Such a move was generally attributed to the high cost and rigidity of labour in the large firms, due to the existence of both a strong trade union movement and to protective industrial legislation (the Workers' Statute) which did not apply to small firms with less than 15 employees. A closer look at these regions showed that firms belonging to a particular industrial sector tended to concentrate geographically in small areas or 'districts' (Bagnasco and Messori, 1975; Becattini, 1979; Brusco, 1986; Fuà and Zacchia, 1983; Garofoli, 1983b). The reasons for this are varied: historical, social and economic factors were brought to light, including the industrial past of many of these areas as far back as the Middle Ages, their tradition of local government and the particular relationship between town and country. It was found that industrial districts existed in many other parts of Italy too, though notably not in the south, and that some of the most successful were neither new nor growing fast.

One of the main characteristics of an industrial district is that of task or process specialization: each firm specializes in one stage of the production process. It is also the feature that most directly contradicts a major theme in the British literature on small firms which equates efficiency and realization of scale economies with large firms. As Burns and Dewhurst (1989, pp. 37–9) have maintained, 'small businesses will not be able to survive, in the long run, in an industry where economies of scale exist and are important', with the exception of: (i) new industries, where economies of scale are still being developed; and (ii) of firms producing specialist products or services for which only a limited market exists. In other words, small firms can succeed where economies of scale exist only if they pursue a 'niche strategy';

> this involves 'filling or creating gaps in the market that large firms find unsuitable for their large investment capacity. *It involves specialising in customers or products, not methods of production'* (emphasis added)

We have quoted Burns and Dewhurst (*ibid.*) precisely because they apparently do not contemplate the possibility that small firms can themselves achieve economies of scale if they adopt a division of labour which is both localized and task-specialized. In this mode of operating, small firms would specialize in methods of production, as well as in products or market segments. Niche strategies would certainly be pursued, but not in the same way as individual, unrelated firms would pursue them. Indeed our own research supports that of others in confirming the importance of these task-specialized niche strategies.

The discovery (or rediscovery, for those who trace them back to Alfred Marshall) of industrial districts implies that each firm is studied not only as an autonomous entity, but also as a part of a whole, the whole being an industrial structure that can be described and analysed in its own right. The existence of such a structure can influence the ways in which individual firms behave, grow, specialize, sell their products and react to market changes. One of the reasons we chose to study three well-known regional agglomerations of small firms was to find out whether they formed a cohesive industrial structure, and if they did, what effects this had on small firm development in the area. In order to discuss these issues further, we need first of all to establish if the industrial district model can inform our understanding of regional agglomerations of small firms outside as well as inside Italy. We also need to consider the viability of other 'development modes' of small firm communities, as an alternative to the industrial district mode.

6.3 INDUSTRIAL DISTRICT THEORY

The economist Alfred Marshall was the first to coin the term **industrial district**, by which he meant 'a concentration of large numbers of small businesses of a similar kind in the same locality' (Marshall, 1966, p. 230). He based his remarks on knowledge of past history and on observation of existing examples of localized industries. According to Marshall, different districts had different origins, primarily due to particular physical conditions. However, they all had a few characteristics in common, namely the concentration and easy availability of skilled labour, the use of highly specialized machinery, the constant spread of technical innovation and a combination of social and economic forces. Marshall attributed the viability of industrial districts to the presence of external economies and to an unspecified 'industrial atmosphere', which guaranteed that vital information and innovation was shared by all. Rediscovering and discussing Marshall, Becattini (1979) emphasized that the industrial district itself, rather than the individual firm or the industrial sector, should constitute the unit of analysis.

Since then, a few up-to-date definitions of the industrial district phenomenon have been put forward, some of them of an operational type, others of a more theoretical nature. Brusco and Sabel (1981) and Brusco (1982; 1986), describing Italian experience, characterized small firms in an industrial district as producing for a national or international market, being connected by subcontracting links yet operating in a highly competitive environment, thus being free to change their clients and/or subcontractors if they so wish.

Collaboration also plays an important part, though mainly among firms whose activities are complementary. Collaboration of this kind is highly conducive to continuing innovation and the acquisition of skills, through a process of learning-by-doing. In addition, they postulate that in an industrial district small firms are largely independent, and that their collective degree of independence can be measured on the basis of two indicators: (i) the percentage of small firms that have a direct sales contact with the external market for the finished products, and (ii) the percentage of subcontractors with a large number of clients (more than twenty), indicating that subcontractors are not dominated by an over-powerful customer.

Garofoli (1983a, 1983b) chose to coin a new term, namely **system-areas**, each containing a high number of small firms producing the same goods or specializing in different stages of the production process, thus complementing each other. Like Brusco and Sabel (1981), he emphasized that a high division of labour characterizes these latter firms, while fierce competition exists between firms which produce the same goods or are involved in the same phase of production. In both cases, innovation spreads rapidly in chain fashion between firms linked vertically (clients, suppliers, subcontractors), or simply by imitation between horizontal firms (competitors). The result is that when a technical innovation is introduced in one firm, it soon becomes common knowledge in the district, to the benefit of all local producers.

More recently, Becattini (1989, p. 128) defined an industrial district in Marshallian terms as:

> a form of industrial organisation and, at the same time, a local community, which results from the synergistic interplay between a population of persons living and working in a certain geographical area and a population of small and medium sized firms belonging to a certain industrial branch (e.g. textiles, shoes and leather, furniture, etc.)

Becattini's definition represents a deliberate attempt to integrate the two existing but different strands of interpretation of the industrial district phenomenon, namely the sociological and the economic. Becattini maintained that this phenomenon defies understanding unless it is approached from an interdisciplinary angle.

The above definitions do not necessarily complement one another as the theory is far from constituting a coherent body. To a certain extent, differences between the various interpretations are inevitable, since each scholar is more familiar with some districts than with others, and has constructed his definitions largely on the basis of direct observations. This could imply that different districts, though having a core of characteristics in common, can also develop their own specific features.

Outside Italy the tendency has been to generalize about the characteristics of existing industrial districts in order to generate new theories of economic development. 'Flexible specialization' theory, for example, argues that Italian industrial districts are one of the many ways in which industrial production world-wide is moving towards 'the manufacture of specialized goods using flexible machinery and skilled labour, in contrast to the mass production of standardized goods using special-purpose equipment and unskilled workers' (Hirst and Zeitlin, 1989, p. 2; on flexible specialization see also Piore and Sabel, 1984; Sabel and Zeitlin, 1985; Regini and Sabel, 1989). The typical flexible firm produces in short runs, therefore it can easily adjust to changing market demands or to special customers' needs. Industrial districts are often singled out as being both flexible and specialized, though the theory itself does not exclusively apply to them. Indeed, Piore and Sabel (1984) have argued that there is a gradual convergence of both large firms and industrial districts towards similar organizational forms. If so, this process started because the large firms strove to imitate and artificially recreate the favourable industrial relations present in an industrial district. We are witnessing, according to them, the unfolding of an historical/ economic phase which will mark the end of mass production and the birth or, at least, the readjustment of existing political institutions to cope with the new forms of capitalist development.

Conversely, the Italian phenomenon has been used to expose posited weaknesses of Williamson's **transaction costs theory** (1975, 1979, 1981), which postulated a dichotomy between markets and hierarchies. According to Williamson, firms choose to operate in a market situation or to organize in large corporations not on the basis of technological considerations as such, but depending on the costs of economic transactions. When the costs of transactions between firms across the market are high, particularly in the case of recurrent, product-specific exchanges between seller and buyer firms, then a customer will proceed to internalize the functions of its regular suppliers, thus growing in size and scope. This tendency is accelerated at times of economic uncertainty and volatility and when there are benefits to be gained by reducing opportunistic behaviour on the part of individual suppliers. This would explain why hierarchical and bureaucratic institutions often replace markets.

Critics have pointed out that Williamson's economic model failed to anticipate new forms of industrial organization, where firms do not integrate vertically yet are closely interrelated across the market (Foray, 1990; Koenig and Thietart, 1990; Lazerson, 1988). The Japanese and Italian models of development, in particular, were cited as evidence that intermediate forms of 'quasi-markets' and 'quasi-firms' are realities (Aoki, 1984; Dore, 1983; Kenney and Florida, 1988). In this context, industrial districts are seen as challenging the transaction costs theory since they are characterized by a large number of small firms which compete and yet also collaborate with each other in the market in some circumstances. In other words, entrepreneurial behaviour in industrial districts is not accurately described as wholly opportunistic. Trusting behaviour arises when either the firms are not in direct competition or their proprietors are related or otherwise 'socially close'. Williamson himself has now considerably altered his position (Aoki, Gustavsson and Williamson, 1990). For him and for others, the industrial district approach and the transaction costs theory are complementary rather than mutually exclusive. Antonelli (1987) argued that the transaction costs theory can explain the formation of both quasi-firms and quasi-markets. The former arise when internalization costs are low but there exists a high level of economic turbulence and uncertainty; the latter – which correspond to industrial districts – emerge when both internalization costs and transaction costs are high. As can be seen, industrial district theory 'connects' with many other theories of economic organization and development.

Yet it would be erroneous to subsume all areas of localized production under a uniform category, irrespective of their differences. Many areas of localized production – particularly those based on sweat-shop conditions of work and pay – simply do not conform to the industrial district 'model' and should not be confused with it (Amin, 1988; Rainnie, 1989). We need therefore to be able to distinguish a genuine industrial district from an *ad hoc*, local industrial area and to gain a better understanding of the workings of geographically contained communities of small firms.

6.4 THE INDUSTRIAL DISTRICT MODEL

On the basis of the definitions by Marshall, Becattini, Garofoli and Brusco, the key characteristics of **industrial districts** can be identified. In addition to the basic feature of the agglomeration of a large number of firms in a defined geographic area, a typical industrial district would manifest a majority of the following:

1. A high level of local entrepreneurship and of firm formation: new firm creation ensures the replacement of firms which cease trading but it also complements a thriving population of older firms (thus innovation and change take place against a background of sustained growth).
2. A geographically self-contained and integrated local production cycle: because the production cycle is integrated and self-contained at the local level, firms can afford to specialize intensively. There exists therefore a high division of labour between firms in the district, so that each specializes in one phase of the production (value-adding) process and remains small or moderately sized. Fully 'self-contained' districts would also include: (a) firms which manufacture the machinery needed at the various stages of production, (b) firms responsible for marketing local production outside the district and (c) a high number of subcontractors, most of which work for a large number of clients – i.e. no firm is wholly dependent on another either for custom or for services.

3. A high degree of collaboration among some local firms (despite intense competition among others): in particular, firms which specialize in different stages of production complement each other and collaborate in a supply-chain. In other words, they are each other's customers/suppliers in a highly vertically deintegrated chain (usually linked through subcontracting arrangements).

4. Innovations spread rapidly around an industrial district – irrespective of the secretive practices of local firms and of their desire to prevent their competitors from gaining access to vital information: geographic proximity undoubtedly helps this process, as does the *ad hoc* exchange of personnel in some cultures like the US 'Silicon Valley' example. Yet the rapid spread of innovations within the district does not prevent the emergence of a few leading firms. Firms can be leaders in two ways: they can be the firms which consistently introduce innovations – technical or otherwise – and keep doing so before others manage to catch up; or alternatively, they are firms which act as mediators/merchants, managing the interface between local production and the outside market. (The important issue of the presence of leading firms within an industrial community will be discussed in detail in Chapter 7.)

5. Social as well as economic cohesion: an industrial district is a community of people as well as of firms. It is a solidaristic community, where the same system of values is widely shared. Networks of family and friends can sustain inter-trading among firms and the emergence of new firms, encouraging and promoting relationships based on trust.

The above features do not, of course, exist in all industrial districts. However, one would expect to find a majority of them occurring in an area if this is to be judged to conform to the model. Accordingly, we now look in detail at the industrial characteristics of our three localities, comparing them with those of the 'archetypal' industrial district. The aim is not simply to ascertain which of the three areas, if any, corresponds to an industrial district, but also to bring to light the relative strengths and weaknesses of each area's industrial organization.

6.5 THE INDUSTRIAL DISTRICT MODEL APPLIED TO COMO, LEICESTER AND LYON

In what combination, and to what extent, do Lyon, Leicester and Como possess the characteristics of the archetypal model described above? Can their industrial behaviour and performance be in any way related to the presence (or absence) of the features typical of an industrial district? Each locality will now be analysed using the five key factors we have just listed.

6.5.1 A high level of firm formation and sustained growth

On the basis of our questionnaire, we were able to classify the firms in each locality according to age (see Table 3.2 , p. 55). The most interesting findings were that in the Lyon sample a majority of firms (56%) had been set up before 1944, with another quarter (23%) established between 1945 and 1959; by contrast, in the Como sample a majority of firms (62%) had been set up between 1960 and 1979 and in the Leicester sample 62% were created between 1970 and 1989.

The above figures indicate that on the criterion of new firm creation Leicester possesses a recent vitality not matched by the other two localities, though Como fares considerably better than Lyon. However, these figures simply tell us that each locality went through a renewed burst of entrepreneurial activity after 1945 – particularly Leicester and Como – but that the timing does not coincide, both for historical and sociological reasons. New firm formation in France was particularly vibrant in the decade or so after the end of the Second World War, and it subsequently stabilized. In Italy too new firm formation in the postwar period was very buoyant, with an ex-agrarian movement making its impact on the level of entrepreneurship from the 1960s onwards. In the UK there was an initially buoyant postwar expansion of new firms, but the process lost all momentum in the 1960s with the ascendancy of the 'big is beautiful' philosophy and punitive capital transfer tax regimes. Revival of the small firm sector was subsequently accelerated by the recessions of the 1970s and early 1980s.

As reported in Chapter 4 (see Table 4.5, here repeated for convenience as Table 6.1), despite their youth Leicester firms were the most likely to be experiencing decline rather than fast growth. Leicester firms are considerably younger than the others, yet almost a quarter reported relative decline, compared with under 10% of firms in the other communities. By comparison, a third of the Italian firms reported rapid growth in recent years compared with a quarter of the French, but only 11% of the UK firms. Taken together with the figures related to firm formation, Table 6.1 presents a picture of

Table 6.1 Growth, stability and decline of the Lyon, Como and Leicester firms

	Lyon	*Como*	*Leicester*
% of firms experiencing:			
Fast growth	24	35	11
Moderate growth	47	44	53
Relative stability	22	16	12
Relative decline	7	5	24

Leicester which is puzzling: is the area stagnating? If so, why have so many firms been started since 1970? This, in turn, raises the question of whether new firm formation, *per se*, irrespective of sustained growth, can be considered a sign of vitality. Arguably, the creation of large numbers of new firms in conditions of precarious survival can foster instability, especially if they engage in free-for-all competitive practices and settle for short-term gains at the expense of research and investment.

The Leicester firms were very under-capitalized compared with the others, as we have seen in Chapter 3. Of course, this could be due at least in part to their relative youth, as well as to the fact that Leicester's activities are more downstream and thus less capital-intensive than the others. Nevertheless, the difference is arguably too substantial to be explained solely on these lines.

Many new firms in Leicester developed in the 1970s in what we interpret as a fairly chaotic and unplanned restructuring of the area in response to macro-economic and sectoral trends (recession, increase of Third World competition), to which the influx of Asian immigrants to the city in those years contributed additional turbulence. Since then a large turnover of firms has become a feature of the Leicester textile industry, as our own respondents were aware. When asked whether they agreed or disagreed with the statement: 'New firms continually come and go in this type of business', 74% of the Leicester respondents said they did, as opposed to 33% and 28% of the Lyon and Como firms respectively. Many of these new firms may in fact not be new at all. Their formation may be part of the phenomenon known as **phoenixism**, whereby 'a company apparently goes out of business, owing money to the taxman or other creditors, and then "rises from the ashes" as a different company, often even operating from the same premises with the same staff' (*Leicester Mercury*, 19 June 1990, p. 3).

This type of firm was most unlikely to figure in our sample, as a majority of our respondents were reputable members of the Leicester and District Knitting Industry Association. Nevertheless, for most of our respondents growth in recent years has been modest or non-existent. Morale of respondents varied: some were confident of the future, but more expressed doubts and pessimism. A number of chief executives were contemplating retirement within the next five to ten years, with no evident succession plan. Even if new firms will subsequently be formed, there is no evidence that they will offer something new, as distinct from taking over (declining) niches from those who leave.

To sum up, if we adopt the criterion of new firm creation allied to sustained growth, then of the three localities studied, Como is the healthiest and the nearest to the industrial district model. Lyon seems to have produced a relatively low number of new entrepreneurs in this sector, while Leicester presents a high degree of entrepreneurship but a worryingly low level of sustained development and growth.

6.5.2   A self-contained local production cycle

The second typical feature of industrial districts listed in subsection 6.4, above, implies that firms are highly specialized and occupy a specific position in the locally concentrated (but organizationally deintegrated) manufacturing cycle. Thus a textile district (such as Prato in Tuscany) would be made up of firms which specialize in spinning or weaving, others in finishing, printing or dyeing and still others in design and wholesaling. A knitwear district (such as Carpi in Emilia-Romagna) would contain firms which specialize in knitting, others in stitching, others in finishing and pressing, others in packing and some in wholesaling. Subcontracting links between the different types of firms ensure the formation of a vertical value-chain.

A textile manufacturing cycle, as described above, operates at Como; and a 'section' of a cycle is present in Lyon; while in Leicester there is no such deintegrated cycle, most firms covering all the major necessary stages of hosiery and/or knitted outerwear garment production.

For Como, our sample included the following types of firm: weavers, printers, dyers, designers and wholesalers, with a few vertical firms carrying out three or more of these activities, usually in combination with wholesaling.

For Lyon, the largest single category in the sample was specialized weavers. Firms carrying out other activities were also present, but they did not trade with each other to any significant degree. There are few signs therefore of a locally contained textile manufacturing cycle. This is probably due, among other things, to the fact that compared to Como, Lyon nowadays presents a low degree of specialization in a single raw material.

In Leicester firms have generally not sustained task/process specialism, but have chosen to locate in market/product niches. Specialisms such as yarn and piece dyeing are now the exception rather than the rule. Thus we would argue that Burns and Dewhurst's (1989) assertion of small firms' viability depending on a strategy of product or market niches and not on task specialization (apart from exceptional cases) has been implemented in Leicester, though not in Como.

On the evidence of our work as presented in more detail in Chapter 7, subcontracting practices were widespread in all three areas. In Como, 64% of the firms we sampled contracted out work, while 47% contracted in. Of these, 27% were subcontractors-only. In Lyon, 84% of the firms contracted out work and 42% contracted in. Unlike Como, virtually none of them were subcontractors-only.

In Leicester too subcontracting was a common practice: 68% of the firms in the sample contracted out work and 38% contracted in. However, 30% of Leicester firms neither used subcontractors nor subcontracted. By contrast, less than 10% of French and Italian firms were independent in this sense. As in the Lyon case, the Leicester sample did not contain any significant number of subcontractors-only.

We wanted to establish whether, beyond the apparent similarities, the nature of subcontracting differed substantially in Leicester from the other two localities. Our findings indicated that in Como and Lyon sub-contracting by specialism was prominent given the degree of task specialization of local firms, while in Leicester it was rather a case of subcontracting by capacity.

The statement 'My firm succeeds because it specializes', received a majority of positive replies from subcontractors, both in Como and Lyon (67% and 65% respectively), while only 30% of the Leicester subcontractors agreed. Moreover, in Como and Lyon – though not in Leicester – the profile of the prime contractors was quite distinct from that of the subcontractors in terms of their functional role. Also each group was aware of its respective strengths (Tables 6.3 – 6.4).

Table 6.2 Median assets, sales and number of staff of the sampled firms

	Lyon £000	Como £000	Leicester £000
Median assets(pounds)	1250	860	250
Median sales (pounds)	4800	1600	1000
Median number of full-time staff	84	20	50

Table 6.3 Responses to the statement: 'My firm succeeds because of its commecial know-how'

	Lyon %	Como %	Leicester %
Prime contractors	81	61	35
Subcontractors	33	20	35

Table 6.4 Responses to the statement: 'My firm succeeds because of its technical know-how'

	Lyon %	Como %	Leicester %
Prime contractors	46	55	47
Subcontractors	67	68	65

The above data together with direct contacts in the respective communities lead us to conclude that in Como and Lyon the prime contractors and the subcontractors are largely complementary in terms of task specialization. The prime contractors have an overtly commercial profile, covering activities such as marketing and design, while the subcontractors have an overtly technical profile, concentrating on technological processes and production. In addition, in both localities a majority of subcontractors see themselves as specialist firms. By contrast, in Leicester there are generally no clear-cut functional differences between the two groups of firms; most subcontractors do indeed see themselves as having a technical profile, but the complementary aspect – i.e. the commercial know-how of the prime contractors – is not as marked. Furthermore, only a minority of the subcontractors consider themselves as specialist firms.

A number of follow-up interviews with Leicester proprietors chosen at random indicated the type of subcontracting that goes on in the locality. They confirmed that they usually subcontract for capacity expansion, not to benefit from each other's specialisms. Significantly, they indicated that when they subcontract, they do so laterally, i.e. where one firm helps out a similar firm on an *ad hoc* basis, to smooth out variations in demand. In short, subcontracting in Leicester appears to be opportunistic rather than systematic. This explains why, in terms of firms' strategies, there were more significant differences between the non-contractors and the firms which were involved in subcontracting than between the prime contractors and the secondary or subcontractors. We will come back to these issues when we discuss their implications for the viability of the Leicester textile industry.

6.5.3 Collaboration between firms in the supply-chain and a rapid spread of innovations within the locality.

Exchange of information and practical help at the trading level was quite common in Lyon and Leicester. Our aggregate data indicated that a majority of Leicester and Lyon firms shared information and collaborated at least at times in a wide range of business areas. Como firms collaborated less often and only in those areas in which they specialized within the district. However, there were more signs of systematic collaboration between subcontractors and subcontracting firms in Como than in the other two localities. Moreover, according to Brusco (1986, p. 188), this type of collaboration 'gives place to small innovations or even important innovations that open up new market prospects'. Tables 6.5 and 6.6 show how firms in each sample related to their customers and suppliers for product design and technical innovations.

For Como, the data are interesting in two respects. First, they indicate that large numbers of firms, including subcontractors, originate technical innovation and product design in-house, which is a sign of strength.

Table 6.5 Origins of product design

	Lyon %	Como %	Leicester %
percentages of firms where design was developed:			
Prime contractors			
In-house only	45	56	12
In association with customers	36	33	70
In association with suppliers	0	11	6
In association with both customers and suppliers	19	0	12
Totals	100	100	100
Subcontractors			
In-house only	12	38	31
In association with customers	59	57	58
In association with suppliers	12	5	0
In association with both customers and suppliers	17	0	11
Total	100	100	100

Secondly, the data are consistent with a vertical chain allowing different types of firms to rely on each others' expertise and indicate that each firm's specialization is to the advantage of all the other firms in the manufacturing cycle. Thus many prime contractors know that technical innovations work their way along the chain, through the suppliers of machinery and the subcontractors (61% of the prime contractors collaborated with or relied on their suppliers for technical innovation). Conversely, product design specifications spread down the chain, from the prime contractors to the subcontractors (57% of the subcontractors collaborated with or relied on their customers for product design).

In the Lyon sample both product design and technical innovations originated either in-house or from customers but the suppliers seemed to play a very marginal role. If we take into account that a large proportion of

Lyon firms made systematic use of market research, a clear picture emerges of autonomous and market-oriented firms.

Table 6.6 Origins of recent technical innovations

	Lyon %	Como %	Leicester %
percentage of firms where recent technical innovations were developed			
Prime Contractors			
In-house only	59	39	67
In association with customers	26	0	7
In association with suppliers	15	61	26
In association with both customers and suppliers	0	0	0
Total	100	100	100
Subcontractors			
In-house only	67	47	21
In association with customers	20	11	26
In association with suppliers	13	42	53
In association with both customers and suppliers	0	0	0
Total	100	100	100

In Leicester the subcontractors relied for the most part on their customers for product design (in line with the other two localities), but they also relied on other firms for technical innovations to a much larger extent than their Como and Lyon counterparts. As for the prime contractors, a majority claimed to originate technical innovation in-house, yet a surprisingly low percentage (12%) originated product design in-house, the majority collaborating with their customers on this. Here the data are consistent with the particular relationship between manufacturers and major retailers which has developed in Britain: the customers of clothing manufacturers are frequently the big retail chains, which provide their suppliers with detailed garment specifications. More recently, according to Zeitlin and Totterdill (1989), retailers have started to see design as a two-way process, and to work in collaboration with their suppliers. It seems to us that in Leicester, compared to Como and Lyon, the predominance of the major retailers has had the effect of reducing the prime contractors to the status of the subcontractors, making it hard for them to develop a crucial creative function such as design.

On the question of a rapid spread of innovations in the locality, we found evidence that Como, and to a lesser degree Leicester, possesses this typical feature of an industrial district. Thus 84% of the Como executives took the view that innovations occur in local firms at **much the same time**, as against 61% of Leicester proprietors and only 44% of the French. Respondents judged intense local competition to be the most likely explanation for this. However, we cannot say whether the timescales perceived by respondents were the same. Specifically, a cycle of innovation may occur much more quickly in one locality than the other, and one would need additional research to explore this possibility.

6.5.4 A common culture

The level of new firm formation in Como and Leicester indicates a thriving entrepreneurial culture. Founder-managers were the norm in both localities, as opposed to Lyon where over half the firms sampled were run by people who inherited them. On the other hand, what could be termed the 'locality factor' – i.e. the sense of belonging to a community with an industrial ethos and a reservoir of skills and expertise – can be detected in all three localities (cf. Chapter 5). The advantages of belonging to such a community were clearly recognized by the firms themselves, particularly in Leicester. When asked whether they agreed with the statement: 'Because this locality has many firms in textiles and/or related activities, customers come from far and wide to find a suitable supplier', 55% of the Leicester firms agreed, compared with 49% in Como and 42% in Lyon.

The Leicester situation, however, is complicated by the fact that the city contains two social communities, each with a cultural identity, one of which is of local and the other of Asian extraction; the latter accounts for 23% of the population of the city. Each community provides a supportive environment for economic and industrial activity but also represents a boundary across which collaborative practices and trust do not normally extend.

We conclude that Como is close to the archetypal industrial district model, while Lyon and Leicester are not, though each possesses some of the features which are deemed typical of an industrial district. Further, the methodology derived from analysis of Italian industrial districts throws into clearer relief the range of possibilities for small firm development existing in different localities and nations. These vary from process specialization linked to a locally concentrated but organizationally deintegrated manufacturing cycle in Como to process specialization without such a locally concentrated production cycle in Lyon, to a locally concentrated and organizationally integrated manufacturing cycle without intensive process specialization in Leicester.

We next discuss what competitive advantages each area derives from its industrial structure and business relationships.

6.6 SMALL FIRM AGGLOMERATIONS: STRUCTURE AND PERFORMANCE VARIABLES

The main advantage a 'classic' industrial district offers small firms is that it encourages innovation and capital investment for three principal reasons. First, the more a firm specializes, the more it can devote its attention to just one industrial activity or product class, and to finding ways to improve, modify, speed up or market its production in a more efficient manner. Secondly, capital investment is less daunting for those firms which can replace or renovate just one or two types of machines without having to worry about the possible effects these changes will have on their other activities or machinery. Thirdly, specialization allows concentration and hence more effective usage of limited financial resources.

Local industrial coherence of the kind manifested in Como and other industrial districts is no longer a prime feature of the Lyon landscape. Nevertheless, we argue that task specialization could be one of those features Lyon has retained from its industrial district past. Thus firms in Lyon appeared to enjoy the advantages conferred by task specialization, even though they no longer operate in an industrial district as defined above. The majority of the Lyon firms appeared to draw extensively on national linkages, while internationalization is a reality for many. Whereas the Como firms have non-regional linkages only for raw materials and end-products, the Lyon firms are characterized by non-regional linkages at intermediary stages too. This explains why our Lyon sample gave a low rate of response to the question about rapid spread of innovation among local firms. If the value-chain is not contained locally, innovation will come to Lyon in part from outside and will also spread to firms in other parts of the world.

In contrast to both Como and Lyon firms, at Leicester there is no obvious division of labour among local firms. Subcontracting is widespread but is not systematic. In recent years the 'locality factor' appears to have been used to the firms' advantage only to attract customers to the area, not to generate `internal' synergies. This is partly due to the fact that despite contributing considerably to new firm formation, the Asian firms have not generally integrated fully into the indigenous industry. Many (perhaps a majority of) Asian firms produce for their own ethnic customers and/or for low-price/low-quality niches. The products of the other firms cater for the middle market, offering acceptable rather than high quality, though they tend to be low in fashion content. In addition, within each broad operating sector firms can follow a variety of business strategies and manufacture different product lines (baby clothes, ladies' and men's garments, socks, underwear, etc.).

Thus the Leicester knitwear industry is very loosely structured, and a major strength lies ironically in a group of firms which deliberately refrain from contracting out to other firms because in part they do not trust them to reach the required standards. These are the firms we termed the 'non-contractors': they are better capitalized than firms which contract out, much more likely to have up-market products and a large number of customers. They generally have product/market specialisms and use specialist managers. They are also better export performers than contractors and their proprietors are more likely to be growth-oriented.

6.7 CONCLUSIONS

On the basis of these findings, one would be justified in concluding that in Leicester a production strategy of 'non-contracting' (leaving aside for the moment the relationship of local firms with the big retail chains) must be counted a positive recipe for growth. It is a strategy which is in line with Burns and Dewhurst's (1989) theory of small firm development and viability and contrasts starkly with that of Como firms and industrial districts in general.

The question is: how sustainable is this strategy in a textiles–clothing locality where most firms are struggling to survive? Many Leicester firms claimed to be in decline and only a few were growing fast. Too many were competing on price rather than quality and in a weak position to withstand the increasing challenge from both European and non-European producers as the tastes and purchasing power of British consumers rise. In the economic recession of 1990–2 many Leicester firms closed down – a short trip through the streets of Leicester revealed large numbers of knitwear and hosiery premises either shut down or for sale. If Leicester begins to lose its knitwear reputation along with its local industrial synergies, what guarantee can there be that customers, especially the large retail chains, will continue to source there at all? For many years the big UK retailers have commissioned a substantial proportion of their purchases abroad, particularly in Hong Kong where producers have more recently moved up-market and become more flexible and reliable (Zeitlin and Totterdill, 1989). In view of the above, even the Leicester 'non-contracting' route to small firm development looks increasingly vulnerable.

The relationship between producers and distributors does not concern Leicester alone but is likely to become prominent in the European Single Market of the post-1993 period (see Chapter 8). As we have already indicated in Chapter 2, there is a high level of concentration in British retail distribution, while in France and Italy retailing is much more fragmented. Yet the growing internationalization of distributors will almost certainly increase the influence of retailers *vis-à-vis* the manufacturing firm. What impact is this development going to have on small firm communities, including those which correspond to the industrial district type? Do even the latter run the risk of becoming dependent on the strategies of the large distributors, despite their internal synergies and industrial organization?

In our opinion a regional concentration of industrial expertise will have a better chance, collectively speaking, to sell its products to the large retail chains if it pursues a coherent strategy at the locality level and sustains in the locality the most creative functions such as design, planning, research and development and marketing. If the firms together cannot do this, the risk of becoming ever more dependent on the strategies of the large distributors and eventually of being replaced by firms or communities operating in other parts of the world will only be magnified. In order to maintain (or regain) the initiative, however, small firm communities will also need to open up to the international business world, if they have not already done so. In other words they must be able to establish direct trading links with the outside world without unduly relying on trade through just a few privileged channels. In order to discuss these issues, the industrial district approach needs to be extended and integrated with a model of interpretation which takes into account extra-regional industry linkages; this will be the theme of Chapter 7.

7

Small firm communities and inter-firm networks

7.1 INTRODUCTION

In Chapter 6 we have discussed the particular advantages conferred on a community of small firms by a cohesive industrial organization based on task specialization allied to a high division of labour between firms. We noted that the typical industrial district structure has been said to encourage innovation and capital investment by these small firms.

Industrial districts, however, are not immune from decline and even atrophy. Indeed it has been argued (Utili, 1989) that the Marshallian industrial district in its nineteenth century version disappeared largely because it was unable to adapt to new market conditions, and stuck rigidly to an obsolete industrial formula. In this context, Camagni (1991, p. 3) has maintained that even the strongest industrial district 'if confronted with rapid and drastic change in the external technological or market development may find difficulties in adaptation and definition of the appropriate reaction strategies'.

This raises the question of the extent to which small firm communities in general, and industrial districts in particular, can change the pace and/or direction of the innovation process when confronted with changing external circumstances. By 'innovation process', we refer not merely to innovation in products and production methods, but more generally to the **transformative capability** of a community, that is, its ability to change fundamentally (if need be) in anticipation of, or in response to, external circumstances (e.g. market trends). With reference to our three textile areas, the question is whether they have been able to develop: (i) effective mechanisms to promote such innovations, and (ii) new economic strategies to withstand increasingly strong competition from outside Europe.

In common with network theorists (Hakansson, 1987; Maillat, 1991), we argue in this chapter that the analysis of innovative behaviour must transcend the in-firm perspective, important though the latter is. Consequently we focus on inter-firm linkages to assess the particular types of (network) relationships that add a strategic dimension to intra-industry behaviour. Whereas in our discussion of industrial districts we considered the locality effectively as a 'closed system', we now explore the innovation process in terms of its internal components (the innovating firms) and also its external ones (innovating, strategic networks involving inter-firm linkages among firms in the local/regional *milieu* and beyond).

We begin by presenting a brief outline of network, particularly **strategic network**, theory. By 'strategic', we impute the meaning commonly invoked in the strategic management literature, namely the quest for long-run effectiveness, as opposed principally to short-run efficiency. Thus strategic network theory naturally emphasizes the importance of the role of **leading firms**. The latter are seen as performing two main roles, namely innovating and stimulating other firms to innovate, and co-ordinating the member firms of the network. Extrapolating from the strategic network literature, we develop four main criteria for identifying leader and follower (satellite) firms which we then apply to our three communities of small firms, with a view to explaining their differing competitive status. We conclude that these three manifest differing network configurations, a conclusion that has a direct bearing on the long-run performance of each.

7.2 INDUSTRIAL NETWORKS: DEFINITIONS

Whereas network analysis originated in the social sciences (cf. Knoke and Kuklinski, 1983), the rapid development and widespread nature of the networking phenomenon have attracted considerable attention in the management literature of recent years. Like the industrial district model, network theory sets out to explain how firms relate to one another: it focuses therefore on groups of firms as opposed to individual firms. Network theory encompasses both large and small firms, firms in geographical proximity as well as those remote from one another.

The **exchange network** of a firm is defined as the companies with which that firm has commercial transactions, in Johannisson's (1987) terms, the 'production network'. These transactions constitute the business and livelihood of the firm: they involve monetary exchanges, engender financial costs (purchase of materials, servicing of debts) and generate income. Thus the core components of the exchange network are the trading contacts of the firm, which therefore constitute an important focus for research on small firms. The exchange network encompasses the specific interactions between firms forming a **value-chain**. The relationships linking trading partners can exhibit equal or unequal bargaining power, be based on trust or opportunism and be strategic or operational in character.

In order to make the network concept operative in the context of small firm communities, three preliminary stages have to be completed. The first involves describing networks in terms of membership and linkages. The second is to establish what goes on within networks in terms of the dynamics of the system of relations between members and to deduce the rules and conventions which condition behaviour. The third stage takes into account the competitive advantages that accrue to small firms by virtue of their precise location and forms of participation in a particular industrial network. The core hypothesis is that certain types of networks are especially successful and confer considerable competitive advantages to member firms. Thus the emergence of small firm communities is likely to be associated with the formation of industrial networks which contribute to the success and well-being of the local industry *vis-à-vis* its national and international competitors.

The nature of the correspondence between industrial districts and networks also needs to be addressed, to avoid confusion and to deepen our understanding of the three communities of firms under examination. An industrial district is itself a combination of networks of firms with varying degrees of overlap. Subcontracting activities establish links between various stages of the production cycle or *filière*. Division of labour, however, is only one aspect of inter-firm linkages. As we have noted in Chapter 5, firms can be interlinked in other ways, for example, via partnerships, joint ventures and consortia, and shared use of resources. Further, Camagni (1991, p. 135) has distinguished between *milieu* **relationships**, namely relations of a mainly informal and tacit nature 'operating better on information circulation and on imitating behaviours' – characteristics of industrial districts – and **network relations**, which he defined as 'a closed set of selected and explicit linkages with preferential partners in a firm's space of complementary assets and market relationships having as a major goal the reduction of static and dynamic uncertainty'. In this terminology, *milieu* relations are always local; whereas networks can be made up of firms predominantly in a given locality, they can equally include firms operating elsewhere, even in different countries. This is properly a matter for empirical study, likewise the degree to which a particular network evidences stability, closure and signs of planned design, as opposed to *ad hoc* evolution.

Generally speaking, an industrial district tends to form a self-contained local production cycle, so we would expect exchange as well as *milieu* relations to be largely confined to the locality, whereas in other small firm communities we may find that local firms have forged close links with external firms in preference to links with one another.

7.3 NETWORK CONSTITUTION

Stage 1 of the proposed analysis means first examining the linear, downstream movement of goods through the manufacturing cycle. Figure 7.1 illustrates a common approach to industry linkages, depicting the route by which garment-related textile products are made, literally the 'value-adding chain'.

Figure 7.1 A typical production route

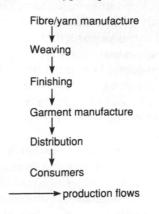

Fibre/yarn manufacture

Weaving

Finishing

Garment manufacture

Distribution

Consumers

⟶ production flows

Though for the sake of simplicity some production processes (such as carding and spinning) have been deliberately omitted, Figure 7.1 describes, *grosso modo*, product flows through the manufacturing and distribution system. However, it fails to capture the complexity of business relations within textiles–clothing; specifically:

1. Intra-sectoral business relationships are only partly described by the linear, downstream movement of goods in the manufacturing cycle: the figure fails to account for information and innovation flows which can travel in both directions along the value-chain.
2. The linear flow of product manufacture does not illuminate market dynamics – i.e. it does not explain which products are being made, why and for whom.
3. The figure depicts production but ignores a major factor in the textiles trade, namely the role of fashion designers and the origins of fashion innovation.
4. The figure also fails to highlight the loci of economic power in the industry – i.e. the 'strategic relevance' (Kamann and Strijker, 1991, p. 155) of the various components of the *filière*; according to this source, strategic relevance refers both to power–dependency relations within the value-chain and to the ability to innovate.

Although it is possible that the loci of economic power are distributed evenly throughout the value-chain, it is more probable that there are a few focal points or nodes which possess and/or regulate vital information and hence enact a major role in stimulating innovation or co-ordinating production flows. The significance of these nodes is that their existence and location may be a crucial factor in determining the extent of competitive advantage of individual firms, and of the community as a whole (stage 3).

Before stage 3, however, it is important to disembed the implicit and explicit rules that regulate the relationships within networks. These generally unwritten rules of conduct can be described in terms of three forms of exchange 'constitution', relationships based on control, co-ordination or co-operation (Szarka, 1990). By 'control' is understood quasi-hierarchical relationships allowing one company to dominate or dictate terms to another, for example, traditional arrangements in the car industry between the major manufacturers and their subcontractors (de Banville, 1982). By 'co-ordination' is understood a situation in which a firm orchestrates the value-adding chain in part or whole; the co-ordinated firms nevertheless have greater room for manoeuvre over design, price and delivery than in the control model. By 'co-operation' is understood a two-sided or multi-sided partnership where, in relation to a specific project, the partners are of broadly equal status, working on the basis of trust stemming from mutual dependence (Pyke, 1988).

Relations based on control tend to produce different results from co-operation, especially from the point of view of the small firm. Network constitution allied to a firm's position in the network materially influences its level of dependence on its partners, hence its ultimate viability. It has been argued, for example, that where networking is limited to subcontracting relationships, the long-term viability of the highly dependent small subcontractor is poor (Sallez, 1980). The dominant contractor squeezes the profits of the small firm to the minimum: the latter's capacity to invest is thereby diminished. Conversely, the possession of extensive assets, both tangible and intangible, can put a firm into a dominating position. Indeed, Mattsson (1986) and Johanson and Mattsson (1987) argued that a firm's network status is predicated on the ownership and availability of assets. By virtue of their greater financial or market power, big firms heavily influence networks in which they are involved (Pyke, 1988).

A complementary view on the consequences of asymmetries in the position of member firms concerns the relationship between the strength and the range of a firm's linkages with other firms. Small firms that rely on a limited number of valued customers may enjoy strong links, yet be disadvantaged by the narrow range these constitute. Strong current links can make it structurally and psychologically difficult to forge new ones, and in the turbulence arising from, say, the loss of a major customer, they will have little experience in forming new bonds. Thus their difficulties in adapting to new production or market conditions may prove fatal. The implication is that small firms which operate in networks where they enjoy a wide range of co-operative links will in general be more viable and resilient.

However, to equate independence with having many clients and dependence with only a few needs qualification. As Porter (1990) has indicated, an important factor in power–dependency relations between firms is their respective bargaining-power. A small subcontractor may possess scarce specialist knowledge and by virtue of owning valuable equipment provide a distinctive, specialist or innovative product or service, in which case it is in a strong position *vis-a-vis* its clients. Under these conditions, the fact that it may have only a limited number of clients does not mean it is a dependent subcontractor. Moreover, in many cases its services may be so specialized that there is little incentive for a customer to internalize them or to abuse the client–subcontractor relationship. Admittedly, there *are* risks in a posture of specialist subcontracting, for example, heavy financial commitment to highly specific, inflexible assets. In practice, on purely economic grounds a specialist subcontractor will need to supply a reasonable number of clients (thereby minimizing the risk of over-dependence on, or takeover by, a major customer) in order to secure a good return on its investments.

But irrespective of firm size and number of clients, entrepreneurs will invariably have to find an acceptable compromise between 'static and dynamic efficacy' (Foray, 1990). Thus the degree of independence allowed the firm by the network constitution and its network status has to be considered alongside its competitiveness, as expressed via its network strategy and performance. From the standpoint of independence, co-operative networks confer greater scope for manoeuvre on member firms, whereas from the standpoint of competitive advantage a controlled or co-ordinated network can often achieve greater overall purposefulness. In other words, a network where relationships between member firms are well-balanced and symmetrical may be less competitive as an entity than one with power asymmetries. Yet co-operation may still be found within asymmetrical networks, provided that the unequal distribution of power is directed to achieving a higher level of overall competitiveness rather than exploiting some network members.

For, at the heart of competitiveness, lies the ability to innovate. Exploitation of some network members by a more powerful partner – e.g. squeezing their profits to a minimum and reducing their capacity to invest – simply hampers their possible contribution to the innovation process. As Kamann and Strijker (1991) have pointed out, the innovation process does not transcend power–dependency relations since it depends on the existence of a firm willing and able both to innovate and work towards a high degree of inter-firm co-ordination and mutual trust.

7.4 STRATEGIC NETWORKS

In this section industrial networks sustaining innovation will be discussed with reference to strategic network theory. This discussion involves the concept of a 'focal' or 'leading' firm and its functions.

7.4.1 Strategic network theory

Although, as Jarillo (1988, p. 31) has remarked, 'strategy scholars have had little use for the concept of networks', a growing body of literature, including Jarillo himself (1988), Miles and Snow (1984) and Lorenzoni and Ornati (1988), has more recently proposed that industrial networks can be more efficient and competitive than either pure markets or hierarchies. The various terms 'strategic networks', 'dynamic networks' and 'planned constellations' have been coined by scholars precisely to emphasize the importance of strategic management and the role of leading/innovating firms.

Based on direct observation of the textile district of Prato (Italy), Lorenzoni and Ornati (1988) conceptualized a 'dynamic network' as a set of firms governed by long-term perspectives, orchestrated or co-ordinated by a leading firm, as opposed to an *ad hoc* group of firms working to achieve only short-term objectives and to solve short-term, contingent problems. They saw the leading firm as performing two main functions: innovating, and co-ordinating the contributions of the member firms in the network. Jarillo attributed a key role to the 'hub firm', defined as 'the firm that, in fact, sets up the network, and takes a proactive attitude in the care of it' (1988, p. 32). Foray (1990, pp. 16–17) also placed the 'innovating firm' at the centre of 'dynamic networks', that is a firm driven by the need to develop new skills and technological know-how without incurring the 'costs of technological irreversibility' (i.e. investing in highly specific assets susceptible to becoming obstacles to change). Such networks are driven by a search for knowledge and skills acquisition and exploitation ('dynamic efficacy'), rather than by a search for cost minimization ('static efficacy').

For many commentators, network strategy appears to depend on fairly rigid and structured relations among member firms in a 'hub-and-spokes' configuration with a 'leading firm' at the hub. But does this interpretation accord with the notion of 'co-operative' networks where member firms have a high degree of independence and so avoid the risk of exploitative behaviour? The answer lies in an equilibrium in the network being reached between a desirable level of independence of satellite firms and their need for guidance and leadership. It can be found through adaptations leading to 'mutual orientation' (Johanson and Mattsson, 1987) or the promotion of trust among network partners (Lorenz, 1988). According to Lorenz, trust need not stem from relations based on equal power, but can result either from the shared values of community members or 'be created intentionally'. The small firm's over-dependency on a large firm can be averted if it extends and diversifies its client base, while clients refrain from placing too many orders on just one subcontractor.

Lorenzoni and Ornati (1988) argued that within a 'planned constellation' firms co-operate with each other and with the leading firm, since the satellites perform important functions, while the leading firm focuses on innovation (albeit this role may require it to make significant investments). By contrast, in an unplanned or 'realized constellation', the role of the satellites is mainly to minimize costs so they are more likely to be controlled and exploited by the leading firm. Arguably, the strategic value of the satellite firms is maximized in a network where each member or partner develops specific and complementary skills and capabilities which are complementary and mutually supportive (Gordon, 1991).

Strategic networks can therefore be defined as inter-organizational sets which emerge because they can confer competitive advantages to member firms when: (i) there is a guiding firm to exercise leadership, and (ii) the satellite firms recognize the merits of being guided by a 'visible hand'. The likelihood of opportunistic behaviour by the leading firm is reduced by the development and consolidation of trust relations among network partners and by the relative independence of the satellite firms in terms of client diversification and/or bargaining power. A network which may have developed using control mechanisms may evolve into a network based on co-operation, given the mutual commitment of the players involved to this change of *modus operandi*.

7.4.2 Strategic networks and industrial districts

Strategic network theory undoubtedly draws its inspiration from those Italian industrial districts where evidence exists of the features described above. But industrial districts do not necessarily contain strategic networks. A high division of labour and widespread subcontracting among firms are conducive to co-ordination by a 'leading' firm, generally a prime contractor, but co-ordination to activate the production chain and satisfy customers' demands may be *ad hoc*. It does not always imply strategic planning or leadership.

In some industrial districts (including Como), the fragmentation of the production process has for some time enabled a 'middle-man' or broker to take a co-ordinating role, managing the interface between upstream producers and downstream distributors. He typically functions by receiving orders from distributors and garment manufacturers and putting work out to local manufacturing companies. Clearly he performs a useful role, allowing for a greater measure of order in the manufacturing chain. Such a merchant/broker may perform routine co-ordination without generating and stimulating innovation and specialization among his subcontractors; conversely, he may provide leadership and foster innovation in such crucial areas as marketing, production methods and product design.

Influenced by strategic network theory (especially Lorenzoni's version) and the impact of recent economic developments, the industrial district literature now attributes much greater importance to networks managed by a 'focal' innovating firm (Nuti, 1989; Utili, 1989). Nuti argued that *ad hoc* operational networks provided a quick, flexible response to changing market conditions in the 1960s and 1970s, while strategic networks are the industrial districts' response to market developments of the 1980s and 1990s (the growing internationalization of producers and distributors, higher quality products, decreasing demand in terms of volume, though not value). Nuti explained this transition mainly as a shifting emphasis from subcontracting **by capacity** (linked to cost minimization) to subcontracting **by specialism** (linked to innovation and product diversification). Subcontracting by specialism implies the need for greater co-ordinating efforts on the part of leading firms to guarantee unity of purpose, particularly at times of great economic uncertainty.

Williamson's transaction costs theory has also influenced the more recent industrial district literature. The difficulties currently experienced by a typical and well-known industrial district such as Prato have led some analysts (Gobbo, 1989; Balestri, 1990) to advance the hypothesis that in a period of dynamic uncertainty when new competitive rules emerge, industrial districts will develop their own form of hierarchy, namely explicit inter-firm linkages, locally and transnationally. Thus, Bianchi (1989) has argued that industrial districts are replacing quasi-markets with co-ordinated quasi-hierarchies. Further, as Nuti argued, the real value of subcontracting links between firms in today's markets should be assessed in terms of their capacity to foster innovation. As regards small firms communities, then, the major determinant of viability may be their capacity to generate and sustain the innovation process, rather than whether firms systematically engage in subcontracting, *per se.*

7.5 EXCHANGE NETWORKS IN COMO, LEICESTER AND LYON

In this section we analyse networking in our three communities of small firms to appreciate more about the innovation process. Typical exchange networks involving Como, Leicester and Lyon firms are described first. We discuss the different ways in which firms trade with each other and with outside firms. By doing this, we try to gain a better understanding of inter-firm linkages, setting the scene for a discussion of the innovation process in the three areas, including information and innovation flows and the role of leading firms in these networks.

7.5.1 Exchange networks in Como

Como's trading networks generally included firms specializing in different stages of the value-chain. Thus a typical trading network within the locality would include at least one firm and probably several from the following categories:

1. Designers (*Disegnatori*): these create the patterns which are then printed on the cloth either at the loom or later.

2. Weavers (*Greggisti*): these make the standard cloth, either independently or as subcontractors to the 'terminal' firms and the 'converters' (see below). They often, in turn, contract out work to other weaving firms. Weavers do not generally have direct access to external markets, except when they produce directly marketable products – e.g. fabrics for furnishing, headscarfs and handkerchiefs.
3. Finishing firms – i.e. finishing, printing and dyeing firms (*Tintostampatori*): these specialize in just one, two or all three of the above activities. They are always subcontractors to the 'terminal' firms and the 'converters'. Like the weavers, they may contract out work to other finishing firms.

Trading networks involving these firms differ in the ways they are linked to their external (often foreign) customers. In most cases, as in other industrial districts, the relationship between the internal network and the external clients is managed by a middle-man, known locally as a 'converter', who receives orders from distributors and garment manufacturers and places orders on local manufacturing companies, thus activating the production chain. In other cases, the links between local producers and external markets is provided by a 'terminal' firm, an integrated or semi-integrated firm which carries out some or all of the different operations present in the district. A 'terminal' firm usually undertakes the most sophisticated weaving work, contracting out the more routine work to other local firms. It also prints and dyes the cloth (and makes use of local specialist firms) and, lastly, markets the final products, whether garment fabrics or headscarfs and other accessories.

In terms of value-chain position, 'converters' are merchants while 'terminal' firms are manufacturers, although the latter also act as wholesalers to other local manufacturers. There are roughly 150 converters in Como, and their number appears to be increasing as young and ambitious managers from local firms become entrepreneurs. Terminal firms are fewer in number; among them are a handful of integrated, medium to large firms with an international reputation and a large sales turnover of £80–£100 million. The best known are Ratti, Mantero, Boselli and Prini.

Over the past two decades, there has been a tendency for the terminal firms to close down their own weaving operations and increase their use of specialist firms via acquisitions, equity holdings and joint ventures. They have also stepped up their research and development. Meanwhile, the converters have strengthened their links with subcontractors via equity holdings, joint ventures and technical co-operation. They have also sought technical co-operation and cross-merchandising arrangements with other converters. According to reliable local sources, there is a clear move towards the formation of 'stable' networks accompanied by increased product–process specialization of the firms which make up the set.

7.5.2 Exchange networks in Leicester

In Leicester the majority of firms are hosiery and knitted-garment manufacturers. They tend to be vertically integrated firms (in a comparatively simple chain). They mostly manufacture their own fabrics, cut panels to size and then sew and finish them in-house. Firms which make fabrics generally do so for their own use and not for resale to other producers. Hosiery makers also tend to have fully integrated facilities. Yet other firms buy in ready-knitted, mainly jersey fabrics, and have few or no knitting-machines.

Unlike the Italian knitwear industry (in recent years particularly associated with Benetton), Leicester firms use mainly pre-dyed yarn; piece-dyeing of 'grey' garments is the exception. Yarn production has never been a local speciality, though there are specialist yarn wholesalers. The advantage of pre-dyed yarn is that a wide variety of natural and man-made fibres can be sourced according to cost and demand dictates from many suppliers around the world. In contrast, piece-dyeing offers the ability to respond to fashion changes very quickly, and for this reason, it conferred an advantage on firms using this technique in the 1980s. The preference of the Leicester firms for using pre-dyed yarns is consistent with their traditional recipes (see below).

Multiple retail chains account for up to 80% of the output of many knitwear merchandise lines. They expect to negotiate directly with Leicester manufacturers, as do the bigger independent retailers. Smaller independent retailers buy from wholesale merchants and from branded suppliers. The latter, including from time to time the major brands (such as Farah and Levi Strauss), buy-in knitwear from the East Midlands for UK resale under their own names, though a good deal is sourced from low-cost overseas manufacturers.

A typical Leicester trading network is relatively simple and tends to a dyadic form. In other words, each firm sells its products to a retail client either directly or through an agent or a branded supplier. In terms of network strategy, recipes appear to be substantially homogeneous, in the sense that Leicester manufacturers sell predominantly into the UK market, offering medium-quality, low-fashion products at competitively low prices and with moderate lead-times. There are a number of firms that cater for the budget end of the market; some are firms set up by Asian immigrants, who rely on comparatively low labour costs (often family labour). Their trading networks differ from those of the other firms; for example, they tend to cater for independent retailers and market stalls, including those that specialize in ethnic or inexpensive clothes. Compared to Como, there is largely an absence of subcontracting by specialism in Leicester.

7.5.3 Exchange networks in Lyon

Firms in Lyon are highly specialized. Specialisms include knitwear and clothing manufacture, but weaving is the predominant activity in the upstream textile segment. As in Leicester, local manufacturers have direct access to their markets and avoid depending on merchants and brokers. Many Lyon firms still invoke the silk tradition of the area to offer high-quality products to sophisticated clients. In this sense, their strategy is similar to that of Como's terminal firms.

Unlike Como firms, however, the Lyon firms in our sample did not trade with each other to any significant degree. Very few of these firms had local trading partners, generally operating nationally or internationally. In this regard, Lyon has largely lost those characteristics usually associated with geographic concentration of industries – i.e. proximity of close customers (and suppliers). However, it appears that collaboration with network partners beyond the locality can successfully substitute for the advantages of geographic concentration.

7.5.4 From exchange networks to strategic networks

Having briefly described the type of relations firms in each locality have forged with their suppliers and buyers, we are in a better position to assess their industrial strategy and performance. We need to establish how many of these same firms exercise a leading role within the exchange networks they belong to. We also need to consider the links between internal and external firms and the 'strategic relevance' of the internal firms in relation to the external ones (see Figure 7.2).

Suppose for the moment that a small firm community encompasses a number of exchange networks, and that these are partly or wholly based on firms in the local community. Suppose also that a given network is 'strategic', that is, it is focused on a leading firm. One can envisage three possible scenarios for this network, each with an associated hypothesis:

1. The leading firm is locally based and strongly integrated within the local economy (Figure 7.2(a)). This scenario suggests a potentially high level of innovation by individual firms (hence by the industrial community as a whole), owing to the close, constructive influence of the leading firm;
2. The leading firm is locally based, but weakly integrated within the local/regional economy, drawing strength from further afield (Figure 7.2(b)). The high level of innovation on the part of the leading firm will probably not translate into a high level of innovation for the community as an entity, because many of its most productive contacts will be with outsiders.
3. The leading firm is located outside the local community (Figure 7.2(c)). This scenario is likely to correspond to a rather low level of innovation by

individual firms in the locality (and hence by the community as a whole) since the driving force for innovation is external.

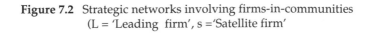

Figure 7.2 Strategic networks involving firms-in-communities
(L = 'Leading firm', s ='Satellite firm'

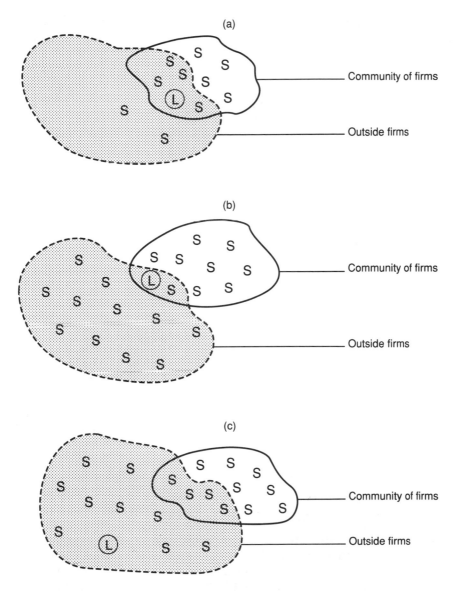

The risk for the locality in scenario 3 is that if for any reason the links between the leading firm (the brain of the network) and its satellites (the body) are cut, the body will probably suffer irreparable damage whereas the brain will not. Certainly the durability of a network cannot be taken for granted. Jarillo (1988, p. 35) emphasized that network relations are still subject to the market test, meaning that network partners are always free in principle to switch to different buyers or sellers, though in practice this freedom is contingent on their degree of dependence on the leading firm or other partners.

The presence or absence of a leading firm in a locality and its degree of embeddedness within the local industrial community have important implications for regional economic effectiveness around the world. For as Bergman, Maier and Todtling (1991, p. 295) have argued, 'depending on the network position of its key actors, a region will in the aggregate be either a controlling or a controlled one'. To discuss these issues further, we now explore the identification of leading and satellite firms and their contribution to the innovation process.

7.6   STRATEGIC NETWORKS: 'LEADING' AND 'SATELLITE' FIRMS

7.6.1   Identifying 'leading' and 'satellite' firms

Definitive criteria for the identification of leading and satellite firms have not been explicitly developed in the strategic network literature. However, a review of the main literature shows that it contains useful potential criteria for identification. Accordingly, we elaborate two different sets of criteria, one for identifying leading firms, the other for satellites. We then apply these criteria to our three samples of firms and discuss the results.

Earlier, we defined the essential attributes of leading or hub firms as being the capacity for innovation and co-ordination. Lorenzoni and Ornati (1988) have defined the innovating role of a leading firm as the ability to:

1. increase and promulgate knowledge of products and markets and their linkages;
2. develop and promulgate crucial technological know-how;
3. respond constructively to technological change;
4. increase the marketing 'clout' of the network.

Lazerson (1988) spoke of the leading–satellite firm structure as conferring on the leading firm control over 'the three key phases of production: design, final assembly and marketing'. Emphasis has also been placed on high-level managerial and strategic skills (Pontarollo and Martini, 1989; Utili, 1989). Drawing on all the above we developed the following usable criteria for identifying leading small firms among the small firm sets in our study:

1. product designs generated in-house, often taking advantage of systematic market research;
2. a chief executive with a 'directing' role: controlling, planning and setting directions, co-ordinating others, delegating to functional specialist managers, etc.;
3. two or more specialist managers, with at least one specialist in design and one in sales/marketing;
4. evidence of recent technical (process) innovation.

We found 12 firms in Lyon (27% of the sample) which tallied with these criteria, 10 in Como (20%), but only 3 firms in Leicester (5%). But in Leicester we found 13 firms meeting three of the four criteria; all of these depended entirely or in part on their customers for design. In passing, it is interesting to note that in the Como sample four of the five firms whose proprietor had replied to the question 'Who are the leading firms in your sector and area?' with an unequivocal 'We are' were captured by our criteria for leaders; two others did not reply to the question, yet were named as leaders by other proprietors.

Turning to possible definitional criteria for satellite firms from the literature, Lorenzoni and Ornati (1988) have referred to 'small entrepreneurs willing to accept only limited subcontracting roles', implying that satellite firms are subservient subcontractors. However, they also point out that satellite firms 'devote great attention to process innovation' but contribute only in a limited way to product innovation. Jarillo (1988) equated satellite firms with subcontractors and defined them as 'risk-averse', partly due to their small size compared to that of the 'hub firm'. Lazerson (1988, p. 338) defined satellite firms as artisanal firms where 'hired managers were normally rejected because of the importance placed on ownership'. These firms were generally created by or associated with another firm through partnerships or invested capital. Also, with specific reference to the fashion sector, Rizzoni (1991, p. 35) has classified as 'traditional' small firms which make use of innovations developed elsewhere, but nevertheless actively take part in **innovation diffusion** and 'introduce incremental innovations, which aim at the improvement of the production process'.

On the basis of the above, we applied the following complementary criteria for identifying satellite firms:

1. design originated by clients or developed in collaboration with them;
2. a chief executive with an 'operational' role, directly involved in the day-to-day running of his business and/or production-oriented;
3. an absence of specialist managers or just one specialist, usually in charge of production;
4. evidence of recent technical innovation.

We found 14 such firms in Como (28% of the sample), 4 in Lyon (8%) and 17 in Leicester (28%).

The characteristics – especially the growth and management strategies – of leaders and satellites will now be examined to establish similarities and differences. We also explore the reasons why Leicester apparently produced so few leading firms, by finding out how – apart from design – the 13 Leicester firms that matched three of the four criteria (from now on called 'sub-leaders') differed from the continental leaders. As we shall see, the Como and Lyon leaders showed remarkable similarities, while the Leicester sub-leaders (though having some commonalities with the Italian and French leaders), differed markedly from them in important ways.

7.6.2　'Leading' and 'satellite' firms in Como

The key characteristics of the 10 'leading' firms in Como are shown in Table 7.1. The data indicate a high degree of homogeneity among them. Aside from the four criteria of 'leadership', they were all well-established firms in terms of assets and employees, had a large number of clients and sold less than 20% of output to their biggest client. Nine out of ten were prime contractors, meaning that they contracted work out to other firms (but did not contract in). They were also export-oriented and had enjoyed moderate to fast growth. Five were 'terminal' firms, two were wholesalers/ converters', three were weavers. All had direct access to outside markets, in the case of the terminal firms and converters by virtue of their roles in the district, whereas the three weavers had made a conscious strategic choice to approach retailers directly.

Table 7.1　Characteristics of Como 'leading' firms

100+ clients	Less than 20% of sales to major client	Export-oriented or international	Contracts out (but not in)
90%	90%	90%	90%
(40%)*	(60%)	(49%)	(44%)

Short-term contracts	Fast/ moderate growth	Median assets (£000)	Median sales (£000)	Median staff
80%	90%	1200	5000	74
(48%)	(79%)	(860)	(1600)	(20)

* The figures in parentheses refer to the entire Como sample and are quoted to facilitate comparisons.

No printing, dyeing or finishing firm was classed among the leaders, but a quarter of wholesalers/converters, a third of weavers and 70% of terminal firms were so classed. The archetypal leading firm therefore is the terminal firm, presumably because it has multi-competences in manufacturing, in marketing and in product design.

The classification of Como's leading firms into these structural subgroups helps us reconstruct information and innovation flows within the most typical exchange networks of the Como firms (Figures 7.3 and 7.4). In a 'converter' network, information related to product technology flows from the fibre/yarn manufacturers to the weavers (and vice versa) and from the latter to the converters. Information related to process technology links the fibre/yarn manufacturers with the weavers and finishers bi-directionally,

Figure 7.3 Information and innovation flows within a converter network

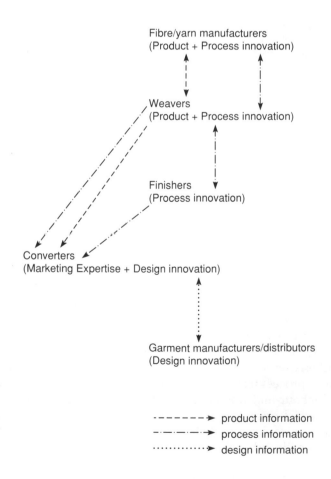

Fibre/yarn manufacturers
(Product + Process innovation)

Weavers
(Product + Process innovation)

Finishers
(Process innovation)

Converters
(Marketing Expertise + Design innovation)

Garment manufacturers/distributors
(Design innovation)

- - - - - - → product information
– · – · – · → process information
· · · · · · · · · · · · → design information

Figure 7.4   Information and Innovation Flows within a **Terminal** firm Network

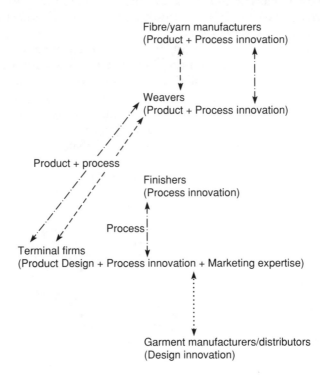

and links the latter in one-way flows with the converters. Uni- or bi-directional information flows regarding design link the garment manufacturers and the converters, depending on whether the latter generate design in-house or depend on their customers for it. It is clear that the 'converter' represents a focal node in the network as it has access to crucial information – *vis-a-vis* its suppliers it possesses information on markets and design; and *vis-a-vis* its clients, it possesses information about local firms' products and process technology. To a large extent, though, it is the high division of labour and fragmentation of the production process among Como firms which creates the need for such a broker, whose very existence and pivotal role are thus closely linked to the 'industrial district' character of the Como textile industry.

It is only when a converter generates design in-house, possesses special marketing skills (rather than relying on long-practised marketing formulae) and develops expertise in product–process technology (directly or indirectly via its partners/subcontractors) that it can exercise a genuine leadership role. The firm is then capable of acting as a catalyst to translate design innovation into new products and/or process technologies, despite its small size. As noted earlier, converters have recently started to establish close partnerships – through preferential agreements or equity holdings – with specialist manufacturers to take advantage of their knowledge and develop new products. Thus more converters could soon emerge as initiators and promoters of innovation. Certainly, according to local sources, converters are attempting to develop a more significant 'leading' role.

By contrast, a terminal firm is more likely to generate or at least exploit radical, as well as incremental, innovation (Unione Industriali di Como, 1983), due to the fact that this type of firm, unlike the traditional converter, has an internal R & D department and possesses in-house knowledge of product and process technologies. The terminal firm gains information on products and process innovations via its network which it then uses to stimulate and develop new industrial expertise. The innovation process works its way back along the network until it eventually prompts imitation by local competitors. Despite their 'leading' role, many terminal firms typically remain small or medium sized.

Table 7.2 Characteristics of Como 'satellite' firms

Fewer than 50 clients	20% or more to major client	Export-oriented or international	Contracts in (and out)
93%	67%	38%	86%
(55%)	(40%)	(49%)	(27%)

Long-term contracts	Fast/ moderate growth	Median assets (£000)	Median sales (£000)	Median staff
83%	86%	750	700	16
(52%)	(79%)	(860)	(1600)	(20)

Secondly, we looked at the characteristics of the 'satellite' firms. These had very similar characteristics to one another, though in marked contrast to those of the 'leaders' (Table 7.2). The typical satellite firm had fewer than 50 clients, sold 20% or more of its production to its biggest single customer, was a subcontractor with long-term or regular, (repeated) contracts and sold predominantly to the regional or national market. In terms of sales and assets, it was smaller than leader firms, a feature which was not attributable to age since the median age of both leaders and followers did not significantly differ.

In terms of power–dependency relations, the picture is mixed. The median percentage of sales by a satellite to its most important customer was 20%, but there were great variations. Slightly more than a third of satellites were relatively independent firms with a fairly wide range of links. Another third could be categorized as relatively dependent firms in terms of number of clients and reliance on their biggest client for orders, and the rest fell in between. Despite their varying degrees of dependence, the majority have enjoyed moderate to fast growth. This may be the result of association with a fast-growing leading firm. However, it may imply that power–dependency relations are less important in determining the viability of small firms than some network theorists believe. Evidently the need exists for more research on this question.

On the whole, we are inclined to attribute the good performance of Como satellites to the presence of two other factors which, as we have already argued in the opening sections of this chapter, minimize the risks of dependency – i.e. bargaining-power and trust. From our data, a majority of Como satellite firms perceived trust, rather than opportunism, as the basis of inter-firm relations in the locality. Also a majority of them were specialists, offering a product or service not easily substitutable in the market-place.

7.6.3 'Leading and 'satellite' firms in Lyon

Key characteristics of the twelve Lyon 'leaders' can be seen in Table 7.3. As in Como, leading firms formed a homogeneous cohort characterized by a high number of clients, a low percentage of sales to their single biggest client, high exports and a prime contractor role. As in Como, they were older and bigger firms than average, in terms of assets, sales and staff employed.

Table 7.3   Characteristics of Lyon 'leading' firms

100+ clients	Less than 20% to major client	Export-oriented or international	Contracts out (but not in)
84%	92%	58%	75%
(63%)	(79%)	(31%)	(51%)

Short-term contracts	Fast/ moderate growth	Median assets (£000)	Median sales (£000)	Median staff
44%	67%	2400	7500	100
(39%)	(71%)	(1250)	(4800)	(84)

The main differences compared with Como leaders were: (i) the type of contracts that Lyon firms had with their clients (mainly regular and long term, while in Como the leaders had predominantly short-term contracts), and (ii) their rate of growth; 67% of Lyon leaders were experiencing fast or moderate growth, the rest showed relative stability.

As regards the position of the French leaders in the value-chain, 40% were weavers/prime contractors, a quarter were vertically integrated firms, while another quarter were knitwear manufacturers. Unlike Como, vertically integrated firms did not appear to produce a particularly high proportion of leaders: only three out of ten vertical firms could be classed as leaders on our criteria.

There were insufficient Lyon 'satellites' in the sample to present meaningful conclusions. Indeed the rest of the Lyon sample was made up of firms whose characteristics were nearer to those of leaders than satellites. To summarize key features of the comparison of Lyon and Como:

1. Leading firms in both localities showed similar characteristics, including above-average size relative to their respective cohorts, and appeared to pursue similar strategies in terms of a broad spread of customers/ markets, and in their use of subcontractors.
2. Vertically integrated firms of above-average size in Como were generally leaders. The exceptions were small non-manufacturing converters. The smaller manufacturing firms were generally in a satellite role.
3. The absence of satellite firms in Lyon may be consistent with the fact that Lyon is no longer a 'true' industrial district, according to our criteria, corroborated by the comparatively low level of local firm interdependencies and complementarities.

7.6.4 'Leading' and 'satellite' firms in Leicester

As noted, the search for 'leading' firms in Leicester turned out to be problematic, with only three in our sample matching the stated criteria. Another larger group matched three criteria, but lacked the 'in-house design' requisite, here called 'sub-leaders'. As British textile manufacturing has often been criticized for a lack of innovative design capability, we looked in some depth at these firms' other characteristics (Table 7.4) to obtain clues as to their 'strategic relevance' in the value chain (Figure 7.5). We wondered, for example, whether the sub-leaders were evolving towards a genuine leadership position or whether they were locked in their present role and status.

The sub-leaders had a relatively low number of customers (half had fewer than 50) and relied on their single biggest client for a high percentage of their sales (the median figure was 26%). They were much older and bigger than the average for the locality, usually employing four or five specialists.

Table 7.4   Characteristics of Leicester 'sub-leaders'

100+ clients	Less than 20% to major client	Export-oriented or international	Contracts out (but not in)
42%	8%	33%	46%
(26%)	(31%)	(9%)	(32%)

Short-term contracts	Fast/ moderate growth	Median assets (£000)	Median sales (£000)	Median staff
18%	54%	400	1850	120
(24%)	(64%)	(250)	(1000)	(50)

A third were export-oriented or international firms. Only half of them were experiencing moderate to fast growth, a somewhat lower proportion than the average for the locality; 38% were actually experiencing decline.

Figure   7.5   Information flows and innovation nodes within networks involving Leicester 'sub-leading' firms.

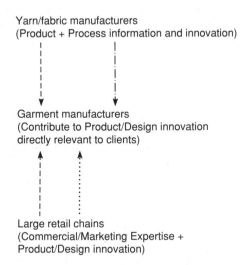

In some respects, the Leicester sub-leaders were similar to Como and Lyon leaders. However, they relied on comparatively few customers for orders (as well as design), at odds with the profile of the Italian and French leaders. They employed a range of specialist managers, as typified by the Lyon leaders, but they lacked the latter's wide-ranging commercial and marketing expertise in export markets, as well as the capacity of Como and Lyon leaders to generate design in-house. In terms of number of clients and reliance on their biggest customers for orders, Leicester sub-leaders were *not* greatly different from the 'satellite' firms there. All except one relied on their biggest single customer for over 20% of their sales.

It is clear that in the UK large retail chains have greatly affected trading relationships in the textiles and clothing sectors. Key functions that elsewhere still characterize textile manufacturers – e.g. creativity and design, marketing and product innovation – have been largely appropriated by the retailers. A strong case can be made that the major chain-store retailers are, in effect, the 'leading' firms for the Leicester knitwear manufacturers. Given that the retailer is well placed to interpret market/fashion trends, and given the historical success of retail chain stores like Marks and Spencer, C & A, Next and the Burton Group, the Leicester firms may have found their own 'strategic' networks, even if this has meant ceding some strategic functions to the multiple retailers. However, the fact that almost half of firms in this category were either stagnating or in decline indicates that membership of such a retail network is no longer rewarding, or that they have already been displaced from the network by a competitor.

The Leicester manufacturers may not have consciously adopted a strategy of working in symbiosis with the large retailers; for the most part, they probably had no obvious alternative, if they were to continue to sell in volume. While it could be argued that the so-called satellite firms would happily accept the role of suppliers to large retail chains despite a high level of dependency, the sub-leaders were firms which might be able to diversify and search for new markets and clients, for they are well-established, with professional proprietors and numerous specialists, some with design responsibilities. Yet these specialist managers appeared to be geared to satisfying the needs of the firms' few major clients, not to expanding in other directions and seeking new markets overseas.

Risk aversion, rather than a desire for autonomy, may explain their continuing commitment to these networks, but risk aversion is one of the characteristics of satellite firms. Further, as Lazerson (1988) has pointed out, large orders from a single client firm in themselves potentially risk over-dependency. A reliable client could in fact be construed as one who maintains a satisfactory level of business, not one who places large orders on a single supplier/subcontractor.

In Como and Lyon many converters and terminal firms have become accustomed to operate in an unpredictable environment, constantly looking for new clients world-wide, whereas Leicester firms established preferential relationships with the large distributors in the 1960s and 1970s in what was probably perceived as a prudent defensive move. The paradox therefore is that operating in an apparently stable environment can lead cumulatively to an unexpected and high-risk situation, a process Johnson (1987) called 'strategic drift'. Conversely, perceived uncertainty can help firms to proact, as they seek to contain and accommodate to their external environment. Thus, as regards information and innovation flows within their exchange networks, the Leicester 'sub-leaders' appear to be weak sources (Figure 7.5).

Table 7.5 Characteristics of Leicester 'satellite' firms (percentage)

Fewer than 50 Clients	20% or more to major client	Export-oriented or international	Contracts in and out
94	76	6	41
(55)	(69)	(9)	(38)

Long-term contracts	Fast/ moderate growth	Median assets (£000)	Median sales (£000)	Median staff
56	65	125	650	21
(76)	(64)	(250)	(1000)	(50)

Turning to the characteristics of Leicester satellites, these were fairly similar to those of the equivalent Como subgroup – i.e. a relatively small number of customers, a high percentage of sales to a single client, weak export orientation and fewer staff than the average for that cohort (Table 7.5). They were, however, more dependent than Como satellites. Almost three-quarters of them had fewer than 20 clients (in Como, two in five) and sold over 20% and often much more of their production to their biggest client. Unlike Como, these firms were also a lot younger than the average for the locality, which may explain their relative dependence on a few customers. Indeed the fact that more than a quarter of firms in this group were experiencing decline may be attributable to their youth, given the high mortality rate among young, small firms generally.

To sum up, the Leicester hosiery and knitwear small firm community contains a large proportion of satellite firms and what we have called 'sub-leaders' – firms in a kind of role **limbo** – but only a few genuine leaders. The real leaders (the large retail chains, we surmise) operate outside the area.

7.7 'LEADING' FIRMS AS CO-ORDINATORS

So far we have identified 'leading' firms in respect of innovation, creativity and marketing clout. Leading firms in strategic networks however, according to Lorenzoni and Ornati (1988), are also co-ordinators. For the network to be effective, innovation must arise throughout the network and this requires the active participation of network members. A leading firm must be able to ensure the mobilization of the network, otherwise its capacity to innovate will have only limited practical application. We now examine the co-ordinating role of the leading firms we have identified and ascertain whether the firms identified as 'satellites' belong to co-ordinated groups.

Specifically, we asked proprietors whether their firms belonged to a group whose activities were co-ordinated, and if their firms did, which firm took the initiative in co-ordinating the group members; their replies are synthesized in Table 7.6.

Table 7.6 Question, 'Does your firm belong to a group of firms whose activities require co-ordination? (percentages)

| | Como | | Lyon | Leicester | |
	Leaders	Satellites	Leaders	Sub-leaders	Satellites
Yes	60	67	83	38	29
No	40	33	17	62	71

A majority of the French and Italian leading firms claimed to belong to co-ordinated groups, five out of every six in the case of Lyon. Two-thirds of Como satellites also claimed to belong to such groups. As regards the co-ordination of such groups, 80% and 70% respectively of Como and Lyon leading firms in co-ordinated groups claimed that they were the co-ordinators. In contrast, well under half of the Leicester sub-leaders and satellites claimed to belong to a co-ordinated group, and of the former, only a handful laid claim to a proactive co-ordinating role.

While the Como leaders generally claimed to be the sole co-ordinators, many Lyon leaders reported a co-ordinating role shared jointly with a supplier or a customer. Because most Como and Lyon leaders are prime contractors, they are *de facto* co-ordinators of a kind and respondents could simply have equated co-ordination with subcontracting practices. In the simplest case, relations between prime contractors and subcontractors do not necessarily need co-ordination. A prime contractor may choose to relate to his subcontractors one-to-one, without ever needing to put any of his subcontractors in touch with the others. On the other hand – and this is the essence of the 'strategic network' concept as applied to the Italian industrial district – contractors (especially sub-contractors) may participate in networks by fulfilling roles not wholly predicated on their formal status. It all depends on the skills the firm has to offer the network and the degree of initiative its proprietor is willing and able to take. This much, we believe, is characteristic of so-called 'dynamic networks' (Foray, 1990). In consequence, the posture of any firm with respect to its innovating, contracting and co-ordinating roles in the network is likely to be context-specific and possibly somewhat idiosyncratic to that firm.

Our findings indicate that a variety of networks operate in the three small firm communities under examination and that some correspond to the 'strategic network' model while others do not. In Como we found locally based networks comprising leaders performing an innovating and co-ordinating role, with satellites in a co-ordinated position, thus in concert manifesting the typical features of so-called 'strategic' networks. When Como firms belonged to co-ordinated groups, the leaders usually took the initiative and acted straightforwardly as the network co-ordinator.

In Lyon local leading firms often appeared to participate in – and co-ordinate – a network, albeit often in collaboration with clients or suppliers. The fact that, despite being prime contractors and innovators, these leaders frequently chose to share the co-ordinating role suggests that they belong to sophisticated networks which go beyond mere superior–subordinate contractor relations and which transcend local/regional boundaries. Furthermore, some of the Lyon firms we sampled did not participate exclusively in the textiles-to-garments *filière* – i.e. a substantial part of their output became inputs to value-adding chains of other sectors such as soft furnishings and industrial products. So one can hypothesize that such firms could be leaders in the textiles *filière*, yet be subordinate in their other relationships, especially *vis-a-vis* dominant clients such as multinational corporations.

So the full picture is evidently complex. The notion that networks may be non-local and manifest shared co-ordination has, we think, been understated in the strategic network literature to date. If innovative and autonomous firms find it rewarding to belong to co-ordinated groups even when the co-ordinating role has to be shared with others, it suggests that the benefits of co-ordination and collaboration are perhaps more widely appreciated and more pervasive than has generally been realized. A historic strength of Como firms was the opportunity afforded their proprietors to draw on well-developed, informal *milieu* relations. The fact that more than a third of all Como firms now claimed to participate in a co-ordinated group could indicate a widespread belief there that milieu relationships are no longer sufficient to ensure the mobilization of trading partners.

Among the Como satellites, two clear patterns emerged. On the one hand, a sizeable number said that the co-ordinating initiative was taken by a local client, indicating that their network was largely contained within the district. On the other hand, some stated that the co-ordinating initiative was undertaken by a consortium of firms, apparently corroborating the notion of shared co-ordination roles in networks, even though such mechanisms have not been noted in strategic network theory thus far. In Como itself various consortia are actively engaged in export initiatives to promote the characteristic products of the area. More research is undoubtedly needed to understand how they operate, what their functions and powers are, and whether a consortium can fully assume the role of a 'leading firm'.

Finally, in Leicester comparatively few firms participated in a co-ordinated arrangement (less than a third). Few proprietors could envision any advantages in co-ordination of the kind we have discussed. This reflects the typical dyadic relationship the Leicester manufacturers have with their retail clients. When one of the partners is greatly dependent on the other for orders and innovations, they are in effect participating in limited, controlled rather than, co-ordinated, networks. No doubt, collaborative practices sometimes exist in these dyad relations, but probably more the result of a conscious attempt by the retailer to encourage the manufacturer to innovate than the reverse. Indeed we hypothesize that any initiative to co-ordinate a multiple-firm network would typically result from initiatives by wholesale merchants and retailers outside the locality.

Can such dyadic networks be labelled 'strategic'? Our view is that they can certainly be competitive in particular cases (one thinks, for instance, of those involving Marks and Spencer), but there would seem little doubt that the benefits arising favour the retailer much more than the typical Leicester manufacturer at the present time.

7.8 COMPETITION AND COLLABORATION WITHIN AND ACROSS NETWORKS

Network theory emphasizes collaboration, whereas free-marketeers such as Porter (1990) stress competition. In an industrial district competition can be fierce yet collaboration and networks also operate. How do we reconcile this seeming paradox? Further, does competition occur within or between networks? According to network theory, competition between rival firms can be replaced by competition between rival networks. Thorelli (1986) argued that the extent of competition depends on the degree of overlap of value-adding activities. If there is complete overlap, then there is likely to be intense competition, while partial overlap can enable collaboration. Competition also inevitably leads to secretive practices on the part of many Como firms, especially those with proprietary knowledge to protect from numerous local imitators.

In Como **vertical collaboration** is common within a network because the activities carried out by network members are complementary, given their tendency to specialize in particular stages of the value chain. **Lateral competition** could, in principle, occur between similar firms within (or across) networks. If, say, two or more firms in a given network had similar specialisms, they would most probably be in competition, perhaps fiercely so. Moderate competition within a network is unlikely to alter its internal characteristics and it is in the nature of a strategic network that lateral competition will be moderated among the partner firms by mutual accommodation, as accepted or proactively engineered by the 'leader', and manifest as preferential collaborative relationships. Otherwise the network will become unstable and one or more of the firms will quit. Given that severe competition may destabilize the network, established network participants who gain from membership have a definite incentive to act so as to restabilize it. In the absence of such action, a new network may emerge, aligned with a new or established 'converter' firm.

There is also the possibility of competition between two networks as entities, should the respective converters aim to serve the same end markets. Competition between such networks in Como can be fierce, precisely because many overlap, both in terms of products and market segments. To the extent that converters are themselves able to specialize, this contains if not wholly eliminates inter-network rivalry.

Collaboration among structurally equivalent firms within a network is conceivable. This form of collaboration is most likely to occur when, for instance, one weaver is recognized to have somewhat differing specialisms than others in the network, hence they complement one another rather than compete directly. Similarly, one might anticipate collaboration across networks, though generally in very specific respects. For example, we found that a majority of wholesalers/converters collaborated over export markets, a majority of finishers over technology/production. Likewise, if we single out 'leaders' and 'satellites', we find that a majority of leaders collaborated over export markets and a majority of satellites over technology production. Collaboration could also take place between firms in different networks occupying differing vertical positions in the value-chain and is fairly common: a finisher or weaver in one network accepts work from converters in other networks, where its specialism gives it an undisputed advantage.

All these practices must obviously take into account the degree of *de facto* competition between equivalent firms in both networks. Further, while mobility of satellites from one network to another is a possibility, leaving a network from a satellite position to become a converter is increasingly rare, as the role now needs considerably greater skills than just the old determination to travel abroad with a pattern book in search of clients. Today converters tend to be ex-employees of the large 'terminal' firms – i.e. people with good qualifications and experience gained in an innovative firm, who believe that they can be successful on their own.

Recently there have been cases of converters agreeing to establish special relationships with each other and each other's regular subcontractors. For example, both converters and weavers could share information with each other and develop new product and/or market strategies. In this way, extra synergies are created between as well as within networks.

In Lyon a majority of firms exchanged information and collaborated in many different ways with other (not always local) firms. Here, unlike

Como, the perceived advantages of collaboration appear to outweigh the perceived disadvantages of possibly damaging leaks of proprietary knowledge. Nevertheless, the Lyon leaders were similar to the Como leaders, in that a majority of them collaborated over sales and markets only.

According to Porter, 'loss of domestic rivalry is a dry rot that slowly undermines competitive advantage by slowing the pace of innovation and dynamism' (1990, p. 170); with reference to geographically concentrated industrial clusters, he argued (p. 171) that:

> 'If rivalry ebbs...there is a tendency for the local cluster to become insular, a closed and inward-looking system. The problem is exacerbated if most firms lack significant international activities and their primary commercial relationships are with each other (for example, suppliers sell almost exclusively to a single domestic industry). Firms, customers and suppliers all talk only to each other. None brings fresh perspectives.'

These observations, one might reasonably think, have relevance to the Leicester context, with its preference for simple and often inwardly focused dyadic network linkages. Our findings suggest that although Leicester firms do share information with others in the community, the process tends to be *ad hoc* and unstructured, not systematic and with a superordinate goal in mind.

A more general question of particular interest is to ask how much of an effect collaboration in and across networks has in **relation to community or network effectiveness** (long-run viability). Porter and others have consistently stated the importance of the competitive mechanism in the survival and 'upgrading' process. We hypothesize, however, that a 'classic' competitive environment prevents firms from creating extra and potentially vital synergies by pooling their (individually limited) resources. Open and easy collaboration, on the other hand, may imply lack (or loss) of dynamism, even complacency. **Thus a mixture of collaboration and competition within and across networks may well provide the best environment for a local industry to thrive.** Equally, it is clear that one should not overstate the intrinsic value of collaboration within an industrial community. Much depends on the value of the shared information and joint actions and whether information exchange and collaboration are used in ways that bring significant competitive advantages to the firms involved in these processes, individually and collectively.

7.9 SUMMARY AND CONCLUSIONS

In this chapter we have discussed exchange and strategic networks from the point of view of small firm communities. Strategic networks imply both leader and follower (satellite) firms. Firms are leaders when they exercise both an innovating and a co-ordinating role. Our network-oriented analysis suggests that Como contains 'strategic' networks co-ordinated by local innovating firms with established synergistic links that have increased the pace and extent of local innovation. As regards power–dependency relations, there are satellite firms with strong links to comparatively few clients and also fairly autonomous, or loosely coupled, satellite firms. Most of these, being specialized, own valuable assets and enjoy considerable bargaining-power *vis-a-vis* their clients. Both leaders and satellites have enjoyed fast or moderate growth in recent years, so network participation seems generally to bring rewards and competitive advantages to member firms, whatever their position and role within the network.

The Lyon sample pointed to the existence of innovating firms belonging to 'dynamic' networks. The innovating role of the Lyon leaders makes them desirable network partners, thus reducing their risk of being displaced from a network. The locality today is not as strong in textiles as in the past, but a number of outstanding firms have survived and prospered. There is also evidence of greater diversification and reduced reliance on the textiles-to-garments *filière* than in the past.

The Leicester sample showed few instances of either innovating or co-ordinating firms, containing mainly satellite firms and what we called 'sub-leaders'. The satellites were heavily dependent firms, having few clients and with a substantial percentage of their sales to a prominent (retail) client. The sub-leaders had a larger client base and arguably more autonomy, but were still strongly coupled to comparatively few clients for a majority of their sales. Despite their relatively greater autonomy than satellite firms, the Leicester sub-leaders were likely to have reported decline, so belonging to 'dynamic' networks 'controlled' rather than 'co-ordinated' by retail chains has been of dubious benefit to them. They run the constant risk of finding themselves replaced by other firms, either on cost grounds or on the basis of superior design and fashion content.

Once an innovative foreign supplier has penetrated the retail chain, the way ahead is shown for others, and once dropped from an existing network, the individual Leicester firm may find that the services it can offer – reliability, stability, capacity to adapt closely to the needs of a few major customers – are in themselves not a substitute for the ability to innovate.

Lastly, as regards strategic network theory, when applied to our three communities of firms it was most informative with reference to locally contained networks in Como. This reinforces the analysis of strategic network theorists such as Lorenzoni and Ornati, whose work has been based explicitly on the reality of Italian industrial districts. Locally contained networks are the ones conventionally advanced as examples of 'strategic' networks in a context of dispersed ownership. When examples of non-local 'strategic' networks have been offered, it is usually in the context of common ownership – i.e. with reference to a large firm whose owned-and-operated units, which may be geographically dispersed, behave as a 'strategic' network. But there is no intrinsic reason to suppose that the theory cannot be extended to non-local, dispersed-ownership contexts.

In Leicester and Lyon we found non-local networks operating in a context of dispersed ownership. For Leicester, networks led by retail chains may have the potential to develop into 'strategic' networks, provided the retailers change the type of relations that pertain between the 'hub' and the contractors, and also among the suppliers themselves. Whether or not this would require a fundamental change in the pattern of ownership of the resources is an open question. For Lyon, independently owned small and medium sized leading firms which do not operate in an industrial district, strictly defined, engage in collaborative practices with outside clients and suppliers without necessarily adopting a static position in the network–not so much a 'quasi-firm' phenomenon, more a loose aggregation of autonomous firms.

To conclude, we affirm the conceptual and empirical validity of the 'strategic' network, defined as a fairly stable set of firms in which a leading firm provides overall co-ordination and each satellite firm in the network 'knows its place' in relation to all the others and behaves accordingly. These networks are found particularly, though not exclusively, in industrial districts.

The 'focal firm' version of a local industrial strategic network is a fair description of what we observed in the Como case, whereas Lyon networks involve partners within and beyond the immediate locality. Moreover, in line with Axelsson (1992, p. 201), we envisage the possibility of networks where – to a greater or lesser degree – strategic action (innovating and co-ordinating) is not **limited to any one focal firm**. Rather, 'it involves part or even most of the network to which the firm is linked'. This means, in principle, that there are no fixed or static roles and positions in the network and each firm has the scope to mobilize the others in respect of new initiatives.

Clearly there is scope for a continuum of organizational approaches and configurations, according to the extent of autonomy ceded (appropriated by) satellite firms in a given network. However, it would be premature to suggest that theoretical developments in strategic network thinking are at an end: there are a variety of fascinating, unanswered questions arising which should justify new research in this area for years to come.

8

The European dimension:
1993 and beyond

8.1 INTRODUCTION

The completion of the **Single European Market** (SEM) was, in principle, scheduled to take effect from 1 January 1993. The underlying aim of this development is to reinforce cross-border trade within the European Community by creating a unified, domestic market. In itself, this is a remarkable ambition and the fruit of several decades of political and economic co-operation between EC member states. Nevertheless, the pace, extent and impact (in terms of production, consumption and employment) of increases in intra-European trade due to the SEM remain to be ascertained.

In this chapter we first set out principles underpinning the completion of the SEM and explore some of the possible consequences of European economic integration by setting out four general models. We then turn to the possible effects of market integration on the textiles and clothing sectors, judged from past performance, and with a view to potential future developments. To analyse some of the differential effects that may occur as European integration deepens, we will present replies from our questionnaire survey of small textile and clothing firms indicating both their awareness of what the SEM is likely to entail and their preparedness for it. Finally, the in-firm perspective will be complemented by analysis of the regional environment in which these firms operate in order to hypothesize development paths for the textiles–clothing industry at broader levels.

8.2 GENERAL MODELS OF EUROPEAN MARKET INTEGRATION

This section will set out and critically analyse four models of European market integration and describe some of their likely consequences.

8.2.1 The revived economy model or 'a bigger cake for all'

The essential mechanism of the revived economy model as set out by Cecchini's influential report of 1988 is market integration by the removal of non-tariff obstacles to trade within the EC. Non-tariff obstacles include barriers due to differences in technical norms, administrative formalities linked to export/import procedures, disparities in national taxation systems and nationalistic preferences in the award of public procurement contracts. Removal of these obstacles should produce a 'supply-side shock', leading to greater competition, downward pressures on costs and prices and a stimulation of demand within the EC. The results are intended to include a better allocation of resources, an increase in output and a decrease in unemployment. In brief, a 'self-sustaining virtuous circle' should stimulate Western European economies and improve European competitiveness in relation to third-party rivals, particularly from the USA and Japan. All of the citizens of the EC are hypothesized to benefit by this process.

The Cecchini Report presented calculations of the likely economic benefits. In many cases they appeared to be significant. Although there has been debate over how convincingly the case was put, the issues to be addressed here will not be whether the mode of calculation was accurate, but the questions of when, **to what extent** and **by whom** the benefits will be realized. Arguably, four factors will militate against a full, speedy and equitable harvesting of benefits.

First, the scale of benefits reaped is likely to vary considerably between industrial sectors. This is because in some sectors – including textiles and clothing – intra-EC trade is already at a high level while it is at a much lower level in sectors such as telecommunications, railway rolling-stock, turbine generators and insurance services. Hence new opportunities created by the completion of the SEM in insurance services, for example, are of a different order to those in textiles–clothing precisely because the markets of the former are at a lower level of Europe-wide integration. Given that the UK has strengths in insurance, national benefits are likely to accrue in that sector and so offset weaknesses in textiles–clothing where Italy has a lead. Hence significant variations exist in current levels of European integration across national sectoral specializations which will have a continuing economic impact during the completion of the SEM. The consequences of these elements will be termed the differential effect.

Secondly, the scale of benefits realized, outlined in the Cecchini Report (1988, 103), as amounting to medium–term gains of 4–7% of gross domestic product, will depend on the degree to which the SEM is successfully completed. The longer the European integration process takes, the slower will be the rate of realization of the economic benefits. This might be termed the 'volume effect'. Successful completion depends largely on political will.

Although '1993' has aroused enthusiasm across Europe, clear signs of resistance continue to be manifested in some quarters. Progress is undoubtedly being made, but the gains are likely to be made slowly over the long term.

Thirdly, the time factor is crucial in appropriating the benefits of the SEM. Punctual completion is problematic. Martin Bangemann (1991), Vice-President of the European Commission, indicated that some 70% of the 107 texts required for the completion of the legislative framework of the SEM have been incorporated into national legislation. Yet only 25% of those texts have been embodied in every one of the 12 EC states. Progress is being made, but in uneven fashion, with the result that inconsistencies in application will inevitably store up future difficulties.

This problem raises the distinction between agreement of principles and implementation in practice. Part of the increase in momentum towards an integrated Europe comes from the move away from community-wide agreements based on unanimity among member states to agreements based on the mechanism of a 'qualified majority'. This is a two-edged blade: although it makes agreements by 'qualified majority' easier (through overriding minority dissensions), it makes community-wide implementation of contentious initiatives less likely. Dissent stifled in the pre-1993 run-up may erupt in the post-1993 period. This fourth problem will be termed the 'submerged polity' factor.

In the medium to long term, the strength of the 'submerged polity' factor will itself be linked to the differential, volume and temporal factors outlined. Each of these factors is extremely difficult to measure, not least because of a certain amount of interdependence among them – positive trends in one can trigger off a favourable reaction in another and likewise with negative trends. In consequence, though it would be premature to make predictions on specific issues, full completion of the SEM is set to extend well beyond 1993.

Moreover, it is possible to foresee a Europe which succeeds in increasing output measured in aggregate terms, a Europe which succeeds in securing all of the medium-term gains of 4–7% of gross domestic product envisaged in the Cecchini report, but which fails to distribute those gains tolerably well to all. The seriousness of the latter worry can be illustrated by two examples. First, the motivation behind the insistence of a number of EC member states on the need for 'a social dimension' is the concern that post-1992 Europe will otherwise lack the appropriate redistributive mechanisms for translating economic expansion into social development. Secondly, the Cecchini Report (1988) acknowledged that 'for business and government ...the road to market integration will be paved with tough adjustments'. If increased competition results in the elimination of inefficient European producers, the thrust to drive prices down will benefit only those consumers who have not been made jobless in the process. Although the completion of the SEM is likely to produce differential gains, it is unclear what balance will be struck between corporate and consumer interests on the one hand, and between the conflicting needs of European nations and regions on the other hand.

In summary, the 'revived economy' model is problematic in that, even if there is to be a 'bigger cake', there is no inevitable association between that bigger cake and benefits for all. This realization animated, a little belatedly, the controversy over the 'social chapter' of the 1991 Maastricht agreement.

8.2.2 The competition model: 'may the best man win'

This model allows for two major variants. First, the competition model at its worst could be the opposite of the 'bigger cake' model since the contest might turn out to be a zero-sum game. In this pessimistic version, market shares would be captured by more powerful firms and/or nations at the expense of weaker firms and nations, leading to aggravated economic polarization within the EC. The scenario is unattractive and probably unsustainable in the long term. Nevertheless given that the international economy has been traversing a period of recession, this unpleasant scenario cannot be ruled out for the 'growing years' of the SEM in the mid-1990s.

Alternatively, in the hypothesis of an expansionary phase later in the 1990s, the competition model could combine with the 'bigger cake' prognosis. In this scenario, firms compete for market share in an expanding market: although the weak go to the wall, the fittest survive and prosper, creating greater wealth which benefits the majority of states and their citizens.

Clearly there is nothing new in these competition scenarios. They are models that business-people generally espouse. The Commission sets great store by the liberal principles of economic competition. Articles 85 and 86 of the Treaty of Rome enshrine market competition at the heart of the project for European economic integration. Taken together, these factors point to the 'competition model' as having great ideological and practical significance in post-1992 Europe.

Of course, competition can be challenging and invigorating. Yet without going so far as Dudley (1989) who claimed that 1992 will be a 're-enactment of the Battle of the Somme', it must also be acknowledged that competition can be deadly serious. A competition model always implies winners and losers. Specifically who will be the producers and consumers that benefit most remains to be seen. A further major issue is whether, on a sector-by-sector basis, increased competition results in a zero-sum game or a bigger cake. Thus the competition model is not incompatible with the revived economy model, but they do not necessarily have identical outcomes. Probably for this reason official EC sources dwell more on the rosier aspects of the 'revived economy' model and less on the thornier implications of the competition model.

8.2.3   The protectionist model: 'Fortress Europe'

The protectionist model holds that, whatever the state of competition between European rivals, it should always be the 'outsider' who is the loser. 'Fortress Europe' has few outspoken advocates. Yet many non-EC firms – not only US and Japanese companies, but also European non-EC firms – have been relocating in EC countries precisely because they fear the barriers to entry will rise (Harrington and Maguire, 1989).

With this model, worst-case and best-case scenarios are again possible. The worst case would posit continued recession in the 1990s: EC barriers might rise in co-ordinated fashion and an experiment in autarchy could follow. The best case is perhaps that of 'Fortress Europe' being little more than a threat to be used to gain leverage against protected third-party economies, including the USA in its more insular instances, but especially Japan. Used wisely, the threat of 'Fortress Europe' may act as a lever to open up trade around the world. However, using this lever involves considerable brinkmanship and may lead to a destabilization in international trade. The inherent dangers are illustrated by the stalemate reached in the 1991–2 GATT discussions between the EC and the USA on agricultural subsidies. As in previous models, there are considerable cross-dependencies among sectors which make prediction difficult. None the less, it seems probable that political pressures to widen the EC will reduce the 'Fortress Europe' mentality.

8.2.4   The 'free-for-all' model or 'importers' paradise'

In this scenario, non-European producers (especially American, Japanese and Far East competitors) will be the main beneficiaries of an 'open' Europe. Clearly this is a worst-case scenario in so far as it assumes that European firms will be unable to withstand the onslaught of third-party producers. Its thrust is that many Japanese and US firms display a higher level of internationalization, economic competitiveness and managerial expertise, and so are better poised to compete in pan-European markets than are European firms generally used to segmented, national markets.

Against this view is to be set the argument that this model describes yesterday's realities, not those of tomorrow. Precisely because of historical, intra-European barriers to trade, European firms have not exploited the scale and organizational advantages enjoyed by non-European competitors. The 1993 initiatives are designed to help remedy this situation. While this is undoubtedly true, the caveats expressed regarding the 'bigger cake' model must be repeated here, namely that differential, volume, temporal and 'submerged polity' factors make outcomes uncertain. In addition, the strengths and weaknesses of EC manufacturing and service industries in relation to international competition vary significantly by sector: for example, in financial services and telecommunications Europe is relatively well-placed but far less so in consumer electronics and information technology.

8.2.5 Overview

The preceding critique of models describing the possible development of the SEM has shown that they all take as their starting-point economic and industrial factors. Crucial as those factors are, they are by no means the only elements to consider in a discussion of the significance of '1993'. On the one hand political and monetary factors will play a significant role, while on the other social and cultural dimensions should not be forgotten. When this mix of broader elements is taken into consideration, the fundamental question of whether market integration equates to a single market arises. It is this question which will now be addressed.

Turning first to the characteristics of European markets, to talk of the EC as a single 'domestic' market-place is still premature. Although it has become commonplace to compare the integration process in the EC to the federal structure of the USA, major differences should not be overlooked. In comparison to the USA, which has a high propensity to market standardization, Europe presents greater variations in consumer demand. Despite the new regulatory environment implied by market integration in the SEM, marketing strategies of firms operating in Europe will still be wise to recognize national and sub-national differences, as well as to identify cross-national trends and market strategies.

Moreover, cultural and linguistic obstacles rank as major non-tariff barriers, especially to the thousands of small firms trading in Europe. There has been very little in the '1993' initiatives which has addressed these problems, nor is it possible to envisage easy solutions. The existence of cultural and linguistic barriers to trade indicates that the analogy between the beneficial effects of the elimination of non-tariff barriers between the federal states of the USA and the elimination of non-tariff barriers between the nation states of Europe is misleading. American society, despite its history of immigration and the importance of other cultures (particularly of the Hispanic communities), remains governed by a common language, English. Although English has world status as the first language of business, it can never be the only language of business. This is particularly clear in the European context. Language barriers will continue to hinder trade in post-1992 Europe unless strenuous efforts are made to improve company executives' proficiency in foreign languages. Japanese firms have taken cognizance of this for some time. Yet many firms have been reluctant to make the considerable investment in human resources that the acquisition of high-level language skills requires. Regrettably, this has been especially true of British firms.

To develop the comparison between market integration in the USA and in Europe, it must be recalled that the US economy is based on a single currency, the dollar, which is also the world's leading currency. These conditions do not obtain in Europe. Progress towards currency exchange stability through the Exchange Rate Mechanism (ERM) has been slow. Great reluctance to participate was shown by Britain in particular. Only after a major policy turn-around within the Thatcher administration did Britain join in the autumn of 1990. At Maastricht in 1991, the Major government still adopted an arm's-length attitude to the next stage of alignment, which would be monetary union. Yet in 1992 the realization dawned around Europe that a number of pro-monetary union EC members will find it practically difficult to achieve the economic prerequisites for monetary unification indicated at Maastricht. The vote in the Danish referendum against the Maastricht Treaty has further slowed, if not halted, the unification process. In addition, the debate over 'widening' of the EC (bringing in central European nations to the EC) vs 'deepening' (real political and monetary union) has further complicated matters. Thus political and economic uncertainties regarding the future of the SEM are far from resolution.

The result of the slow progress to full monetary union (understood as an effective single currency) has been continued difficulty for intra-European trade due to risks induced by parity fluctuations and to the costs of currency conversion. Even within the ERM, permitted exchange fluctuations are still sufficiently large to wipe out small profit margins, while converting currency through the banking sector carries a further financial penalty. These problems arise on a scale sufficient to necessitate currency 'hedging' by large companies and to dissuade many small, less financially sophisticated firms from direct exporting. While such problems will inevitably exist on the world economic stage for the foreseeable future, they detract from the credibility of a single domestic market in Europe. With multiple national currencies set to persist for the remainder of the 1990s, trade between European countries will be perceived in terms of foreign, not domestic, markets. For all these reasons – monetary, political and cultural – business-people are likely to find that the so-called 'single' European market will remain extremely heterogeneous.

8.3 THE EUROPEAN TEXTILES AND CLOTHING INDUSTRY AND THE SEM

The Cecchini Report (1988, p. 64) described the textiles and clothing industries as having received 'the medicine of EC market integration earlier than most', making it 'perhaps the outstanding example of a manufacturing sector which has already reaped considerable benefits from progress towards home market conditions in Europe'. Certainly textiles–clothing firms operate in market conditions more like those planned for the SEM than those currently obtaining for sectors in Europe such as road haulage or insurance. The extent to which this has resulted in 'considerable benefits' is, however, open to debate. Accordingly, each of the four theoretical models outlined above will be compared to the reality of developments in the textiles–clothing sector.

To take them in reverse order, Europe as an 'importers' paradise' is a reality. The penetration of European markets by non-European producers has been proceeding at an alarming pace, as we have indicated in Chapter 2. To stem the tide and allow structural adjustment in the EC, member nations have to greater or lesser degrees invoked protectionist measures under the various Multi-Fibre Arrangements (MFAs). Yet the lack of a systematic, uniform approach to the MFAs due to national differences in the nature and extent of protectionism, as well as the possibilities available to ignore or undermine it, have so far excluded talk of a 'Fortress Europe'. Additionally, imbalances in trade in textiles–clothing among European countries – particularly between Italy and her neighbours – are frequently more significant than those between the EC and the developing nations. Thus differential benefits are clear. Single market competition (or close approximation thereto) in the EC has resulted in winners and losers. In bald terms, Italy and perhaps Germany can be classed as winners, France and Britain largely as losers.

But has the 'cake' grown bigger? Measured by volume, EC output of textiles and clothing grew by approx. 1.5% between 1963 and 1973, but remained static between 1973 and 1979 (GATT, 1980). Between 1980 and 1987, textiles production in constant prices increased by 8% while that of clothing increased by 18% (*Panorama of EC Industry*, 1990). Thus there are signs that the size of the 'cake' has increased. However employment fell by 401 000 in textiles and 254 000 in clothing in the EC between 1980 and 1988 (*ibid.*).

In summary, although elements of all of the models have so far applied to some extent, the major components have been increased competition (model 2) and increased market penetration by non-European suppliers (model 4).

Turning to future developments, two broad scenarios will be envisaged here for the European textiles–clothing industry in the post-1992 years. The first is that of no significant change as a result of the SEM, while the second explores the possibility of further significant change. These issues will be addressed by reference both to the literature and to the authors' surveys.

8.3.1 The 'no-change' scenario

The Cecchini Report (1988) predicted that only few or minor changes would take place in textiles–clothing due to the SEM; it made the judgement that firms were not experiencing significant difficulties in conducting intra-

Community trade and that the removal of any remaining non-tariff barriers was 'only likely to have marginal effects' (p. 65). Some cost reductions and savings were envisaged, but these totalled only 0.7% of costs. This is a modest figure given the latitude appropriate to statistical prediction. Indeed the report acknowledged that production and transport savings may simply be captured in distributors' margins.

Table 8.1 Respondents' views on how the Single European Market will affect their firm (percentage of firms)

	Lyon	Como	Leicester
Little or no change	36	7	23
Favourably	42	51	16
Unfavourably	2	2	16
Not sure	20	40	45

The 'no-change' scenario was explored in our three-country survey (Table 8.1). The view that patterns of trade in the 1990s would mirror those of the 1980s was indeed embraced by many of our French and British respondents. Some respondents specifically commented that they considered the European market in textiles–clothing to be already integrated. Many firms believed that the status quo would continue. Some firms, particularly in Leicester, seemed to believe that their domestic markets would not come under new threat.

Firms having a significant exports orientation usually believed either that the SEM would have little effect or adopted a favourable attitude to post-1992 trading conditions. Table 8.2 gives figures on levels of export activity at the time of the survey.

Table 8.2 Exports orientation of surveyed firms (percentage)

	Lyon	Como	Leicester
Firms with 50%+ export sales	20	24	2
Firms with 26–49% export sales	15	27	7

The generally more favourable attitude of the French and Italians as compared to the British may be explained by the optimistic belief that the post-1993 period will preserve their advantages. The French, who foresaw either no change or change favourable to themselves, seemed to be saying:

'We can at least hold our own or indeed do better.' The hidden message from the Italian respondents seemed to be: 'We are already among the winners and we'll keep it that way.' Conversely, most of the firms stating they were unsure were those with little or no exports profile. In summary, even a favourable attitude towards the SEM can simply indicate a belief in a maintained and beneficial status quo.

8.3.2 Significant change as a result of the SEM

As has been acknowledged by industry representatives (Blum, 1989), the possibility of significant change occurring within the textile and clothing industries due to European integration cannot be ruled out. This does not necessarily contradict the assumptions of the previous section. The Cecchini Report (1988) was concerned with industry-wide gains and losses in the EC. Nevertheless, it is feasible (likely even) that significant change will occur differentially, that is, due to shifts among particular nations, regions, size categories of firms and/or subsectors.

For example, the Leicester knitwear sector appears vulnerable. As indicated in Table 8.2, the British sample had a lower experience-base in international markets. Thus the lower export levels of the British firms was reflected in a greater number of unfavourable views and the near majority of 'don't knows' recorded in Table 8.1. The lower level of internationalization correlated with the lower experience base of the UK firms, measured in terms of their younger age, smaller assets and turnover. Having less current experience in intra-Community trade, the British cohort was understandably uncertain about future developments. Here our findings accorded with those of Nerb (1988, p. 196), whose summary of a major survey of European industry's perceptions of 1993 indicated that the balances of textiles–clothing firms perceiving opportunities to be greater than risks were 52% for Italy, 34% for France and 31% for Britain The British were in fact the least positive national group in the Community as a whole in relation to the Single Market programme. If British firms prove unable or unwilling to seek out export markets or to parry threats to home markets, then greater penetration of British markets and larger deficits in the balance of trade will result.

The Nerb survey (1988, pp. 8–9) also showed that textiles and clothing firms considered that administrative barriers and frontier delays were the major non-commercial obstacles to trade. This view reflects the structure of the textile and clothing industries in that small and medium sized firms make up their bulk. The costs associated with bureaucratic obstacles tend to weigh relatively more heavily on small than on large firms, since the former rarely have the specialist skills and the financial resources of the latter. Accordingly, the removal of administrative barriers becomes proportionately more beneficial and more urgent.

Changes in retail distribution systems due to European integration are likely to have a major impact on manufacturing firms. One highly probable development in the 1990s is a cross-community extension of national and multinational distribution companies. Marks and Spencer and Benetton have led the way, and more retail multiples are following. Concentration and internationalization of distribution have already had, and will continue to have, repercussions on sourcing patterns. Manufacturers who already either supply own-label products or subcontract to the chains will find themselves in conditions of increased international competition. They will need to defend acquired markets against predators. Conversely, dynamic firms looking for new opportunities will seek to link into new patterns of distribution, either by direct dealings or through intermediaries. By implication, they will need to extend their information-gathering methods, to identify opportunities beyond their home customer base and find efficient ways of exploiting them. Developing local and international networks – particularly of the 'strategic' type discussed in Chapter 7 – is one solution to these needs. Indeed changes in the linkages between manufacturers and distributors may well constitute the major innovation within EC markets over the coming years. Here too differential trends are likely, with balances of losses and gains stacking up unevenly around the regions of Europe.

Finally, the completion of the internal market will probably have repercussions on the real impact of the MFA. Under current arrangements, restrictions on imports from developing countries vary among EC member states due to differing bilateral agreements between individual European importing countries and non-European exporters. Faini and Heimler (1991) have argued that: (a) these variations have led to significant price differentials between sales of equivalent products around Europe, and (b) national variations in import restrictions will necessarily disappear in the SEM, leading to increased import penetration of the hitherto more protected economies. Much depends, however, on the renegotiation of MFA IV, a theme to which we return in Chapter 9.

Notwithstanding the uncertainties that the textile and clothing industries face during the decade of the 1990s, we conclude from the foregoing that the completion of the internal market *is* likely to have a significant impact, principally because competition within the EC will increase. Issues related to the development of the SEM therefore matter. Thus we next present detailed analysis of levels of awareness of and preparedness for 1993 among our surveyed firms.

8.4 AWARENESS OF 1993 AMONG THE FIRMS CONTACTED

8.4.1 Availability of information on 1993

We hypothesized that small firm strategy formulation for the SEM depends on adequate information flows. Questions probing the availability and value of information on SEM issues produced disquieting answers. To give a complete picture, results on information availability are reported in Table 8.3.

Very few information sources – ranging from local, national and EC agencies to business and personal contacts – have fulfilled their potential. The sampled small firms were frequently underinformed: their needs had only partially been met by official bodies. These findings accord with a major survey undertaken in March–April 1991 by Gray (1992, p. 19) which revealed that the single main problem perceived by UK small firms in relation to the SEM was lack of information.

The limited extent to which EC agencies have been perceived as active no doubt reflects the fact that information dissemination about EC issues has been decentralized to national and local levels for sound, logistic reasons. In Britain and France national agencies have done much to increase awareness. In comparative terms, the British Department of Trade and Industry's 'Europe: Open for Business' campaign appears to have been successful in this respect. On the other hand, Italian respondents viewed their government's contribution to lifting awareness of the SEM as poor. In contradiction to traditional interpretations of the French system as being highly centralized, in this instance the most successful decentralization of information dissemination occurred in France. A majority of French respondents considered their Chamber of Commerce to have been a worthwhile information source, a finding not paralleled elsewhere.

Availability of information from non-official sources registered broad parallels in Britain and France. Interestingly, Italy has the highest percentage of positive responses on every non-official source. This suggests that information flows follow significantly different patterns in Italy as compared to Britain and France.

The cross-national comparison shows that a great number of options have been available for both information dissemination by official channels and information collection by small firms. These possibilities have been exploited to different degrees in the three localities: our findings suggest that there are striking elements of success and failure in channel usage. Given that European issues are likely to assume ever-increasing importance, it would make sense for governments, at national and local levels, to reassess their communication links with their various publics in order to improve performance in these areas.

Table 8.3 Sources of information on the Single European Market and its implications for respondent's firm (percentage of firms)

	None	A little	A great deal
European agencies			
Lyon	74	26	0
Como	100	0	0
Leicester	76	22	2
National government			
Lyon	58	40	2
Como	97	3	0
Leicester	38	38	24
Local government agencies			
Lyon	67	30	3
Como	88	12	0
Leicester	71	25	4
Chambers of Commerce			
Lyon	34	47	19
Como	78	22	0
Leicester	55	38	7
Trading contacts			
Lyon	56	33	11
Como	44	44	12
Leicester	56	29	15
Consultants/other non-trading contacts			
Lyon	74	14	12
Como	42	47	11
Leicester	82	16	2
Media			
Lyon	30	35	35
Como	19	72	9
Leicester	40	54	6

8.4.2 Usefulness of information on 1993

The availability of information forms only half of the issue here: the usefulness of information for strategy formulation is also crucial. While a number of factors influence the mediocre levels of strategy formulation indicated in Table 8.4, among them must rank low **availability** of information and low **usefulness** of knowledge in the eyes of our respondents. A major criticism to emerge from our survey is the relatively general nature of the information provided. For information to be operationally useful, it must be directly relevant to the sector and sufficiently detailed to support strategy formulation. For the most part, our respondents took the view that these requirements had not been met.

Table 8.4 Whether as a result of contacts with information sources, respondents had worked out a strategy to meet the challenge of 1993

	Yes %	No %	No reply %
Lyon	9	89	2
Como	18	70	12
Leicester	29	66	5

Certain caveats do have to be sounded. We could not ascertain how hard our respondents concentrated on availing themselves of existing information sources. Neither can we comment on their expertise in making use of potentially relevant information, especially where data required reworking and analysis. Making long-term strategy for the small firm is notoriously difficult. It may not be an area in which many of these firms can devote much time. Omissions and hesitations may relate as much to managerial limitations in the small firms themselves as to the availability and quality of information, sources. In consequence, the need is not just for more information, but also for advice in interpreting it. Many respondents, rightly or wrongly, did not perceive such help to be readily available.

If small firms are to compete seriously in the Single Market, there is a compelling need for the rapid construction of data-banks tailored to their needs. The Euro-Info Centres set up under the auspices of the EC are probably the most logical agencies for such an endeavour. However, successful promotion of such a project necessitates more resources and better co-operation from firms providing the necessary information. The major clients for this type of service would probably be established small firms, rather than start-ups which have tended to receive most policy attention in the past.

8.5   READINESS FOR 1993

8.5.1   Company readiness

Despite the difficulties of foreseeing developments related to the completion of the SEM, many of the companies surveyed were taking action. A large majority in each country claimed to be prospecting new markets: 76% in France, 63% in Italy and 75% in the UK. Yet despite initial appearances of consistency in readiness for the SEM, close analysis revealed a number of differences in response within the subsamples. Intensive dealings with European markets are likely to require firms to have specialists in fields such as design, marketing and sales, yet numbers of such specialists varied markedly, as Table 8.5 shows.

Table 8.5   Employment of specialists

	Lyon %	Como %	Leicester %
Exporting	56	30	19
Marketing/sales	71	53	45
Product design	78	43	40

The percentage of French firms having a specialist specifically for sales and even for exports was high. It provided an instance of the international orientation of the Lyon sample. At the opposite extreme were the Leicester firms who had far fewer specialists, with the skills weakness being particularly apparent in exporting.

The Italian firms occupied intermediate positions, a finding which must be read in the light of differences in the role of the CEO (discussed in Chapter 5), and due to differing regional industrial structure (discussed in Chapters 6 and 7). Italian 'industrial districts' are characterized by a high local division of labour between firms, manifested in task specialization in relatively small components of the value-adding chain. Hence specialization within firms has to be understood in relation to specialization between firms. An exports orientation is often realized through intermediaries such as 'leading' manufacturing firms or non-manufacturing 'converters' who take orders and commission production.

These trends were confirmed by responses to a question on the use of sales/marketing agencies. Only 5% of French firms considered the latter to be very important as compared to 36% of British firms and 49% of Italian firms. In consequence, significant export strategy differences emerged between the national samples, with the French adopting a highly self-reliant stance and the British and Italians tending to rely on intermediaries.

Arguably, a greater proportion of small firms in all three countries should develop specialist expertise to deal with the intricacies of export markets. Not only do administrative procedures and financial technicalities have to be tackled, but at a more fundamental level, in-depth knowledge of the demands of overseas markets has to be acquired by persistence over the medium and long term. There are real causes for concern here, particularly in relation to the British sample. Small firms who access foreign markets must develop (or be able to draw on) expertise at a series of levels. An exports orientation involves much more than finding foreign buyers. There are implications in terms of product design, in logistics (in terms of production, transport and delivery constraints) and in communications (the languages and cultures they deal with). Too many firms undervalue or ignore linguistic skills and so compound the cultural barriers to trade. Without further reinforcement of the European Monetary System, currency exchange fluctuations and conversion costs will continue to present problems, especially for small firms who are often financially vulnerable but lacking in financial expertise. While such problems are overcome by seasoned exporters (by definition), they act as a disincentive to others.

In consequence, 'prospecting' and a 'sales' orientation are worthwhile starting-points but are merely the tip of the iceberg when it comes to trading in the SEM. A thoroughgoing business plan for operating in the SEM is a desirable strategy. Similar proportions (between 56% and 60%) of firms in each country were making specific plans. These were far higher rates of preparation than those reported by Gray (1992, p. 14), who found in a large 1989 survey of a wide range of UK small firms that only 33% had made preparations for 1993. However, Gray also indicated that small manufacturers of finished consumer and industrial goods have more frequently taken action than other types of small firm (p. 4), thus our findings are not atypical. None the less, sizeable numbers of small firms have been slow to make preparations – surely a short-sighted and dangerous position – though successive surveys by the Small Business Research Trust have shown that levels of preparedness in Britain are increasing over time (*ibid.*).

Among those firms in our survey who were making plans (Table 8.6), an emphasis on sales and marketing was as expected the most common response for each country. Nevertheless, a number of firms were aware that the challenges of the SEM required complementary strategies. Many firms realized that product design will be a key feature. Though ideally marketing strategy should be integrated into the product from the design stage – as opposed to being appended later as a sales 'pitch' – a majority of firms sampled gave no clear indication that they realized this.

Table 8.6 Preparation strategies for 1993 (percentages based on those firms who had made plans)

	Lyon %	Como %	Leicester %
Marketing/sales	62	40	53
Product design/specifications	31	36	28
Production technology	19	52	3
Sources of new finance	23	20	7
Legal	12	0	3
Other	8	0	3

Responses to the issue of technological upgrading proved particularly revealing. Of the total sample, one in three Italian firms was reassessing production technology, as compared with one in nine French firms and one in twenty-four British firms. This strategy accorded with one of the generally acknowledged drivers of Italian success in textiles–clothing: investment in up-to-date manufacturing equipment. Emulation of this approach might be useful advice to the other cohorts. The tiny number of British firms in the survey who were reassessing their production technology implied short-sightedness in relation to the future upgrading of manufacturing equipment. This is particularly important inasmuch as the British sample had low levels of productive assets. Lack of investment has been one of the classic causes of British industrial decline: it is a matter for concern that this characteristic shortcoming might continue in Leicester.

Clearly exporting incurs financial problems (e.g. access to sufficient working capital, payment delays, currency movements, insurance, etc.) which should not be underestimated. Indeed, in two extensive surveys of small firms, financial issues were identified as the major difficulty in exporting (Bannock and Peacock, 1989, p. 32). Yet very few of the British firms were looking into alternative, cheaper continental sources of finance as a means of enhancing their competitive strategy. Though exchange rate movements affect the total cost of borrowing from abroad and hence create a risk factor, it is a sign of strategic myopia that European financing was not being explored by more firms, given the prohibitively high levels of interest rates in Britain that obtained at the time of the survey. On the other hand, some of the French and the Italians were reassessing their financial strategies.

To summarize, a number of small firms in our research showed foresight in planning for the SEM, but a number of lags and leads in export competences have been identified across the three localities. Many firms have concentrated on the obvious marketing/sales avenues. Interestingly, a minority of more adventurous firms have been exploring other ways of improving their competitive advantages – notably by improved design, by diversifying sources of finance and by investing in production technology. On the other hand, a number of firms were failing to prepare. In the medium to long term, this is likely to cause them problems. Developing the marketing mix and resourcing its logistic implications must be top priorities.

Having discussed the firm-level perspective, we next turn to the question of regional readiness for 1993.

8.5.2 Como: prepared for 1993?

Depending on year, the Como textiles and clothing sectors already export between 50% and 70% of production (Associazione Serica Italiana, 1982–90). Thus the region appears well placed to sustain successful competition in the SEM. None the less, the effects of the Single Market programme have to be related to other change catalysts. As indicated above, European producers face the challenge of increasing concentration in retail distribution. Large chain stores offering quality products with medium-to-high fashion content expect ever higher flexibility, shorter delivery times and better managerial skills on the part of their suppliers. For Como firms to become suppliers of large stores on a Europe-wide basis, they need a higher level of co-ordination and unity of purpose within the region. The higher the fashion content and the shorter the delivery time, the greater will be the need to improve information flows and transport arrangements. The logistical implications are for equipping with the latest information technologies and possibly for siting production units close to distribution centres. This would involve careful planning, new investments and possibly joint ventures or setting up of subsidiaries abroad. Individual firms may find it hard to achieve these targets: local consortia may provide solutions. In Como, consortia already exist for specific tasks: there is a consortium to promote exports, another to analyse the sourcing of raw materials, etc. Such consortia, which are promoted by employers' organizations or the Italian Silk Association, may see their role enhanced in the future.

Deepened European market integration is likely to affect the relationship between the different groups of textiles–clothing firms in the Como area. In principle, three types of change in the industrial structure of the area are possible, namely:

1. Greater vertical integration and the creation of larger, multi-competence firms.
2. Greater inter-firm collaboration with small firms themselves taking initiatives to collaborate.
3. More frequent and systematic co-ordination among small firms than at present, orchestrated by 'leading firms' (such as the larger manufacturers or the 'converters'), in terms of the 'strategic network' model outlined in Chapter 7.

In each case, a reduction in levels of independence enjoyed by individual firms is likely. It is as yet unclear which of the three directions will predominate. In line with the trends indicated in Chapter 7, we hypothesize that the advantages of the third, namely sharing a common, purposeful strategy while maintaining the adaptability of decentralized structures, are likely to prove crucial.

An increase in the impact of fashion cycles linked to greater internalization of distribution is welcomed by Como's industrialists. Many see the fashion challenge as providing an opportunity for Como to become a European centre for quality cloth and services. However, there are adverse side-effects. Demand for standard fabrics will continue. Indeed weaving firms producing standard cloth have already reduced in number. If the district shifts more towards design and specialist services at the expense of weaving, employment in textiles–clothing will decrease further.

Equally, there may be beneficial external effects. In interview with one of the authors, a spokesman for the local textiles association expressed the view that the main effect of the SEM on the regional economy could come not from within the textiles–clothing industry itself, but from a reorientation of the banking system. Easier availability of credit would enhance the investment potential of local firms.

8.5.3 Lyon: prepared for 1993?

The readiness of the textiles industry in Lyon and the surrounding area will partly be determined by existing strengths and weaknesses. As indicated in earlier chapters, the strengths of the region are drawn mainly from relatively high capital intensity, high value added per employee, medium to top quality products, a high level of exports and a professional approach to management. In the survey there were few new entrants, indicating that barriers to entry are high, with the exception of the medium to low quality end of clothing manufacture where new firm creation in the inner city has been fairly strong (Montagné-Villette, 1990, pp. 125–8). The small firms in our research had increased their capitalization and level of internationalization over the long term. This acquired momentum of the Lyon textiles firms makes it probable that their position is defensible on a medium-term basis at national and international levels.

However, the longer-term prospects must be assessed in relation to the small size and independent nature of many of firms in Lyon and Rhône-Alpes. These factors indicate vulnerability. While amalgamation and concentration could enhance their ability to compete in world markets in the long term, of necessity this would reduce the small firm population, should it occur. Alternatively, the advantages of flexibility attaching to small size may continue to be exploited, for example, by entering into new trading partnerships. The growth of the retail multiples brings a need for small firms to identify and exploit international networks in distribution. As indicated in Chapter 7, the Lyon firms frequently entered into collaborative arrangements with other producers and with clients outside the locality. This tendency is a major non-tangible asset, being potentially capable of both ensuring small firm independence and flexibility by stabilizing inter-organizational ties. It is unclear, however, whether their more loosely structured relationships will be as effective as the tightly coupled networks of Como firms indicated in Chapter 7.

Inevitably, there have been signs of uneven performance among firms. Though a number of firms in the sample appeared to be well prepared for the SEM, many were not. Further, as competition from 'developing' countries has been stronger in clothing than textiles, the upstream situation of many of the Lyon region's specializations has given some protection from new producers but this situation is unlikely to continue indefinitely. The threat exists of newly industrialized and of developing countries using earnings from clothing sales to finance investments in high-quality textiles production. Such moves would increase supply, increase competition and depress prices: new producers would capture a bigger share of downstream demand currently serviced by European producers and reduce the market opportunities of the latter.

Textiles in the Lyon area have fared better in recent years than in other parts of France such as the Nord-Pas de Calais where decline has continued apace (Chirot, 1989). Yet this should lead to vigilance, not complacency. Competition in both the SEM and world markets may force firms to decide between enhanced collaborative arrangements or takeovers. Clothing firms in particular, face a round of restructuring as import penetration has been increasing.

In brief, Lyon firms draw strength both from production prowess and from independent marketing skills. But should they trip up, there is little to break their fall in terms of a supportive local industrial structure of the Italian type. The Italian example of a high degree of local industrial synergy points to the desirability of industrial cohesion at local/regional level. In the Lyon area this no longer exists to such a degree. In the long term, the porous nature of local linkages in textiles–clothing may prove to be a source of disadvantage for the region, even though a number of firms are individually well-poised for the SEM.

8.5.4   Leicester: prepared for 1993?

Despite their small size, many of the Leicester firms have as trading partners the major retail chains, though the size disparity emasculates their bargaining-power. None the less, a majority prefer to negotiate independently. Whatever the impact of size disadvantages when dealing nationally, the absolute lack of scale appears to be even more significant in export performance, at least on the evidence of the firms surveyed.

Future plans (where they existed) were generally predicated on a no-change scenario. Many Leicester firms seemed to assume that British retailers will not change suppliers. These assumptions are open to question given that other EC suppliers will increasingly target the lucrative end-markets the big British retailers can offer. Yet in the short to medium term this type of opportunity does not exist on a reciprocal basis elsewhere in the EC for British firms, since the level of concentration in retail distribution of textiles and clothing is lower outside Britain. This creates practical market entry problems for small British firms seeking to enter relatively disaggregated continental distribution systems.

These problems are exacerbated by the product–market strategies of the Leicester firms in our sample. Firms were characterized by a preference for self-sufficiency in value-adding. Where collaboration occurred, it tended to be lateral, apparently for reasons of expediency, rather than aimed at a systematic fostering of synergy between task-specialized firms as was often the case in Italy. Further, the combination of specialization and collaboration in the Italian 'model' both encourages and demands an export orientation, in that larger markets are required to make specialized investments pay off and because the coordinating role of 'leading' firms provides a launching-pad for smaller partners. It is significant that virtually no Leicester firms in our sample perceived such leading firms existing locally.

Leicester firms have preferred to specialize in particular market niches, mostly in products characterized by low fashion content and middle-of-the-road quality, thus seeking to avoid contest both with high-priced fashion goods and low-priced exports from Turkey, China, etc. They have aimed for value for money, rather than low price. From a short term managerial perspective, marketing logic is possibly on their side. Yet because the concept of specialization is perceived by many British respondents in terms of market niches, they tend to underestimate the potential for specialization in terms of value-adding processes. This is particularly important as the size and durability of their niches will come under increasing threat from both within the EC and from the continuing movement up-market of producers such as Hong Kong.

Long-term success can be understood in different ways. Many respondents apparently equated success merely with survival not growth. We contend that growth of the business activity is crucial. Thus we draw a distinction between business activity and the organizational unit. It would be in the interests of the Leicester entrepreneurs to increase the size of their business activity without automatically increasing employment within the firm, thereby generating higher productivity and profitability. But achieving greater levels of specialization and of innovation to compete with foreign competitors will require heavy investment, yet our survey shows that the typical level of capitalization of the Leicester firms is low. This is a major handicap when facing international competition, both from high productivity and low-labour cost sources.

The situation is the more worrying as other routes to improvement seem blocked. A renewal of Leicester firms by a new generation of entrepreneurs might be hoped for, but though the rate of firm creation has been high, new firms are often run by middle-aged owners in traditional niches rather than young entrants with new ideas. Though Britain has many talented graduates of art and design, few signs of their pursuing an entrepreneurial career in Leicester were traced. Further, family support in terms of both personal and financial inputs were found to a greater extent in Italy and France than in Britain. With the exception of the Asian community, the extended family is not generally involved in the family business today, leaving the entrepreneur to follow a somewhat isolated path.

Given this range of concerns, it is difficult to express great optimism for the future of the Leicester community of firms in relation to its EC competitors, though undoubtedly there are some progressive firms in Leicester who will continue to achieve a great deal in the Single Market of the 1990s.

8.6 CONCLUSIONS

The textiles and clothing sectors have experienced marked changes over the past two decades and there seems every reason to assume this will continue. Of the post-1993 scenarios outlined in this chapter's first section, we contend that the competition model is the most likely. Internationalization of sourcing and distribution has become widespread. Even without the initiatives for an integrated European market, this trend was already increasing in momentum. With the SEM pushing in the same direction, it will be surprising if there are no major changes in distribution systems or no shakeout in textiles and clothing manufacture in the mid to late 1990s.

Such a shakeout is likely to be precipitated by upgrading of equipment and products by the more effective EC producers and by increased competition from low-cost sources beyond Europe. The latter developments, together with increasing consumer affluence, will precipitate a new round of structural adjustment as a kind of ratchet-effect pushes internationally oriented production further up-market. The volatility of fashion markets, in particular, will entail different relationships between creativity, quality and volume: the winning strategies of the 1980s are likely to become outmoded in the late 1990s.

The Single Market may lead to an improvement in trading conditions for a wide range of small textiles and clothing firms, provided they are efficient and outward-looking. Yet as shown by our research, some firms and subsectors are better prepared than others for 1993. Many, but by no means all, firms contacted clearly had significant individual strengths. Moreover, Italian and French firms generally revealed a broader experience base in exporting, as well as greater readiness and greater enthusiasm for 1993, than British firms. Thus many of the continental firms have a head-start. These differential effects are likely to be amplified in the post-1993 period: they will impact not only on the performance of individual firms, but also on the regions in which they are located, with the result that weaker communities of firms may not remain viable. Yet firms and communities specializing in consumer manufactures have no option but to adapt. A European dimension is no longer an option but a necessity.

9

The dynamics of change

9.1 INTRODUCTION

Going beyond the European perspective espoused in Chapter 8, in the present chapter we will consider the wider future prospects of the textiles and clothing industries in general, and of the three localities surveyed in particular. We examine major catalysts of change coming from both inside and outside the textile and clothing industries and analyse ongoing patterns of adjustment within the three communities surveyed.

The first section of this chapter disembeds five major trends, each of which currently has the potential radically to modify the global trading environment of textile and clothing producers and condition their medium to long term viability. Against this background of incipient change, we will examine in the second section the question of whether the firms and regions surveyed have been converging towards comparable development paths. Examination of their respective current strategies, structures and styles will allow future trajectories to be traced. This will enable the book's general conclusions to address policy-making issues in relation to development tracks.

9.2 CATALYSTS OF RENEWAL

It is perhaps inevitable that near to the end of the millennium the future looks more uncertain than ever. In all likelihood, the textile and clothing industries will traverse another major period of change over the coming decades. A number of factors already point to significant developments, though we are mindful that it is too early to ascertain with any certainty the scale and pace of their effects. In this section we outline five catalysts of renewal, namely:

1. the renegotiation of MFA IV;
2. new regional influences;
3. environmental issues;
4. technological issues;
5. issues related to firm size.

While we cannot be sure that all will have a large impact on the world textiles industry, or even on the localities we surveyed, it would be extremely surprising if none of them generate major challenges.

9.2.1 Renegotiation of MFA IV

For most textiles producers in developed countries, the single most important element of policy in the recent period has been the several Multi-Fibre Arrangements (MFAs) which have offered a degree of protection of domestic markets from penetration by suppliers from developing countries (the reader is referred to p. 22 for discussion of the history of the MFAs). In a survey conducted by Kurt Salmon Associates, an overwhelming majority of industry respondents indicated that they considered the renegotiation of the MFA to be more important than the completion of the European Single Market (Larcombe, 1990).

Debate has long raged among economists over the deleterious effects on free world trade of the various MFAs (see e.g. Curzon *et al.*, 1981; Hindley and Nicolaides, 1983; Keesing and Wolf, 1980). As a result of the controversies, world policy-makers at the start of the 1990s were as far as ever removed from agreement. Trela and Whalley (1990) indicated that in the considerable uncertainty around the real effects of the various MFAs, some developing nations would prefer renewal of the system since it offers a measure of protection for their market outlets in the developed world.

As regards Britain, Silbertson (1991) estimated that were the MFA to disappear, UK prices to consumers would fall by 5% while employment would decline by 7%, with some 33 000 job losses. The fear of job losses, falls in output and company closures has prompted the Apparel, Knitwear and Textiles Alliance (AKT), formed by the British Clothing Industry Association, the British Textiles Confederation and the Knitwear Industries Federation, to lobby in favour of renewing the MFA. The AKT has called for 'fair' trade, arguing that more rigorous GATT agreements are required to end trade distortion due to dumping, unfair subsidies, trade barriers to UK exports and thefts of brand names and designs in order to safeguard Britain's fifth largest manufacturing sector (AKT, 1992; Harrison, 1989). French trade lobbies have taken similar pro-MFA views (Lewis, 1990a).

MFA IV was negotiated in 1986 to conclude in July 1991. However, due to the breakdown in GATT discussions during the Uruguay Round (consequent on disagreements between the USA and the EC over agricultural subsidies), no new agreement was signed in 1991. Rather, MFA IV was extended for one year and a transitory period of twelve years was put forward for its phasing-out (*International Textiles*, 1991). Unfortunately, as this book went to press, deadlock continued making estimates of the scale of future change impossible. Nevertheless, the likelihood is that trade barriers blocking imports from developing countries will be reduced, resulting in increased competitive pressures on textile–clothing firms in developed nations.

9.2.2 New regional influences

The globalization of world textiles markets has already resulted in the penetration of Western markets by a range of producers situated on the other side of the world. One of the key questions over the coming decade in connection with trade liberalization will be the extent to which countries such as India and China will be granted greater access to Western markets and, moreover, prove capable of producing goods that Western consumers want. The case of China is made more complex by the fact that it regains possession of Hong Kong in 1997, with unpredictable compounded effects. Hong Kong is, of course, already a major world player in textiles–clothing and could serve as a 'launch pad' for Chinese exports.

Yet recent events nearer to home in central and Eastern Europe have introduced new elements into the equation. For too long, the Cold War and the Iron Curtain debarred extensive, mutually beneficial exchanges between East and West Europe. With the collapse of the communist system in most of central and Eastern Europe at the end of the 1980s, a number of the old impediments to trade vanished. In 1990, Bulgaria, Czechoslovakia, Hungary, Poland and Romania were integrated into the 'general system of preferences', liberalizing their textile and clothing trade with the EC (Silbertson, 1991). Central and Eastern European countries have since been reassessed by textile and clothing manufacturers and distributors in terms both of exploiting new markets and of setting up new production centres.

For Western firms accustomed to dealing with distant parts of the world, the opportunity to forge production links with Eastern Europe would at face-value offer an ideal combination of relatively low labour costs, a skilled workforce and close proximity. These factors, together with the enthusiasm of Hungary, Poland and former Czechoslovakia for EC membership, make increases in trade in textiles and clothing a foregone conclusion.

The likely extent of those increases does, however, merit close examination. A study by the Hungarian economic consultancy ECHO (1991) threw light in some overlooked corners. First, in the Eastern European textile and clothing industries an inverse relationship holds between market size on the one hand, and advanced technology and good product quality on the other. Thus the largest markets are those of the ex-USSR, while the most advanced producers are in (former) Czechoslovakia, Poland and Hungary (in that order). Secondly, the development of their textile and clothing sectors is intimately linked with the general state of their economies. Although full official statistics have not yet become available for 1990–1, observers have pointed to catastrophic decline. Domestic demand has decreased due to falls in living standards resulting from high prices and contracting real wages. In 1991 a collapse in foreign trade within the former Comecon countries – especially towards the ex-USSR – was not offset by penetration of new Western markets. The switch to convertible currency trading in January 1991 actually resulted in more difficult trading conditions due to slower and more complex procedures, making containment of foreign debt even more problematic. Industrial restructuring in Eastern Europe has become more essential than ever.

As regards restructuring of the textile and clothing sectors, ECHO (1991) reviewed possible models for change. The report concluded that neither a 'northern European model' (based on medium-sized firms as found in Western Germany) nor a 'southern European model' (based on small firms in Italy) is likely to prevail in Eastern Europe. Thus the 'industrial district' or regional agglomeration model was not even envisaged in the ECHO report, probably a sign of its limited perceived transferability. Rather, it predicted a mixed model in which large state firms would be broken up by privatization into medium-sized firms, together with an increase in small firms as large companies hive off activities and as entrepreneurs bring in new capital. None the less, the continued existence of large firms is likely, taking the form of joint ventures with Western companies in central Europe, while in the ex-USSR domestic capital firms will continue to operate at the cheaper end of the market in high-volume, standardized production. In general, Eastern European companies face the same problems, namely loss of markets, capital shortages, large accumulated debts and outdated assets.

Due to these characteristics and problems, Eastern Europe probably presents a different order of threats and opportunities in textile and clothing than is sometimes envisaged. A number of reasons can be advanced to explain this:

1. Eastern European products are currently often uncompetitive.
2. Large volumes of textiles and clothing are produced in the ex-USSR but these are largely unsaleable on Western markets.
3. The central European countries (Poland, former Czechoslovakia, Hungary) are relatively small, in terms both of demography and of GDP.
4. In circumstances of capital shortage, it is by no means clear that the textile and clothing industries will be a priority for stepped-up investment. The industrial structures of Eastern European countries are not those of the developing nations – as is sometimes erroneously believed – but are closer to the West than commonly appreciated. Consequently,

industrialization via the textile and clothing industries is not the major development path it has been in East Asian countries. Wages are lower than in the EC but much higher, especially in central Europe, than in Asia. Further, the aim of Middle Europeans is to improve their living standards, which can only be achieved by exploiting high value-added industries.

None the less, inward investment by Western textiles-related enterprises appears to be increasing. While predictions are hazardous, there are grounds for believing that such investment will be highly targeted and in specialized niches, rather than in high-volume, standard goods. Thus our contacts with Italian producers have indicated that some are investigating production opportunities in Hungary, due to the attractive combination of lower wage levels, high skills and particularly close proximity. German firms have developed a tradition of resorting extensively to 'outward processing'. This involves exporting semi-finished products such as uncut fabric, adding value abroad then reimporting the goods duty free for finishing or for sale. Thus in a number of garment-manufacture stages, considerable savings have been made in the past by subcontracting to low-wage Eastern European neighbours and developing countries. Looking to the East has indeed been a general strategy of German industry and is set to continue. To give one measure, of the 327 joint ventures existing in a range of sectors in 1989 between EC countries and the ex-USSR, France was responsible for 32, the UK for 54 and Germany for 139 (Andries, 1990).

Taking these various factors together, the textile and clothing industries of Eastern Europe are in line for major restructuring. However, Western producers will do well to envisage these changes as presenting opportunities and threats for them in discrete niches, rather than as across-the-board. Thus localities such as Leicester, making medium-quality, low-to-medium priced goods, can expect to see Eastern European competitors strongly challenging their markets, while up-market, specialist producers in Como and Lyon will feel relatively insulated, or indeed should seek out new export or production opportunities.

9.2.3 Environmental issues

Issues related to the environment impact on the textile and clothing industries in several ways. First, consumers and policy-makers have become increasingly aware of the environmental effects of various types of industrial production. Recent trends have been towards consumers wanting more 'environmentally friendly' processes and products and consequently towards tougher legislation. The textiles and clothing industries cannot remain aloof from the problems of waste and pollution management and must address them in the short to medium term. Secondly, if we are indeed witnessing a period of climatic change as some environmental experts claim, then textiles output will modify dramatically in the medium to long term.

Turning first to the environmental responsibilities of the textile and clothing industries, fashion by definition means a rapid turnover in products. Consumers usually discard fashion items not for functional reasons but because they are no longer in vogue. Although according to Watson's (1991) estimates textiles form only 5% of domestic waste, many textile products are not biodegradable. To reduce the problem of waste, two avenues are open. One is for consumers to reduce effective consumption by ignoring short-term fashions and buying fewer longer-lasting garments. The second is to recycle textiles to a far greater extent than at present. A major shift in this direction would have major, but differential, consequences on textiles producers. Firms capable of high construction quality would receive a boost, and new niches might be created in recycling activities. However, per capita textiles–clothing consumption would reduce, leading to decline of output for the industry overall, at least in markets in the developed world where demography is largely static. This would exacerbate known trends towards an ageing population in countries such as Britain and France.

The pollution problems caused by the textiles and clothing industries are serious, with wet processes posing significant difficulties (*ibid.*). Activities such as dyeing and finishing are particularly reliant on chemical additives which are sources of air- and water-borne pollution. Indeed, a 1990 conference organized by the UK Textile Institute was provocatively entitled: 'Are Textiles Finishing the Environment?', and US data for 1987 placed textiles as the sixth most important source of industrial pollution (*Textile World*, 1989, p. 23). Waste management has become a key issue for all firms connected with the chemicals industry. Tougher legislation is being developed in Europe and North America to counteract the build-up in toxic gas and water emissions.

Cleaning up industry has a cost: by and large, the 'polluter pays' principle has been invoked, yet in reality matters are rarely simple. The issues go beyond the behaviour of consumers or of individual firms to embrace whole sectors. Dempsey (1991, p. 42), reporting on the Davros Conference of that year, signalled the need to 'develop and use ecological balance sheets over the whole value chain to compare alternative [production] routes'. There is no doubting the good sense of the proposition: the difficulty is in identifying paths to its implementation. In industries such as textiles and clothing, where the level of vertical integration is often low but the level of international sourcing is extremely high, co-ordination of the kind suggested is extremely difficult. Indeed the major danger of tougher environmental legislation is a flight of capital to those locations where economic and social exigencies prevail over ecological desiderata.

To effect change, consumer pressure may prove as necessary as the statute book. Certainly by the start of the 1990s, the idea of 'green textiles' had become fashionable among some consumers. However, recent consumer preferences for 'natural' materials (i.e. cotton, wool, silk) have led to the erroneous idea that synthetics cause more pollution. The reality is more complex: synthetics are not biodegradable but production tends to require less energy and water, while natural fabrics, though biodegradable, give off toxic gases on decay particularly once treated in finishing processes (Watson, 1991). Whether consumers *en masse* are willing to pay higher prices for 'environmentally friendly' products is as yet unclear in Britain, though the trend is stronger in countries such as Germany and Denmark.

Furthermore, commentators such as Elson (1990) have drawn the distinction between 'green' consumers and 'ethical' consumers. The former are concerned with the natural environment. The latter group tend to share those concerns, but are also preoccupied with the social environment – with fair wages and acceptable working conditions in both the developed and developing countries. Since so many imports are sourced in low-wage countries, often in sweat-shop conditions, a strong consumer movement towards 'ethical' purchases would have a major impact on the garment industry, creating niches for retailers promoting an 'ethical' image and potentially altering the balance of advantage in favour of local production in the developed world. Judged from the viewpoint of the developing nations, this would of course constitute a perverse effect.

Lastly, should it be proved that the environment has indeed been irredeemably altered by industrialization and that 'global warming' has become a reality, then the long-term consequences for the textiles–clothing industry will be massive. Without going to the extremes of certain press reports claiming that high-technology, all-over body protection will be required when exposed to ultraviolet light, the 'global warming' scenario entails that clothing in a different style, weight and quantity will be required in the next century. Fresh opportunities are likely to arise which will rejuvenate the industry and generate first mover advantages to firms who anticipate new trends. Meeting those challenges will require innovative production methods and lead to new industry structures within textiles–clothing.

9.2.4 Technological issues

Technological progress has been swifter and more decisive in upstream fibre and textiles manufacture than in downstream clothing assembly. In Chapter 2 we indicated that the strengths of the developed countries generally lie in capital- and skill-intensive textiles manufacture than in clothing where the low-wage costs of developing nations have proved crucial in ensuring superior competitiveness.

Technological progress may, however, be eroding the lead of developing nations in cut-and-sew operations, although the evidence to date is partial and sometimes contradictory. Already during the 1980s, the Japanese attempted to overcome local labour shortage and cost problems by capital investment in automation. Under the aegis of MITI, highly proficient Japanese equipment manufacturers, such as Juki and Brother, were encouraged to develop the so-called Automated Sewing System project: the aim was to produce an entirely automated garment-manufacture shop. Progress has been slow but to turn the vision into reality in the twenty-first century is no longer science fiction. Were the project to succeed and gain currency, it would erase most of the competitive advantage enjoyed in clothing production by low-wage countries. Indeed the United Nations Centre on Transnational Corporations (1987, p. xii) noted that there was considerable potential in the automated production of hosiery, knitted garments, children's clothes and men's shirts.

However, the OECD (1989) emphasized that the development of the automatic sewing-shop was still slow due to the intrinsic 'resistance' of fabric to machine-handing. It concluded that although automation had an important role in parts of the industry (such as automated warehousing systems as in Benetton), the high-wage countries were likely to become ever less competitive compared to low-wage suppliers.

In consequence, different trends are emerging within downstream manufacturing operations. In subsectors where automation has become, or is becoming, feasible, such as knitwear and hosiery, there is a need for producers to invest in new manufacturing equipment. Ominously, in the case of the Leicester knitwear and hosiery firms, we have seen that capital investment has been low. In operations requiring a large labour input, the grounds for 'delocalization' of production remain as strong as ever. Given high Italian labour costs, it is unsurprising that Como producers have been investigating production opportunities in lower-wage Eastern European locations. Thus in the former group of activities, the ability to generate capital and to manage high technology processes will be the criteria for survival. In the latter, the ability to plan and co-ordinate will be crucial.

Finally, it is important to emphasize that technological innovation from within the textile and clothing industries is *not* the only source of renewal. Apart from the continuing but well-known transversal effects of information technology across manufacturing industries, the environmental issues discussed in the previous subsection will themselves provoke modifications in technologies and work practices.

9.2.5 Issues related to firm size

Taken in conjunction, market trends, environmental questions and technological change all point towards radical change within the textile and clothing industries. This raises the question of the relationship between firm size and long-run competitiveness.

Industry trends in the 1980s largely favoured small and medium sized firms, but reasons are emerging to believe that the balance of advantage is altering. Thus, Anson (1991) reported that returns on investment were lower than 0.2% in firms with less than £500 000 turnover, but around 15% in companies with over £50 million in sales revenue. Furthermore, given the interplay between environmental and technological issues discussed above, the firms best placed to meet the R & D and investment challenges are those with the largest financial reserves: they are usually medium to large sized companies. Thus the highly concentrated UK textiles and clothing industries may yet accrue relative gains in competitiveness against countries with more fragmented industries.

Internationalization of sourcing and distribution likewise points to the importance of large firms. The United Nations Centre on Transnational Corporations (1987, p. xi) noted that although barriers to entry have been low in garment production, barriers are significant in the international marketing and distribution of clothing. Producers in developing countries have been largely dependent on large Western corporations for their market outlets. Indeed we have seen that many British manufacturers have likewise become dependent on the multiples. With the development of the Single European Market, with the probable softening of the MFA and with the rise of new regional producers (such as Eastern Europe), the importance of international co-ordination of sourcing and distribution will be reinforced.

Clearly major distributors will seek to take advantage of new international opportunities. However, no one model of internationalization can be assured inevitable predominance. Alongside the **external sourcing model** where a distributor directly commissions or buys in goods from around the world, can be cited the **internal control model**, such as has largely obtained among medium-sized German firms. Thus German industrialists have been able to retain their influence within German markets by their organization of the production cycle through the practice of 'outward processing', described above. Whereas in the 'external sourcing' model the distributor monopolizes production savings, in the 'internal control' model the industrialist and the distributor share the benefits. The crucial feature is, of course, that the latter strategy is more likely to ensure the survival of indigenous manufacturing firms and jobs. Hence producers in other nations, including France and Italy, have been experimenting with this approach.

In effect, the major success factors – high creativity, anticipation of market trends, fast response and low costs – can be utilized in a number of combinations. Distributors and producers can now enter into complex arrangements allowing maximization of strengths and minimization of weaknesses, such as Third World sourcing of cheap, standard products but home production of capital-intensive components; retention of design and marketing but use of 'outward processing' for labour-intensive operations;

local production of skill-intensive, high value-added or fast turn-round products etc. The permutations of strategic options are already extensive.

Although large firms more frequently have the financial and managerial expertise necessary to exploit those permutations, a total return to a 1970s style 'big is beautiful' philosophy is not feasible. The relationships between company structure and behaviour no longer obey the same equations. Large companies have been learning to emulate small and medium-sized firms by decentralizing into slimmer, more autonomous units displaying the same organizational and technological flexibility demonstrated by the best small firms while retaining advantages of scale related to finance, logistics, R & D and market power.

In time these developments may remodel the textile and clothing industries. While optimum size of production **units** can be specified by industrial engineers for particular processes, the balance of market opportunities may no longer be weighted to any particular size of **firm**. It now appears that size, *per se*, has become a less important determinant of success, while the strategies of individual firms, the relationships among producers and the interface between suppliers and distributors have become more important. Strategic networks of the type analysed in Chapter 7, where 'leader' firms both promote and profit from the complementary expertise of smaller production units, may prove to be the optimum solution.

In summary, small firms acting in isolation are likely to find the global trading environment increasingly difficult. Yet large size will not automatically assure success. A sea-change in both industry structure and attendant interpretations is taking place since the benefits of scope can be achieved in ways other than large size. Thus the traditional analysis of company size in terms of direct ownership of assets is itself modifying. Behaviour has become more important than structure. The complexities of today's markets require a new degree of organizational flexibility, hence the paradigm is shifting to inter-organizational strategies in conditions of diffused ownership. The various catalysts of change described above can only reinforce the need for flexibility in terms of products, processes and structures.

9.3   THE VECTORS OF CHANGE

Although the catalysts of change discussed above assume a number of forms whose future effects cannot be predicted, it is instructive to ask whether recent developments have pushed in the same direction or whether differentiated, semi-autonomous evolutionary processes operate within industries such as textiles and clothing.

Acceleration in the process of European integration at the end of the 1980s has raised the question of the nature and extent of economic and social convergence within EC countries (Cressey and Jones, 1991). In textiles–clothing, broad-brush descriptions would point to convergence resulting both from supply-side factors such as capital and worker mobility and rapid innovation diffusion, as well as market-driven phenomena such as increased homogeneity of tastes within European markets and rapid fashion dissemination, comparable disposable income and patterns of purchasing underpinned by cultural and socioeconomic similarities. Yet closer inspection raises questions about the meaning and extent of convergence.

Taking the case of fast-growth firms, we consider the issue of convergence at two levels. At one level is the question of whether convergence exists within regional agglomerations of small firms. Variables here include predominant production activities and types of specialization in a locality, its industrial traditions and reputation, as well as its outside markets. At another level is the question of cross-national convergence of 'best practice' in terms of the strategies pursued by individual firms across the three districts.

More specifically, can convergence on quality, design and innovation along Italian lines be taken as the most valid business strategy for small textiles firms in other parts of Europe? Evidence does exist which points in this direction. However, local and national specificities are also strong and continuing sources of divergence. The case for each of these propositions will now be considered.

9.3.1 Convergence in small firm strategies

Questionnaire responses revealed that most firms in the three localities have sought to adapt to changing conditions. The vast majority of firms in each locality had upgraded their operations recently in terms of improved production quality, improved equipment standards, increased product variety, increased flexibility towards customers and faster delivery times. Yet even if a number of similarities across localities are evident in the frequency of changes (measured in terms of the proportions of firms making changes), the rate of change is by no means identical. Analysis of the data (for details see Table 4.7, p. 82) revealed that under several rubrics the proportion of Como firms which had **not** introduced recent changes was the highest, while in Lyon it was the lowest. Firms in Como may now have reached a more shallow gradient on the learning curve and hence are now changing at a slower pace than those in Lyon and Leicester. This suggests that some convergence for the 1990s is possible.

But was the move to a strategy of higher quality a rewarding one for the firms which have effected it? Were improvements in quality of output, standard of equipment and levels of flexibility associated with good performance and growth? To answer these questions we compared the fastest-growing firms in each area to those which were either stable or in decline. In particular, we sought to establish how the most and the least successful strategies differed, and whether there was a formula that was successful in all three areas.

Contrary to expectations, flexibility towards customers did not stand out as an important growth factor. In Leicester only a third of the fast-growers claimed to have increased their flexibility to customers' needs, compared to over three-quarters of stable or declining firms. In Como and Lyon the percentages were almost the same for the fast-growers and for stable or declining firms.

The main finding of the analysis was that in all three localities the fast-growers relied on high-quality output to a larger extent than did stable or declining firms. In Como three-quarters of the fast-growers produced up-market products. This compared with only 40% of stable or declining firms. In Leicester half of the fast-growers offered high-quality products. Only a third of stable or declining firms produced for the top end of the market. In Lyon the difference was much smaller, the percentages being 36% and 33%. Most important, a policy of improving product quality was usually found in the fast-growth firms (e.g. 82% in the case of Lyon, 88% for Como and 67% for Leicester).

Improvements in product quality among fast-growers were also linked to higher levels of investment in machinery and better equipment standards. Roughly half of the fast-growers in all three areas reported assets in equipment and machinery worth more than £500 000, compared with a much smaller proportion of stable or declining firms. In all three countries a higher proportion of the fast-growers said they had recently improved the standard of their equipment. (In Leicester, 100% for the fast-growers and 45% for stable or declining firms; in Como the percentages were 75% and 60% respectively, while in Lyon they were 82% and 50%.)

Although it may seem self-evident that the firms achieving greater growth were those which invested more, textile and especially garment manufacturing firms in Britain have had a poor record on investment. Old machinery was used to produce low-quality goods. Though this reduced costs, it also depressed the value-added, thereby leaving producers short of capital for investment. Extrapolating from our findings, generating more business by moving up-market and making appropriate capital investment are allied responses that small firms can successfully adopt.

A diversified customer base is a third feature of the Leicester fast-growers: 66% had more than 100 clients, as opposed to only 11% of the firms indicating stability or decline. Moreover, 83% of the Leicester fast growers sold less than 20% of their production to a single customer. Conversely, 89% of stable or declining firms sold 20% or more of output to one customer. Likewise, in both Como and Lyon many fast-growers reported increases in the number of customers to a much larger extent than did stable or declining firms. Extrapolating from the data, firms which pursue an aggressive

The vectors of change

marketing and sales policy based on quality production can succeed in finding new customers and increasing their output.

This analysis is reinforced by a review of the characteristics of the least successful firms. The profile of the quarter of Leicester firms experiencing decline is singularly unambiguous, as is indicated in Tables 9.1 and 9.2. Few customers, lack of design flair, low investment levels and down-market products are associated with declining firms. The data in Table 9.2 suggest that some firms have tried to adapt to new conditions by increasing product variety, but without a corresponding emphasis on quality and investment.

Table 9.1 Characteristics of Leicester firms experiencing decline (percentages)

Fewer than 50 clients	87
More than 20% of sales to single client	81
Externally generated design	87
Assets of £150,000 or less	62
Middle- or down-market products	75

Table 9.2 Recent changes made by Leicester firms experiencing decline (percentages)

	Constant/decrease	Increase
Product variety	6	94
Standard of equipment	63	37
Quality of output	57	43
No. of regular clients	80	20

To sum up, despite some differences across localities, these findings indicate that there were signs of convergence in terms of a formula for growth both within and across localities. Thus in all three areas, firms are likely to grow faster if they step up their investment, improve product quality and increase their marketing effort towards entering new markets and servicing a wider spread of customers.

9.3.2 Divergence due to locality-specific styles and structures

Entrepreneurs cannot readily escape conditioning by their macro and micro environments. Three key arguments will be advanced to justify this thesis. They stem from sociocultural milieu effects, from regional economic structures and from the particularized or idiosyncratic nature of commercial and technical knowledge within a given small firm community. Each of these factors has major conditioning effects on competitive strategies within each locality: they simultaneously confer differential opportunities and constrain in-firm strategy formulation.

Our research suggests that the impact of the *milieu* effect occurs via informal channels of communication, including families and social circles, as well as trading contacts (cf. Chapter 5). These embedded, often unrecognized, influences create a style of doing business that is particular to the locality in question.

As indicated in earlier chapters, major regional differences exist in industrial structures and these specificities likewise condition perceived opportunities within a locality. For example, the scope for subcontracting by process specialism is high in Como and Lyon, but low in Leicester. In consequence, entrepreneurs in Como are likely to perceive the need for – and value of – such specialization in order to create a niche in their industrial community. Likewise, the concomitant asset-specific investments of Italian firms make them vulnerable unless they have either a big market share, great bargaining-power *vis-à-vis* suppliers and customers, or otherwise have reason to trust them.

From a more theoretical perspective, the notion of a unique trajectory of economic and technological competence which cannot be readily emulated in the short term is now well-documented (e.g. Pavitt, 1989). While the arguments have typically been advanced for firm-specific idiosyncratic knowledge (Nelson and Winter, 1982), it is highly probable that the knowledge characterizing particular communities of small firms conforms in each case to a similar pattern. In other words, know-how within a community remains largely specialized to it. In simple terms, this means that although proprietary knowledge may 'leak' out of the firm or district, would-be competitors cannot necessarily exploit that knowledge to advantage, given that its owners will continue the innovation process that generated the proprietary knowledge in the first place; Lippman and Rumelt (1982) called this phenomenon 'uncertain imitability'. Rate of leakage or 'diffusion' of new knowledge is a function of internal structures and behaviours within the firm and the community. Moreover, firms will go to great lengths to protect knowledge that is a critically important strategic asset, even to the extent of refusing to seek patent cover, since this is an obvious way for competitors to find out what advances are being made (Winter, 1987).

A complementary consideration is sometimes called 'codification' of knowledge, by which is meant the degree to which knowledge is presented in a widely recognized structure, format or paradigm (Boisot, 1986). Codification is generally a facilitator of diffusion (whether formally or informally). Boisot (drawing on Ouchi, 1980) argued that the form of knowledge prevailing in a sector has a major influence on the kind of organizational structures which are likely to be most effective. At one extreme, well-codified and diffused sectoral knowledge is consistent with disaggregation of the means of value-adding, since outputs and services can be bought via spot-contracts in the market-place (Williamson, 1975). At the other extreme, idiosyncratic and uncertain knowledge (in form or quality) militates in favour of a secretive, hierarchical 'feudal' organization within (and perhaps among) competing firms, where each controls those strategic value-adding activities necessary to extract the full commercial returns available. The more typical positions lie between the two poles. Thus conventional vertically integrated bureaucracies have been the classic response to controlling the external diffusion of knowledge resident in them and so underpinning their positions of competitive advantage. Conversely, well-diffused but substantially uncodified knowledge is likely to best match an informally structured federation of small units, having clan-like qualities.

Clan structures appear to characterize Italian industrial districts quite well. Preceding analyses of Como firms indicate that firms jealously guard **high-level** proprietary skills and information, sharing them only when unavoidable or in risk-free situations such as where collaboration within the vertical production chain has been accepted. The disaggregated nature of the textiles and clothing industries in Lyon together with the specialized output of many firms point to similar patterns. In each case, local know-how appears to be of an uncodified, largely semi-diffused type.

The Leicester case seems different, however. Although the surface impression is again of disaggregated, uncodified knowledge, the reality is arguably different. First, the extent of highly particularized knowledge contained in the products and processes that typify the Leicester firms (hosiery, knitted, cut-and-sew garments) may be comparatively modest. Secondly, and potentially of greater significance, the systematic transfer of designs from major UK retailers to Leicester producers points to a codification of industry knowledge. These elements of generalized diffusion of knowledge mean that Leicester producers have far less particularized knowledge to guard jealously and are less able to link into networks where such knowledge develops. Since they deal largely in 'common knowledge', they again prove to be extremely vulnerable. Consequently, in the terms of Clarke and DeBresson (1990), Leicester could be losing its 'innovation-design capability'.

If, as we suggest, long-run community success depends on creating idiosyncratic and locally contained knowledge and expertise, relatively secretive, clan-like federations of small firms are one means of protecting that success. On the other hand, the desire to access and control all the information necessary for success explains the prevalence of hierarchies (as in vertically integrated firms) or quasi-hierarchies (as in the Benetton case). Certainly we should not be too optimistic about the prospects for relatively egalitarian industrial communities. There seems to be a need for powerful leading firms, of the kind Leicester arguably does not contain. Leading firms outside a community cannot be relied on to have the best interests of the community at heart, for example in taking and implementing strategic choices in marketing, in the structuring of production, sponsoring training centres, stimulating and financing R & D, and other sorts of informal co-ordinating and lobbying on behalf of the community.

9.4   CONCLUSIONS

In Como the strategies pursued by individual firms and at district level have reinforced the area's high-quality profile and enhanced its international competitiveness. In Lyon many firms never abandoned their high-quality, up-market profile, while among the others current moves in that direction represent a return to tradition. That tradition makes an affirmation of the high-quality approach associated with Lyon's history as a centre of silk production credible.

However, Leicester sends confused signals to the outside world. The area appears to fall between two models of development. One is to pursue the 'traditional' path of value-for-money production, a strategy that runs the risk of slipping ever further from middle-market to down-market goods. Here UK producers are becoming increasingly uncompetitive in relation to developing countries in terms of labour costs. The other model is to embrace a 'high-quality' strategy, though how realistic this might be for many Leicester firms can be questioned. Under 10% of the Leicester sample were fast-growers, while firms in decline accounted for a quarter. Of the latter, a majority do not appear to be making major efforts to change their business strategy. Even the most successful firms may be held back by the depressed economic environment.

Yet to encourage a switch from price competition to competition on non-price factors at the level of the district is a major task. That some of the best-performing firms are converging towards an up-market, high-quality strategy is therefore no guarantee that the district will come to be associated with this strategy. First, local producers may not perceive the necessity of changing their course but hope instead for an improvement in macro-economic conditions. Such an improvement may produce short-term comfort but will not resolve structural shortfalls in competitiveness. Secondly, small UK firms are often hampered by a lack of capital, little training in management skills and a total unfamiliarity with export markets. Thirdly, they are strongly influenced by national demand characteristics, particularly the emphasis placed by UK consumers on price. Fourthly, the inertia of industrial tradition and established practices limits innovation. This is particularly clear as regards changes in the inter-firm division of labour (such as a move to subcontracting by specialism), where collective momentum or clear leadership rather then individual initiative would be required to effect change.

These features make the extent of genuine convergence problematic. Elements of cross-national convergence exist in terms of individual firms' strategies, specifically in terms of producing more up-market products sold to a greater number of customers, an outcome requiring higher levels of design skills, of investment and marketing effort. But fewer signs of convergence can be discerned across the three *localities*. Moreover, similarities in development paths should not disguise dissimilar starting- points. The baseline from which we judge whether different regional groups of firms are moving up-market is different in each case. The baseline for Leicester is low compared to the more prestigious baselines conferred on Lyon and Como by their history of silk production. In consequence, each of the three areas may show signs of moving up-market, yet if each steps to higher rungs of the ladder, their respective positions will be maintained or even further separated.

By extrapolation from these observations, two conceptions of European convergence emerge. In one sense, convergence suggests a meeting of equals coming together at the same point: this would imply a reassuring outcome. But in another sense, convergence can refer to the process of following the same trajectories in space, but with substantial time lags between the various actors. This conception evokes the image of a race, which indeed market competition usually *is*. But like all races, it has winners and losers. Patently, this is a less comfortable outlook, particularly for areas such as Leicester which lag behind.

In summary, European producer localities are implementing a strategy of differentiation on quality and/or fashion but may not be doing so quickly enough *vis-à-vis* non-European producers, many of whom are already hurrying along the same road. Without changes in strategy, the long-run survival of some textiles and clothing localities may be in doubt.

Yet as the discussion on the catalysts of change has suggested, the textiles and clothing industries of the twenty-first century will differ as radically to today's version as has been the case over previous centuries. The ability to make rapid structural and behavioural adjustments will prove crucial for ensuring survival. Firms and localities that are too tightly locked into yesterday's development paths cannot hope to compete. The only formula for success will be a strategy of continuing change, based on the qualities of flexibility and vision.

10

General conclusions

10.1 THE COMPETITIVENESS OF SMALL FIRM COMMUNITIES

The main aim of our research has been to address the issues of the competitiveness and innovativeness of small firm communities in a mature industrial sector. At one level, the competitiveness of a community of firms depends entirely on the competitiveness of the individual firms which constitute such a community. In this sense a community is no more than the sum of its components. Indeed one of our major findings is that there is a high degree of individuality in the firms surveyed, both in terms of ownership and of market/process/product specializations. Yet the fact remains that they operate in traditional textiles localities each with its own cultural and social milieu, which means that regional specificities and constraints and established industrial practices largely shape the range of future options open to these firms. Thus proprietors are likely to utilize local recipes and conform to local norms of small firm behaviour and local structures.

The process is essentially circular, in that past and current developmental choices inevitably shape the growth paths and internal structures of the community itself which, in turn, condition the scope of future choices perceived and implemented by local entrepreneurs. The implication is that communities are on long-run developmental tracks which are both particular to the locality and largely incapable of significant change in the short to medium term. Each community represents a unique combination of both economic and social features, and although it can obviously try to develop (or 'import') new strategies and managerial styles, these have to be successfully 'implanted' into an established body. It would be totally unfeasible, for example, to suggest that any one of the three local communities analysed in this book can adopt *en bloc* the strategies and growth paths of either of the other two. However, this does not exclude the possibility that a community imitates and recreates selected elements which have been identified as conducive to economic success in other areas, provided these are compatible with its existing base of human skills, economic resources and accumulated knowledge. This poses the question of whether particular tracks make sense in economic terms and whether and by what means they can be diverted towards more successful outcomes. It has, in short, important policy implications.

The heart of the matter is that economic success requires innovativeness which, in turn, is community-specific and cannot easily transcend local models and patterns of growth. Before we discuss the relevance and feasibility of policy measures that would enhance the competitiveness and prosperity of small firm communities we need therefore to highlight the different models of development epitomized by Como, Lyon and Leicester.

10.2 THREE MODELS OF DEVELOPMENT

The three industrial communities compared in the book undoubtedly follow three different development tracks. Whichever 'window' we opened to survey the characteristics and behaviour of the firms, we discovered systematic differences among them. We conducted three different levels of analysis: the level of the firm (and its owner/manager), the level of the local community (both in terms of its social milieu and in terms of its industrial organization) and the level of the global trading environment, which directly or indirectly affects the strategy and competitiveness of locally based clusters of firms.

At the level of the firm, we found evidence of success and failure factors in all three localities, though these were not equally distributed. The Lyon firms sampled were generally doing well (only 7% were experiencing decline) and their industrial success was linked, at least in part, to the prevalence of industrial recipes which local firms appeared to have in common, namely high-quality products, extensive use of professional managers, good levels of capital investment and a diversified client portfolio, with many firms being export-oriented.

In Leicester firms pursued relatively homogeneous recipes (as in Lyon), but unlike Lyon this was not particularly conducive to industrial success, as shown by the fact that a quarter of the Leicester firms sampled were in decline while only a few were experiencing fast growth. Local recipes included medium-quality and low to medium fashion products, a relatively low number of customers per firm, high reliance on a few clients for the majority of orders and a low export profile.

Como firms pursued mixed recipes. At one extreme were well established and professionally run firms with a large number of clients and low reliance on a single client for orders, at the other extreme were firms run by artisan or family entrepreneurs, employing no professional managers, having fewer than 30 clients and selling more than 20% of their output to their single biggest customer. However, fashion and quality content tended to be high across the board and levels of exports were particularly good. Only 5% of Como firms were experiencing decline, indicating that the area's particular mix of recipes worked to the advantage of the local textiles and clothing industries.

At the level of the community, the exploration of industrial organization led to the conclusions that Lyon and Leicester were not industrial districts, though they had a few characteristics in common with them, but that Como was indeed one. This discovery added a new albeit not entirely unexpected dimension to our previous findings. We were now in a better position to explain why Como firms did not follow common recipes and why they were highly specialized and strongly competitive. Inter-firm complementarity was the locality's key to success. Como, as an industrial district, was characterized by process specialization linked to a locally concentrated but organizationally deintegrated production cycle. In Lyon we found process specialization without a locally concentrated production cycle, while Leicester was characterized by a locally concentrated and organizationally integrated manufacturing cycle without intensive process specialization.

The lessons to be drawn from a three-way comparison which makes use of the industrial district model are the following:

1. The greatest advantage an industrial district structure offers small firms is a sectoral structure based on a high division of labour. This allows each firm to specialize in one phase of the production process and/or to concentrate on just one industrial activity or market. Specialization encourages, indeed in a competitive environment dictates, investment and innovation. Conversely, having a limited activity set makes investment and innovation affordable even for very small firms. In addition, specialization in small units of production encourages flexibility. Thus Como can offer many different combinations of products, processes and design to its clients.

2. As in the Lyon case, firms which do not operate in an industrial district can also enjoy the advantages conferred by process specialization, provided they link up with firms carrying out complementary activities on a national or even international basis.

3. The Leicester case indicated that small firms covering more than one activity and a variety of products and markets tend to suffer the disadvantages of limited size and enjoy few of the advantages that specialization can offer them. While market specialization ('niche focus') is theoretically a viable option, it is hard to sustain over the long term. Being in close geographical proximity does not give local firms the extra synergies they might achieve if they complemented each other by forming an integrated vertical chain.

At the level of the community, we also took into consideration the innovative behaviour of local firms. In Como and Lyon, though not in

Leicester, innovative firms made up a substantial percentage of the total samples. The difference between Como and Lyon concerned the degree of integration of 'leading', innovating firms into the regional economy. This was high in Como, where leading firms co-ordinated largely local networks, but low in Lyon, where these firms participated in non-local networks. When leading firms are strongly integrated within their community, they perform the following crucial roles:

1. they look outwards, scan environments for threats and opportunities and act on these messages;
2. they innovate and stimulate innovation in other local firms, a consequence of which is that activity is intense and experimental. These are the firms that learn most and promote the cause of learning in the community;
3. they weed out the complacent and inefficient firms by either channelling business away from them or offering it to them only if they too are prepared to invest, innovate and take considered risks (the co-ordinating role);
4. they foster convergence between their own perceived interests and those of the community to which they belong.

In short, these leading firms are in effect the entrepreneurial leaders of their respective communities. When leading firms are only weakly integrated into the local industrial community, they play a less directly supportive and stimulating role among their local peers, although peer-group rivalry may still be strong. None the less they contribute to building up and promoting a positive image of their industrial region to the outside world.

Thus to the question: 'What makes a small firm community innovative and thriving?', the answers provided by our research can be summarized as:

1. a dynamic set of 'leading' firms;
2. a range of complementary processes, as well as market-product specializations;
3. a high number of local firms with a wide range of customers, an export profile and low reliance on just a few clients for orders.

However, this still begs the question whether a community of essentially small firms will perform better than a few big firms over the long term. Linked to this is the question of whether a small firm community can successfully manage (or even just survive) the process of internationalization of sourcing and distribution discussed in the course of this book. The advantages that some small firms have over many large ones in the textiles and clothing sectors tend to be seen in terms of flexibility, creativity and fast response to fashion changes. However, small firms acting in isolation from one another cannot replicate the all-round competence of the best larger firms. As we have argued in previous chapters, the growing internationalization of production and distribution now allows for an extensive range of strategic options, many of which require the breadth and depth of managerial expertise and financial commitment expected of most large firms. In recent years, large firms have increasingly learnt to imitate the flexible style of management and organization of production typical of innovative and successful small firms operating in industrial network structures.

Can small firms operating in local industrial communities, in turn, strive to take advantage of those factors which traditionally work in favour of large firms – e.g. high levels of managerial skills, internal co-ordination and investment? Our findings indicate that this is indeed possible if small firms pool together their resources and knowledge and combine in forming strategic networks. These networks, whose formation appears increasingly to characterize Italian industrial districts like Como not only profit from flexible specialization, but also promote the innovation process and achieve a degree of mutual co-ordination which resembles that of large firms, while retaining their capacity to instigate innovation and react to change. Internationalization is assured by specialist firms ('converters' and 'terminal' firms) which manage the interface between local manufacturing and outside markets. In acting on their own behalf, they also ensure the livelihood of their suppliers.

In so doing, they do not act out of altruism. The need to keep costs down will in all probability lead both converters and terminal firms increasingly to source certain products from abroad (e.g. the more standard fabrics), thus putting pressure on the local industry. However, their networking within the community will to a certain extent cushion local producers from the worst consequences of this process, by offering them the opportunity to diversify further and specialize in higher value-added output. More important, despite the pivotal role played by some Como firms (the 'leaders') and the possible demise of some activities currently carried out within the community, local industry as a whole should be able to manage the internationalization process to its own advantage by retaining *in loco* the most creative and strategic activities.

Lyon, though no longer an industrial district, offers an example of a different but probably no less viable way of dealing with the small firm/ large firm issue and with the internationalization process. The strategy of individual Lyon firms has been to build up a strong management team and high levels of investment in specialist assets. Within the locality each firm functions as a 'mini-large firm', whereas outside the locality it has developed preferential linkages with national and international suppliers and customers.

The situation of Leicester's small firms is more problematic. They do not appear able either to emulate the behaviour of large firms individually or collectively, to achieve the advantages associated with size by coming together as co-ordinated quasi-firms. Their autonomy *vis-à-vis* their clients is fairly limited. The interface between local manufacturers and outside markets is largely managed by outside organizations, namely large retailers and wholesale distributors. The former, however, apparently regard the Leicester textiles industry as external sourcing, in the same light as other manufacturing areas around the world. Thus the internationalization process has unquestionably increased the precariousness of the Leicester textiles community, a long-run trend for which the community has thus far not found an adequate response.

10.3 POLICY IMPLICATIONS

There can surely be no doubt that the key to future success at the local community level is to combine scale of output with productivity (hence acceptable unit cost), flexibility and responsiveness towards market needs, non-scale advantages such as design flair, well-promoted brand names and wide appeal to international tastes. Continuing innovativeness (knowledge diffusion and application) must be a crucial individual and communal responsibility to compete effectively in the broader context. But this latter comment needs clarifying. We are not suggesting collectively negotiated solutions in the manner of traditional cooperatives. Rather, we have been impressed, in the Como case particularly, by the ability of what we call 'leading firms' to show the way forward by example and by orchestrating conventional exchange processes in networks of small and medium sized firms. Further, this co-ordinating ability is mirrored by the apparent willingness of other firms to be co-ordinated. In short, we note a pragmatic communal acceptance of the benefits of mutual accommodation of skills and outputs. Readers with an interest in the organization behaviour literature may recognize parallels with Mintzberg's (1979) conceptualization of an 'adhocracy', but applied to a set of resources under dispersed ownership.

How such networks can be sustained is another matter. The application of information technology as exemplified by Benetton is a positive force for preserving decentralized ownership of co-ordinated production resources. In general, however, there must also be an appropriate degree of organizational coupling to ally market responsiveness to production facilities. In addition, it is not surprising that Benetton emerged from an Italian region where the cultural and social milieu and industrial traditions produced small firm communities of the industrial district type.

The above discussion raises the question whether and how an ineffective community other than an industrial district might restructure and innovate which, in turn, leads inevitably to considerations of future trends in the textiles and clothing industries and of broader industrial policy.

The different scenarios outlined in Chapters 8 and 9 underline the uncertainty surrounding future economic developments and so indicate the difficulty inherent in developing adequate policy measures at national and regional level. One scenario which is likely to have great significance in post-1993 Europe is the 'competition model', implying that there will be winners and losers and that some industrial localities may succumb altogether. On the positive side (from the small firm perspective), greater competition can also limit the influence of large firms. The freedom of multinational firms to exploit EC markets in a cavalier fashion has come in for much scrutiny. Concerns over the market power of large firms seem likely to grow. Thus it is not unreasonable to suppose that controls on large corporations allied to policy objectives of economic 'levelling-up' via regional policy will actually encourage the survival of small firm communities distributed across the regions. Achieving this aim can be facilitated by imaginative local governmental agencies seeking central funds for continuing regional development.

A knottier issue concerns the EC's relations with Third World countries and NICs. While the EC may wish to protect indigenous industries, it will be under continuing pressure during GATT and particularly MFA negotiations (despite a deadlock as we write) to make concessions to developing countries. In so far as import quotas and tariffs on textiles decline, competition from outside the EC will increase, making the situation of European textiles and clothing producers more difficult.

At overall EC policy-making levels, politicians and commissioners alike are bound to feel pressured to make concessions that will tend to abandon or discourage low-technology sectors in favour of higher-technology sectors with better perceived future prospects, not least to promote inward investment by the Japanese and others. So it would seem very unwise to think that indigenous textiles industries can expect overly generous assistance or even much sympathy from Brussels.

Furthermore, it would seem reasonable to suppose that large corporations will progressively de-emphasize their own reliance on European production, as indeed has been their strategy in recent years. This offers, albeit indirectly, further support to the argument for local industrial communities in textiles and clothing to seek self sufficiency, based on the models and mechanisms we have described at length in the book, and where appropriate to diversify their economic base. Currently EC policy-making is in line with these objectives, mainly through its RETEX scheme, set up in December 1991, and modelled on policies already implemented in steel, coal and shipbuilding, with a budget of 500 million ECUs over a five-year period (*Euro-info*, 1991; *Target 1992*). The aim, however, is not to prop up an ailing industry, but to target small viable firms in order to improve managerial skills and vocational training, increase inter-firm co-operation (in research, marketing, etc.) and reduce pollution (*Euro-info*, 1992). Most important, the scheme aims to diversify the economic base of regions heavily dependent on the textiles industry in order to decrease their level of dependence.

Leicester has appealed for EC funding under RETEX (*Leicester Mercury*, 6 March 1992), a further indication of the precarious position of the textiles–clothing community there, but also a positive sign of action on the part of the city's local government institutions. As it stands, however, the RETEX scheme is ambiguous and its outcome uncertain. On the one hand, it appears to offer little hope to the weaker European textiles industries, pushing them towards closure. On the other hand, it seems to offer communities such as Leicester a lifeline and a chance to restructure and innovate. Ultimately, though, it is up to individual communities to assess their future prospects with a view either to restructuring or simply winding down.

More generally, it is worth emphasizing that not all local industrial communities have the same organization of production, nor the same needs. Formulae for providing support and stimulus to growth – as opposed to disengagement – have therefore to be modified to local circumstances. This points to an important role to be played by local and regional agencies, both in assessing the failings of the local industry and in highlighting appropriate measures to overcome them by continuing collaboration with local firms.

The need to develop specific policy measures for each industrial locality has, for example, been translated into the provision of collective services (e.g. data-banks, technical advice, shared resources), an approach that proved particularly effective in Italian industrial districts. In consequence, the collective services approach was advocated in the UK by Zeitlin (1985) for the London clothing industry, and it was influential in the setting up of fashion centres in Hackney and Nottingham (Davenport and Totterdill, 1986; Johnstone *et al.* 1988). In industrial districts, however, firms are linked to each other through systematic subcontracting links and so form a loose industrial organization. In this context, the value of collective services is augmented since positive inputs percolate through the community. However in Lyon and Leicester quite different types of organization exist. If, as in Leicester, local firms pursue individualistic strategies, equate success with self-sufficiency and do not value co-ordination, then the provision of collective services is unlikely to improve the competitiveness of local industry. More recently, Zeitlin and Totterdill (1989, p. 183) accepted the inherent contradiction of 'imposing from above an industrial strategy which depends on co-operation and mutual trust among the parties involved' and concluded that the tendency to centralization in the UK during the 1980s had compounded the difficulties for local policy-making.

The distinctiveness of the Italian context has indeed been the incentive to local firms to 'form a system'. Initiatives so far promoted to this end have included encouraging local business managers to discuss the development and exploitation of complementarities in the production process, organizing public debates and publicity on 'the way forward' for the local industry, publishing regular business reports and data of interest to small firms and promoting research on local industrial structures, as well as organizing fairs and exhibitions with a local/regional emphasis. At the least, these initiatives have increased the mutual awareness of local business people.

Similar consciousness raising would be beneficial in Leicester and possibly in Lyon. The aim would be to develop new strategies to deal with external competitors, as well as with major distributors. A general pattern for future effectiveness might lie in contracting out more activities, leading to increased task specialization and a more mutually beneficial division of labour among firms. In the Leicester case, the question of design flair is crucial, for without it, local producers lose their bargaining power and possibly even their attractiveness as suppliers to the retail chains. Although in theory individual firms could improve in-house design by employing more specialists, arguably the typical Leicester firm already tries to be too autonomous by carrying out too many activities. It is doubtful whether they could extend the range of their operations and competences while concurrently improving quality of output and increasing investment. This would seem a prime example of where independent design houses should flourish. The training of highly skilled textiles and clothing managers and would-be entrepreneurs is also crucial. In this context, the recent initiative by Marks and Spencer and other leading textiles and clothing manufacturers to sponsor degree courses in Textiles Studies at the University of Leeds, UMIST and Leicester's new De Montfort University should be welcomed. Although many graduates will eventually work for the large retailers and manufacturers, these courses should also produce a number of young and dynamic entrepreneurs with professional training and creative ideas.

Clearly our suggestions concern both the market and policy initiatives. We contend that the policy process has quite properly an important objective of structuring a mutually beneficial local trading environment. Community agents and local government institutions can play a crucial role in this respect. Indeed the issue of regional restructuring is tightly bound to the existence of the will and the means to implement effective, tailored strategies. There is now a growing body of evidence that effective regional government initiatives can be crucial to long-run regional economic health. One thinks here, for example, of the efforts of the Welsh and Scottish Development Agencies. Ironically, no such regional authorities with corresponding powers exist to promote the interests of the English regions. Possibly the nearest equivalent is to be found in the so-called new towns (such as Milton Keynes Development Corporation) which have played a very positive role in local economic development, notably the encouragement of inward investment and the spawning of opportunities for small firms to emerge and grow. The weakness of the English regions in this respect is very much in evidence when seen against the European experience. Eastern England simply does not contain regional institutional structures comparable to those in Rhône-Alpes or Lombardy. As integration within the EC develops, the regional tier of government will arguably become even more significant. Yet the current Conservative government has embarked on dismantling such elements of regional government as currently exist (e.g. at metropolitan county level). This undoubtedly restricts the scope for local industrial policy.

As things stand presently, we are more optimistic for textiles communities in Como and Lyon than in Leicester. Indeed it is possible to see the Leicester knitwear industry as a sad case of a community drifting towards oblivion – one of the many casualties of the new international division of labour. Against this view, our findings indicate that there are ways forward, though pain-free prescriptions for achieving success in the short term simply do not exist. Any way forward for Leicester and similar industrial communities is, however, subject to the following conditions, pertaining both to market forces and to policy-makers:

1. An effective input from regional government taking a long term view; also national government-sponsored agencies for regional development.
2. Local/regional agencies with sufficient resources and prestige (e.g. more effective Chambers of Commerce, dynamic trade associations promoting debates and encouraging new initiatives among local entrepreneurs).
3. A stock of enthusiastic and committed entrepreneurs.
4. Exploration of mutual self-interest and collaboration among the entrepreneurs themselves and between them and local/regional agencies.

In brief, there is a need to recognize and accept leadership potential from whatever source it emerges.

Abstracting from our particular industry example, we critique the proposition that unconsidered encouragement to small firm communities is an appropriate means to facilitate the competitiveness and prosperity of mature manufacturing industries in the post-1993 European Community. Subsidizing industrial localities with fundamental structural or motivational deficiencies is a lost cause. However, we contend that encouraging innovative and entrepreneurial communities is a desirable policy objective in order to demature and revitalize a number of so-called 'sunset' industries. Precisely because, as our own book shows, each community shows an identifiable developmental path, its particular weaknesses should be relatively easy to assess. Acting on this knowledge is, of course, much more problematic, but intensive collaboration between locally based agencies and the entrepreneurs themselves is the only way, in our view, to galvanize individual industrial communities towards more successful and rewarding tracks.

Ultimately, we would emphasize the importance of entrepreneurial leadership. With greater European market integration as a result of the `1993' initiatives, with the probable softening of the MFA, the risks posed by new regional competitors and the need to invest in the right products and processes for tomorrow's markets all pushing towards radical change in the textiles and clothing industries, time is running out for communities who prove incapable of far-sighted adjustments.

References

Abernathy, W. (1978) *The Productive Dilemma: Roadblock to Innovation in the Automobile Industry*, John Hopkins University Press, Baltimore, Md.

Abernathy, W., Clark, K. and Kantrow, A. (1983) *Industrial Renaissance: Producing a Competitive Future for America*, Basic Books, New York.

Ackoff, R. (1970) *A Concept of Corporate Planning*, Wiley Interscience, New York.

AKT (1992) Trade Distortion – an International Affair, *International Textiles*, **732** April, 71–2

Alcouffe, A. *et al.* (1987) Propriété et pouvoir dans l'industrie, Tome 2: Le secteur privé, *Notes et études documentaires*, No. 4832, La Documentation Française, Paris.

Aldrich, H. and Whetten, D. A. (1981) Organization Sets, Action Sets and Networks, in Nystrom, P.C. and Starbuck, W. H. (eds) *Handbook of Organizational Design*, Oxford University Press, London.

Amar, M. (1987) Dans l'industrie, les PME résistent mieux que les grandes entreprises, *Economie et Statistique*, **197**, 3–11.

Amboise, G. d'. and Muldowney, M. (1988) Management Theory for Small Business: Attempts and Requirements, *Academy of Management Review*, **13**, (2), 226–40.

Ambrose, D.M. and Koepke, G. *(1984) Networking: Building Strength from the Collective Resources of Small Businesses*, Proceedings of the Small Business Institute Directors' Association.

Amin, A. (1988) Specialization without Growth: Small Footwear Firms in an Inner-city Area of Naples, Working Paper, CURDS, Newcastle upon Tyne.

Amin, A., Johnson, S. and Storey, D. (1986) Small Firms and the Process of Economic Development, *Journal of Regional Policy*, October–December, 493–517.

Andries, M. (ed.) (1990) *The Future of Relations between the EEC and Eastern Europe*, Club de Bruxelles, Brussels.

Anson, R. (1991) Small May No Longer be Beautiful, *Textile Outlook International*, November, 3–6.

Anson, R. and Simpson, P. (1988) *World Textile Trade and Production Trends*, Special Report No. 1108, Economist Intelligence Unit, London.

Antonelli, A. (1987) Dall'economia industriale all'organizzazione industriale, *Economia Politica*, 4(2), 277–320.

Aoki, M. (1984), Innovative Adaptation through the Quasi-Tree Structure: an Emerging Aspect of Japanese Entrepreneurship, *Zeitschrift für Nationalokonomie*, 4, 177–98.

Aoki M., Gustavsson B. and Williamson, O. (eds) (1990) *The Firm as a Nexus of Treaties*, Sage, London.

Arnaud, R. (1990) *La France en chiffres*, Hatier, Paris.

Associazione Serica Italiana (1982–90) *Rapporto sulla industria serica italiana*, Associazione Serica Italiana, Rome.

Axelsson, B. (1992) Corporate Strategy Models and Network-Diverging Perspectives in Axelsson, B. and Easton, G. (eds) *Industrial Networks : a New View of Reality*, Routledge, London.

Axelsson, B. and Easton, G. (1992) *Industrial Networks. A New View of Reality*, Routledge, London.

Aydalot, P. (1983) Crise économique, crise de l'espace et de la pensée, in Planque, B. and Wever, C. (eds) (1983) *Le Développement décentralisé: dynamique spatiale de l'économie et planification régionale*, Litec, Paris.

Aydalot, P. (1984) The Reversal of Spatial Trends in French Industry since 1974, in Lambooy, J.G. (ed.) *New Spatial Dynamics and Economic Crisis*, Finnpublishers, Tampere.

Baden-Fuller, C. (1989) Exit from Declining Industries and the Case of Steel Castings, *Economic Journal*, 398(99), 949–961

Baden-Fuller, C., dell'Osso, F. and Stopford, J. (1991) Competition Dynamics behind the Mask of Maturity, in Faulhaber, G. and Tamburini, G. (eds) *European Economic Integration: The Role of Technology*, Kluwer, Boston.

Bagnasco, A. (1977) *Tre Italie. La problematica territoriale dello sviluppo italiano*, Il Mulino, Bologna.

Bagnasco, A. (1985) La costruzione sociale del mercato: strategie di impresa e esperimenti di scala in Italia, *Stato e Mercato*, 13, 9–45.

Bagnasco, A. (1988) *La costruzione sociale del mercato*, Il Mulino, Bologna.

Bagnasco, A. and Messori, M. (1975) *Tendenze dell'economia periferica*, Valentino, Turin.

Bagnasco, A. and Trigilia, C. (eds) (1984) Società e politica nelle aree di piccola impresa. Il caso di Bassano, Arsenale, Venice.

Bagnasco, A. and Trigilia, C. (1985) *Il caso della Valdelsa*, Angeli, Milan.

Balestri, A. (1990) *Cambiamento e politiche industriali nel distretto tessile di Prato*, Angeli, Milan.

Bamberger, I. (1983) Value Systems, Strategies and the Performance of Small and Medium Sized Firms, *International Small Business Journal*, **1**(4), 25–39.

Bamford, J. (1984) Small Business in Italy – the Submerged Economy, in Levicki, C. (ed.) *Small Business: Theory and Practice*, Croom Helm, London.

Bangemann, M. (1991) Further Progress on the Road to a Single Market – as well as Delays in Certain Key Sectors, *Target 1992*, January, 1.

Bannock, G. (1980) *The Promotion of Small Business: a Seven Country Study*, Economists' Advisory Group, London, Vol. 1.

Bannock, G. and Peacock, A. (1989) *Governments and Small Business*, Paul Chapman, London.

Banville, E. de and Chavent, Y. (1980) L'Industrie de l'habillement dans la région Rhône-Alpes, CRESAL, Saint Etienne.

Banville, E. de and Roux, J. (1980) Groupes, petites unités et nouvelles bases de légitimité, in ADEFI *Les Restructurations industrielles en France*, Economica, Paris.

Banville, E. de (1982) La sous-traitance pour l'automobile et le poids lourd, *Revue d'économie industrielle*, **19**, 34–40.

Banville, E. de (1984) L'entreprise entre la PMI-sation et l'évolution de réseaux de solidarité, CRESAL, Saint Etienne.

Barbagli, M., Capecchi, V. and Cobalti, A. (1988) *La mobilità sociale in Emilia-Romagna*, Il Mulino, Bologna.

Barber, J., Metcalfe, J. and Porteous, M. (1989) Barriers to Growth: the ACARD Study, in Barber, J. *et al.* (eds) *Barriers to Growth in Small Firms*, Routledge, London.

Barber, J., Metcalfe, J. and Porteous, M. (eds) (1989) *Barriers to Growth in Small Firms*, Routledge, London.

Barreyre, P.-Y. (1984) The Small Firm in the French Economy, in Levicki, C. (ed.) *Small Business: Theory and Practice*, Croom Helm, London.

Beaver, G., Faulkner, T., Lewis, J. and Gibb, A. (eds) (1986) *Readings in Small Business*, Gower, Aldershot.

Becattini, G. (1979) Dal 'settore' industriale al 'distretto' industriale. Alcune considerazioni sull'unità di indagine dell'economia industriale, *Economia e Politica Industriale*, **1**, 7–21.

Becattini, G. (ed.) (1987) *Mercato e forze locali: il distretto industriale*, Il Mulino, Bologna.

Becattini G. (1989) Riflessioni sul distretto industriale marshalliano come concetto socio-economico, *Stato e Mercato*, **25**, 118–28.

Becattini, G. (1990) Italy, in Sengenberger, W., Loveman, G. and Piore, M. (eds) *The Restructuring of Small Enterprises: Industrial Restructuring in Industrialised Countries*, International Institute for Labour Studies, Geneva.

Berger, S. and Piore, M. (1980) *Dualism and Discontinuity in Industrial Societies*. Cambridge University Press, Cambridge.

Bergman, E. M., Maier, G. and Todtling, F. (eds) (1991a) *Regions Reconsidered. Economic Networks, Innovation and Local Development in Industrialised Countries*, Mansell, London and New York.

Bergman, E. M., Maier, G. and Todtling, F. (1991b) Reconsidering Regions in Bergman, E., Maier, G. and Todtling, F. (eds) *Regions Reconsidered: Economic Networks, Innovation and Local Development in Industrialised Countries*, Mansell, London and New York.

Berrier, R. J. (1978) The Politics of Industrial Survival: the French Textile Industry, unpublished PhD thesis, MIT.

Bertolini, G. and Tudway, R. (1982) Création d'entreprises et création d'emplois: maïeutique industrielle et ingénierie de la création, *Economie et humanisme*, **263**, January–February, 16–28

Beteille, R. (1978) L'industrie en milieu rural en France, *L'Information Géographique*, **1**, 28–43.

Bianchi, P. (1989), Concorrenza dinamica, distretti industriali e interventi locali, in Gobbo, F. (ed.) *Distretti e sistemi produttivi alle soglie degli anni '90*, Angeli, Milan.

Biffignandi, S. (1987) *Il Sistema industriale della Lombardia*, Il Mulino, Bologna.

Binks, M. and Coyne, J. (1983) *The Birth of Enterprise: An Analytical and Empirical Study of the Growth of Small Firms*, Hobart Paper No. 98, Institute of Economic Affairs, London.

Birley, S. (1985) The Role of Networks in the Entrepreneurial Process, *Journal of Business Venturing*, **1**, 107–117.

Blim, M. (1991) *Small-Scale Industrialization and its Consequences*, Greenwood Press Praeger, London.

Blum, C. (1989) Europe 1992 – the Most Important Reforms in the Eyes of the European Textile Industry, *Textile Leader*, **4** April, 48–59.

Boisot, M. (1986) Markets and Hierachies in a Cultural Perspective, *Organization Studies*, **7** (2), 135–58.

Bolton, J. (1971) *Small Firms: Report of the Committee of Inquiry on Small Firms*, HMSO, London.

Bonnet, J. (1987) Lyon et son agglomération, *Notes et Etudes Documentaires*, No. 4836, La Documentation Française, Paris.

Bonnetin, M. (1987) Sainte-Sigolène: une conversion industrielle réussie, in Mifsud, P. (ed.) *Milieux urbains et développement local*, CREUSET, Saint Etienne.

Boswell, J. (1973) *The Rise and Decline of Small Firms*, Allen and Unwin, London.

Bosworth, D. and Jacobs, C. (1989) Management Attitudes, Behaviour and Abilities as Barriers to Growth, in Barber, J. *et al.* (eds) *Barriers to Growth in Small Firms*, Routledge, London.

Boudeville, J. (ed.) (1968) *L'Espace et les pôles de croissance*, PUF, Paris.

Boudon, A. and Boss, J.-F. (1976) Analyse du système textile, *CESA Cahiers de recherche*, No. 52, Jouy-en-Josas.

Brusco S. (1982), The Emilian Model: Productive Decentralization and Social Integration, *Cambridge Journal of Economics*, **6**, 167–84.

Brusco, S. (1986) Small Firms and Industrial Districts: the Experience of Italy, in Keeble, D. and Wever, E. (eds) *New Firms and Regional Development in Europe*, Croom Helm, London.

Brusco S. and Sabel C. (1981), Artisan Production and Economic Growth, in Wilkinson, F. (ed.), *The Dynamics of Labour Market Segmentation*, Academic Press, London.

Bucaille, A. and Costa de Beauregard, B. (1987) *PMI. Enjeux régionaux et internationaux*, Economica, Paris.

Burgelman, R. (1983) A Process Model of Internal Corporate Venturing in the Diversified Major Firm, *Administrative Science Quarterly*, **28** (2), 223–44.

Burns, P. and Dewhurst, J. (1989) *Small Business and Entrepreneurship*, Macmillan, Basingstoke.

Buzzell, R. and Gale, B. (1987) *The PIMS Principles*, The Free Press, New York.

Caizzi, B. (1952) *Vicende storiche della tessitura serica comasca*, Noseda, Como.

Camagni, R. (1991a) Introduction: from the Local Milieu to Innovation through Cooperation Networks in Camagni, R. (ed.) *Innovation Network: Spatial Perspectives*, Belhaven Press, London.

Camagni, R. (ed.) (1991b) *Innovation Networks: Spatial Perspectives*, Belhaven Press, London.

Carland, J.A. and Carland, J.W. (1991) An Empirical Investigation into Distinctions between Male and Female Entrepreneurs and Managers, *International Small Business Journal*, **9** (3), 62–72.

Carland, J. W., Hoy, F., Boulton, W. and Carland, J. A. (1984) Differentiating Entrepreneurs from Small Business Owners, *Academy of Management Review*, **9** (2), 354–59.

Cayez, P. (1980) *Crises et croissance de l'industrie lyonnaise*, Editions du CNRS, Paris.

Cecchini, P. *et al.* (1988) *1992: The European Challenge. The Benefits of a Single Market*, Wildwood House, London.

Cento Bull, A. and Corner, P. (1992) *From Peasant to Entrepreneur: the Survival of the Family Economy in Italy*, Berg, Oxford.

Central Statistical Office (1975–88) *Monthly Digest of Statistics*, HMSO, London.

Chaplin, P. (1982), Co-operatives in Contemporary Britain, in Stanworth, J., Westrip, A., Watkins, D. and Lewis, J.(eds) *Perspectives on a Decade of Small Business Research: Bolton Ten Years On*, Gower, Aldershot.

Chassagne, S. (1981) Industrialisation et désindustrialisation dans les campagnes françaises: quelques réflexions à partir du textile, *Revue du Nord*, **63**, 35–57.

Chell, E. (1985) The Entrepreneurial Personality: a Few Ghosts laid to Rest?, *International Small Business Journal*, **3** (3), 43–54.

Chell, E. (1986) The Entrepreneurial Personality: a Review and Some Theoretical Developments, in Curran, J., Stanworth, J. and Watkins, D. (eds) *The Survival of the Small Firm*, Aldershot, Gower, Vol.1.

Child, J. (1972) Organizational Structure, Environment and Performance: the Role of Strategic Choice, *Sociology*, **6**, 1–22.

Chirot, F. (1989) Le textile perd le Nord, *Le Monde*, 3 November, p. 35.

CISL Informazione (1988) *Atti del convegno 'Como e la seta: sviluppo o declino?'*, 17 October.

Clarke, P. and DeBresson, C. (1990) Innovation-design and innovation poles, in Loveridge, R. and Pitt, M. (eds) *The Strategic Management of Technological Innovation*, Wiley, Chichester.

Clutterbuck, D. and Devine, M. (1985), Why start-ups start, *Management Today*, July, 58–63.

Conseil Economique et Social (1982) Le devenir des industries du textile et de l'habillement, *Journal Officiel*, 5, 25 February, 195–257.

Cooke, P. and Imrie, R. (1989) Little Victories: Local Economic Development in European Regions, *Entrepreneurship and Regional Development*, **1** (4), 313–27.

Cornforth, C. (1986) The Role of Local Co-operative Development Agencies in Promoting Worker Co-operatives, in Beaver, G. *et al.,* Readings in Small Business, Gower, Aldershot.

Courlet, C. (1986) Dynamiques industrielles locales en Savoie, *Economie et Humanisme,* **289** May–June), 37–45.

Cressey, P. and Jones, B. (1991) A New Convergence?, *Work, Employment and Society,* **5** (4), December, 493–5.

Creusat, J. and Richard, A. (1987) Une approche des systèmes industriels régionaux. Les cas de l'Alsace et de la Haute-Normandie, *Economie et Statistique,* 199–200, May–June, 65–81.

Cromie, S. (1987) The Aptitudes of Aspiring Male and Female Entrepreneurs, in O'Neill, K., Bhambri, R., Cannon, T. and Faulkner, T. (eds) *Small Business Development: Some Current Issues,* Gower, Aldershot.

Cromie, S. (1991) The Problems Experienced by Small Firms, *International Small Business Journal,* **9** (3), 43–61.

Cromie, S. and Ayling, S. (1989) The Motivation, Satisfaction and Company Goals of Business Proprietors in Mansfield, R. (ed.) *Frontiers of Management,* Routledge, London.

Cross, M. (1983) The United Kingdom, in Storey, D. (ed.) *The Small Firm: an International Survey,* Croom Helm, London.

Curran, J. and Stanworth, J. (1984), Small Business Research in Britain, in Levicki, C. (ed.) *Small Business: Theory and Practice,* Croom Helm, London.

Curzon, G. *et al.* (1981) *MFA Forever? Future of the Arrangement for Trade in Textiles,* Trade Policy Research Centre, London.

Cyert, R. and March, J. (1963) *A Behavioural Theory of the Firm,* Prentice-Hall, Englewood Cliffs, NJ.

Daly, D. and McCann, A. (1992) How Many Small Firms?, *Employment Gazette,* February, 47–51.

Darwent, D. F. (1969) Growth Poles and Growth Centers in Regional Planning – a Review, *Environment and Planning,* **1**, 5–32.

Davenport, E. and Totterdill, P. (1986) Fashion Centres: an Approach to Sector Intervention, *Local Economy,* **1** (1), 57-63.

Davies, S. (1990) Job Losses in UK Textiles, *Textiles Horizons,* March, 8.

Delanoë, G. (1975) *Etude sur l'évolution de la concentration dans l'industrie du textile en France,* CEE, Luxembourg.

Dempsey, E. (1991) Davros: Global Forum for Business and Industry Leaders, *Textile Leader,* **8**, 38–43.

Devilliers, M. (1987) Performances et comportements comparés des petites et grandes entreprises depuis le second choc pétrolier, *Problèmes Economiques*, **2031**, 1 July, 6–11.

Dore, R. (1983) Goodwill and the Spirit of Market Capitalism, *British Journal of Sociology*, **34**, 459–82.

Dudley, J. W. (1989) *1992: Strategies for the Single Market*, Kogan Page, London.

Durand, P. (1972) *Industrie et régions. L'aménagement industriel du territoire*, La Documentation Française, Paris.

Dyvrande, B. (1980) L'industrie oyonnaxienne à l'ère des craquements, *Revue de Géographie de Lyon*, **4**, 343–72.

ECHO (1991) Textiles and Clothing in Eastern Europe: Industries in Crisis, *Textiles Outlook International*, November, 9–29.

Elson, D. (1990) Marketing Factors Affecting the Globalisation of Textiles, *Textiles Outlook International*, March, 51–61.

Eme, B. and Laplume, Y. (1981) Les nouveaux entrepreneurs en France, *Futuribles*, **49**, November, 35–50.

Euro-info (1991) Textile Industry; an Overall Strategy to Increase Competitiveness, *Euro-info*, **44**, 4–5.

Euro-info (1992) RETEX: Aids to Small and Medium-sized Enterprises, *Euro-info*, **47**, 7.

Faini, R. and Heimler, A. (1991) The Quality and Production of Textiles and Clothing and the Completion of the Internal Market, in Winters, L.A. and Venebles, A. J. (eds) *European Integration: Trade and Industry*, Cambridge University Press, Cambridge.

Favaretto, I. (1986) Mutamento tecnologico ed economie di scala nei sistemi di imprese, *Economia Marche*, **7** (3), 355–83.

Filta-Cisl Lombardia and Filta-Cisl Como (1988), *Como e la seta: sviluppo o declino?*, Como.

Foray, D. (1990) 'The secrets of industry are in the air'. Coopération industrielle et équilibre organisationnel de la firme innovatrice, Discussion Paper, Institut International d'Etudes Sociales, Geneva.

Forni, M. (1987) *Storie familiari e storie di proprietà*, Rosenberg and Sellier, Turin.

Fortune (1991) The Fortune Global 500, *Fortune*, **124** (3), 29 July.

Fourcade, C. (1984–5) The Demarrage of Firms: International Comparisons, *International Small Business Journal*, **3** (2), 20–32.

Frey, L. (1974) La problematica del decentramento produttivo, *Economia e Politica Industriale*, **11**, 6

Fuà, G. and Zacchia, C. (eds) (1983) *Industrializzazione senza fratture*, Il Mulino, Bologna.

Gallagher, C. and Stewart, H. (1985), Business Death and Firm Size in the United Kingdom, *International Small Business Journal*, 4 (1), 42–57.

Ganguly, P. and Bannock, G. (eds) (1985) *Small Business Statistics and International Comparisons*, Harper and Row, London.

Ganne, B. (1983) *Gens du cuir; gens du papier*, CNRS, Lyon.

Ganne, B. *et al.* (1988) Milieux industriels et systèmes industriels locaux. Une comparaison France–Italie, GLYSI, Lyon.

Garofoli, G. (1983a), Le aree-sistema in Italia, *Politica e Economia*, 11, 37–60.

Garofoli, G. (1983b) Aree di specializzazione in Europa, *Economia Marche*, 2 (1), 3–46.

Garofoli, G. (1986) Le développement périphérique en Italie, *Economie et Humanisme*, 289, May–June, 30–6.

GATT (1980-1990) *International Trade*, GATT, Geneva.

Gerelli, E. (1983) *Per una politica dell'innovazione industriale*, Angeli, Milan.

Gibb, J. (ed.) (1985) *Science Parks and Innovation Centres: Their Economic and Social Impact*, Elsevier, Amsterdam.

Gibb, A. and Scott, M. (1986) Understanding Small Firms' Growth, in Scott, M. *et al.* (eds) *Small Firms' Growth and Development*, Gower, Aldershot.

Gobbo, F. (ed.) (1989) *Distretti e sistemi produttivi alle soglie degli anni '90*, Angeli, Milan.

Goffee, R. and Scase, R. (eds) (1987) *Entrepreneurship in Europe: the Social Processes*, Croom Helm, London.

Goldthorpe, J. (ed.) (1984) *Order and Conflict in Western European Capitalism*, Oxford University Press, Oxford.

Gordon, R. (1991) Innovation, Industrial Networks and High-technology Regions, in Camagni, R. (ed.) *Innovation Networks: Spatial Perspectives*, Belhaven Press, London.

Grant, R. (1986) Business Strategies for Adjusting to Low-cost International Competition in Mature Industries in McGee, J. and Thomas, H. (eds) *Strategic Management Research: a European Perspective*, Wiley, Chichester.

Gray, C. (1992) *Small Business in the Big Market. Small Firm Owners' Views on the Likely Effects of the Single Market*, Small Business Research Trust Monograph, Milton Keynes.

Graziani, G. (ed.) (1975) *Crisi e ristrutturazione dell'economia italiana*, Einaudi, Turin.

Greiner, L. (1972) Evolution and Revolution as Organizations Grow, *Harvard Business Review*, July–August, 37–46.

Hakansson, H. (ed.) (1987) *Industrial Technological Development: a Network Approach*, Croom Helm, London.

Hall, G. (1989) Lack of Finance as a Constraint on the Expansion of Innovatory Small Firms, in Barber, J. *et al.* (eds) *Barriers to Growth in Small Firms*, Routledge, London.

Hannan, M. and Freeman, J. (1977) The Population Ecology of Organizations, *American Journal of Sociology*, **82** (5), 929–64.

Harrington, J. and Maguire, S. (1989) 1992: the Regional Impact, *European Management Journal*, **7** (2), 235–9.

Harrison, P. (1989) AKT: a Powerful New Voice, *Textile Horizons*, April, 55–6.

Harrison, R. and Mason, C. (1987) The Regional Impact of the Small Firms Loan Guarantee Scheme, in O'Neill, K., Bhambri, R., Cannon, T. and Faulkner, T. (eds) *Small Business Development: Some Current Issues*, Gower, Aldershot.

Hedberg, B. (1981), How Organizations Learn and Unlearn, in Nystrom, P. and Starbuck, W. (eds) *Handbook of Organizational Design*, Oxford University Press, London, Vol. 2.

Henderson, B. (1979) *Henderson on Corporate Strategy*, Abt Books, Cambridge, Mass.

Herpin, N. (1986) L'habillement: une dépense sur le déclin, *Economie et Statistique*, **192**, October, 65–74.

Herpin, N. (1987) L'habillement et le corps, *Economie et Statistique*, 196, February, 55–63.

Heseltine, M. (1989) *The Challenge of Europe: Can Britain Win?*, Weidenfeld and Nicolson, London.

Hindley, B. (1984), Economics and Small Enterprises, in Levicki, C. (ed.) *Small Business: Theory and Practice*, Croom Helm, London.

Hindley, B. and Nicolaides, E. (1983) *Taking the New Protectionism Seriously*, Trade Policy Research Centre, London.

Hirst, P. and Zeitlin, J. (eds) (1989) *Reversing Industrial Decline? Industrial Structure and Policy in Britain and her Competitors*, Berg, Oxford.

Hitchens, D. and O'Farrell, P. (1987) The Comparative Performance of Small Manufacturing Firms in Northern Ireland and South East England, *Regional Studies*, **21** (6), 543–53.

Hofstede, G. (1980) *Culture's Consequences*, Sage, Beverly Hills, Calif.

Hough, J. (1982) Franchising – an Avenue for Entry into Small Business, in Stanworth, J., Westrip, A., Watkins, D. and Lewis, J. (eds) *Perspectives on a Decade of Small Business Research: Bolton Ten Years On*, Gower, Aldershot.

Houssel, J.-P. (1971) Les petites villes textiles du Haut-Beaujolais. De la tradition manufacturière à l'économie moderne, *Revue de Géographie de Lyon*, **1**, 329–47.

Houssel, J.-P. (1980) Les industries autochtones en milieu rural, *Revue de Géographie de Lyon*, **4**, 305–341.

Hunt, D. and McVey, B. (1984) 'Fishing Co-operatives – What Are We Really Talking About?, in Lewis, J., Stanworth, J. and Gibb, A. (eds) *Success and Failure in Small Businesses*, Gower, Aldershot.

Hutchinson, P. and Ray, G. (1986) Surviving the financial stress of small enterprise development, in Curran, J., Stanworth, J. and Watkins, D. (eds) *The Survival of the Small Firm*, Gower, Aldershot, Vol. 1.

INSEE (1988) Textile-habillement: Rhône-Alpes dans le peloton de tête des régions, *Bref Rhône-Alpes*, **1018**, 21 September, 3.

INSEE (1990a) *Vingt ans de comptes nationaux 1970–1989*, INSEE, Paris.

INSEE (1990b) *Annuaire rétrospectif de la France. Séries longues (1948–1988)*, INSEE, Paris.

International Textiles (1991) Uruguay Half-round, *International Textiles*, **729** December, 6.

International Textiles (1992) EEC Prepares to Cope with Shrinkage, *International Textiles*, **732** April, 6.

ISTAT (1985) *VI Censimento generale dell'industria, del commercio e dell'artigianato, Vol. II, Tomo 1, Fase 13 (Como)*, ISTAT, Rome.

Istituto Tagliacarne-Censis (1989), *Localismi e nuove strategie d'impresa. I casi di Bari, Padova e Prato*, Angeli, Milan

Jacomet, D. (1989) *Le Textile-Habillement. Une industrie de pointe!*, Economica, Paris.

Jarillo, J. (1988) On Strategic Networks, *Strategic Management Journal*, **9** 1, 31–41.

Johannisson, B. (1986) Network Strategies: Management Technology for Entrepreneurship and Change, *International Small Business Journal*, **5** (1), 19–30.

Johannisson, B. (1987) Beyond Process and Structure: Social Exchange Networks, *International Studies of Management and Organisation*, **17** (1), 3–23.

Johanson, J. and Mattsson, L.-G. (1985) Marketing Investments and Market Investments in Industrial Networks, *International Journal of Research in Marketing*, 2 (3), 185-195

Johanson, J. and Mattsson, L.-G. (1987) Interorganizational Relations in Industrial Systems: a Network Approach Compared with the Transaction Cost Approach, *International Studies of Management and Organization*, **17** (1), 34–48.

Johnson, G. (1987) *Strategic Change and the Management Process*, Basil Blackwell, Oxford.

Johnstone, D. *et al.* (1988) *Developing Businesses*, HMSO, London.

Jones, T. and McEvoy, D. (1986) Ethnic Enterprise: the Popular Image, in Curran, J., Stanworth, J. and Watkins, D. (eds) *The Survival of the Small Firm*, Gower, Aldershot, Vol. 1.

Kamann, D.-J. and Strijker, D. (1991) The Network Approach: Concepts and Applications, in Camagni, R. (ed.) *Innovation Networks: Spatial Perspectives*, Belhaven Press, London.

Keesing, D. B. and Wolf, M. (1980) *Textile Quotas against Developing Countries*, Trade Policy Research Centre, London.

Kenney, M. and Florida, R. (1988) Beyond Mass Production: Production and the Labour Process in Japan, *Politics and Society*, **16**(1), 121–58.

King, R. (1985) *The Industrial Geography of Italy*, Croom Helm, London.

Knoke, D. and Kuklinski, J.H. (1983) *Network Analysis*, Sage, Beverly Hills, Calif.

Koenig, C. and Thietart, R.-A. (1990) The Mutual Organization: a New Form of Co-operation in a High-technology Industry, in Loveridge R. and Pitt M. (eds) *The Management of Technological Innovation*, Wiley, Chichester.

Kroeger, C. (1974) Managerial Development in the Small Firm, *California Management Review*, **17**(1), 41–6.

Labasse, J. and Laferrère, M. (1966) *La Région lyonnaise*, PUF, Paris.

Laferrère, M. (1960) *Lyon ville industrielle. Essai d'une géographie urbaine des techniques et des entreprises*, PUF, Paris.

Lafuente, A. and Salas, V. (1989) Types of Entrepreneurs and Firms: the Case of New Spanish Firms, *Strategic Management Journal*, **10**(1), 17-30.

Larcombe, K. (1990) Survey of Attitudes to 1992, *Textile Outlook International*, March, 98–103.

Lassini, A. (ed.) (1984) *Competitività e cooperazione nei processi innovativi dell'impresa*, Angeli, Milan.

Lassini, A. (1986) *Opportunità tecnologiche, piccola dimensione e strategie innovative*, Il Mulino, Bologna.

Lataste, J. (1982) La place des PME dans l'économie française, *Economie et PME* (1er trimestre), 6–12.

Lazerson, M.H. (1988) Organizational Growth of Small Firms: an Outcome of Markets and Hierarchies?, *American Sociological Review*, **53**, 330–342.

Leicester Mercury (1992) Textile Industry Bids to Win Euro Cash, 6 March, p. 18.

Lenglet, F. (1991) Le Sentier défend son modèle, *L'Expansion*, 3–16 October, 164–71.

Leveson, J. (1986) The Phenomenon of Strategic Collaboration, *Directors and Boards*, **10**(4), 20–23.

Levicki, C. (1984) *Small Business: Theory and Practice*, Croom Helm, London.

Lewis, M. (1990a) Profile of the French clothing industry, *Textile Outlook International*, March, 62–97.

Lewis, M.(1990b) The French Textile Industry, *Textile Outlook International* July, 53–83.

Lewis, J., Stanworth, J. and Gibb, A. (eds) (1984) *Success and Failure in Small Businesses*, Gower, Aldershot.

Lindblom, C. (1959) The Science of Muddling Through, *Public Administration Quarterly*, **19** (2), 78–88.

Lippman, S. and Rumelt, R. (1982) Uncertain Imitability: an Analysis of Interfirm Differences in Efficiency under Competition, *Bell Journal of Economics*, **13**, 418–38.

Lorenz, E.H. (1988) Neither Friends nor Strangers: Informal Networks of Subcontracting in French Industry, in Gambetta, D. (ed.) *Trust: Making and Breaking Cooperative Relations*, Basil Blackwell, Oxford.

Lorenz, E.H. (1989) The Search for Flexibility: Subcontracting Networks in British and French Engineering, in Hirst, P. and Zeitlin, J. (eds) *Reversing Industrial Decline?*, Berg, Oxford.

Lorenzoni, G. and Ornati, O. A. (1988) Constellations of Firms and New Ventures, *Journal of Business Venturing*, **3**, 41–57.

Loveman, G. and Sengenberger, W. (1990) Introduction: Economic and Social Reorganisation in the Small and Medium-sized Enterprise Sector, in Sengenberger, W., Loveman, G. and Piore, M. (1990) (eds) *The Re-emergence of Small Enterprises: Industrial Restructuring in Industrialised Countries*, International Institute for Labour Studies, Geneva.

Loveridge, R. and Pitt, M. (eds) (1990) *The Strategic Management of Technological Innovation*, Wiley, Chichester.

Lowe, J. (1986) Competitive Strategy through Technology Licensing for the Small Firm, in Scott, M., Gibb, A., Faulkner, T. and Lewis, J. (eds) *Small Firms' Growth and Development*, Gower, Aldershot.

McGee, J. (1989) Barriers to Growth: the Effects of Market Structure, in Barber, J. *et al.*, *Barriers to Growth in Small Firms*, Routledge, London.

Maillat, D. (1991) The Innovation Process and the Local *Milieu*, in Bergman, E.M., Maier, G. and Todtling, F. (eds) *Regions Reconsidered: Economic Networks, Innovation and Local Development in Industrialised Countries*, Mansell, London and New York.

Marchesnay, M. (1984) Small Business in the New French Industrial Policy, *International Small Business Journal*, **2**(2), 25–34.

Marshall, A. (1919) *Industry and Trade*, Macmillan, London.

Marshall, A. (1966, 1st edn 1890), *Principles of Economics* (8th edn), Macmillan, London.

Mattson, L.-G. (1986) Indirect Relations in Industrial Networks – a Conceptual Analysis of their Strategic Significance, paper presented at the Third International IMP Research Seminar, ESC de Lyon.

May, N. (1986) Constitution d'un regard. Fordisme et localisme, *Les Annales de la recherche urbaine*, **29**, 5–13.

May, T. (1987) *An Economic and Social History of Britain 1760–1970*, Longman, Harlow.

Mee, A. (1937) *The King's England: Leicestershire and Rutland*, Hodder and Stoughton, London.

Meilhaud, J. (1991) Industrie lyonnaise: l'alliance réussie de la spécialisation traditionnelle et de l'innovation, *Problèmes économiques*, **2207**, 27 September, 6–9.

Miles, R. E. and Snow, C. C. (1984) Fit, Failure and the Hall of Fame, *California Management Review*, **26**(3), 10–28.

Milne, T. and Thompson, M. (1986) The Infant Business Development Process, in Scott, M., Gibb, A., Faulkner, T. and Lewis, J. (eds) *Small Firms' Growth and Development*, Gower, Aldershot.

Ministère de l'Industrie (1987) *Le Secteur textile-habillement*, SESSI, Paris.

Ministère de l'Industrie (1990) *Les Chiffres clé de l'industrie*, SESSI, Paris.

Mintzberg, H. (1973) Strategy Making in Three Modes, *California Management Review*, **16**(2), 44–53.

Mintzberg H. (1979) *The Structuring of Organizations*, Prentice Hall, Englewood Cliffs, NJ.

Montagné-Villette, S. (1990) *Le Sentier, un espace ambigu*, Masson, Paris.

Morse, R. (1977) Entrepreneurial Initiatives and Community Need Fulfilment, in Neck, P. (ed.) *Small Enterprise Development: Policies and Programmes*, International Labour Office, Geneva.

Mounfield, P. (1972) The Foundations of the Modern Industrial Pattern, and The Modern Industrial Scene: Changing Patterns of Manufacturing in the Post-war Period, in Pye, N. (ed.) *Leicester and its Region*, Leicester University Press, Leicester.

Mytelka, L. K. (1982) In Search of a Partner: the State and the Textile Industry in France, in Cohen, S. and Gourevitch, P. (eds) *France in the Troubled World Economy*, Butterworth, London.

Nanetti, R. (1988) *Growth and Territorial Policies. The Italian Model of Social Capitalism*, Routledge, London and New York.

Nelson, R. and Winter, S. (1982) *An Evolutionary Theory of Economic Change*, Belknap Press, Cambridge, Mass.

Nerb, G. (1988) *The Completion of the Internal Market. A Survey of European Industry's Perception of the Likely Effects. Research on the 'Cost of Non-Europe': Basic Findings*, Commission of the EC, Luxembourg, Vol. 3.

Newman, B. (1968) *Portrait of the Shires*, Robert Hale, London.

Norburn, D. (1989) The Chief Executive: a Breed Apart, *Strategic Management Journal*, **10**(1), 1–16.

Nouvel Economiste (1991) Crise sans précédent, *Nouvel Economiste*, **812,** 20 September, 55.

Nueno, P. and Oosterveld, J. (1988) Managing Technology Alliances, *Long Range Planning*, **21**(3), 11–17.

Nuti, F. (1989), Sistemi articolati di produzione e 'rapporti tra imprese'. Lo stato dell'arte dell'analisi dei rapporti tra imprese nell'industria manifatturiera: riconsiderazione della letteratura e aggiornamenti, in Gobbo, F. (ed.) *Distretti e sistemi produttivi alle soglie degli anni '90*, Angeli, Milan.

O'Neill, K., Bhambri, R., Cannon, T. and Faulkner, T. (eds.) (1987) *Small Business Development: Some Current Issues*, Gower, Aldershot.

Oakey, R. (1984) *High Technology Small Firms: Regional Development in Britain and the United States*, Pinter, London.

Oakey, R., Rothwell, R. and Cooper, S. (1988) *The Management of Innovation in High-technology Small Firms: Innovation and Regional Development in Britain and the United States*, Pinter, London.

OECD (1982) *Innovation in Small and Medium Firms*, OECD, Paris.

OECD (1983) *Textile and Clothing Industries. Structural Problems and Policies in OECD Countries*, OECD, Paris.

OECD (1989) The Importance of Technological Innovation in the Clothing Industry', *Textile Leader*, **5**, 103–118.

Ouchi, W. (1980) Markets, Bureaucracies and Clans, *Administrative Science Quarterly*, **25**, 129–141.

Paci, M. (1973) *Mercato del lavoro e classi sociali in Italia*, Il Mulino, Bologna.

Paci, M. (1975) Crisi, ristrutturazione e piccola impresa *Inchiesta*, **5**, 20.

Paci, M. (1980) *Famiglia e mercato del lavoro in una economia periferica*, Angeli, Milano.

Panorama of EC Industry (1990) Office for Official Publications of the EC, Luxembourg.

Pavitt, K. (1989) Strategic Management in the Innovating Firm, in Mansfield, R. (ed.) *Frontiers of Management*, Routledge, London.

Pecqueur, B. (1987) Tissu économique local et systèmes industriels résiliares, *Revue d'Economie Régionale et Urbaine*, **3**, 369–78.

Perrin, J.-C. (1984) La reconversion du bassin industriel d'Alès. Contribution à une théorie de la dynamique locale', *Revue d'Economie Régionale et Urbaine*, **2**, 236–54.

Perroux, F. (1950) Economic Space: Theory and Applications, *Quarterly Journal of Economics*, **64**, 89–104.

Perroux, F. (1955) Note sur la notion de pôle de croissance, *Economie Appliquée*, 307–20.

Perry, C. (1986) Growth Strategies for Small Firms: Principles and Case Studies, *International Small Business Journal*, **5**(2), 17–25.

Peterson, R. and Schulman, J. (1987) Capital Structure of Growing Small Firms: a 12-Country Study on Becoming Bankable, *International Small Business Journal*, **5**(4), 10–22.

Piore M. and Sabel, C. (1983) Italian Small Business Development: Lessons for U.S. Industrial Policy in J. Zyman, J. and Tyson, L. (eds) *American Industry in International Competetion*, Cornell University Press, Ithaca, NY.

Piore, M. and Sabel C. (1984) *The Second Industrial Divide: Possibilities for Prosperity*, Basic Books, New York.

Pitt, M. (1989) Corporate Birth, Crisis and Rebirth: the Emergence of Four Small UK Service Firms, in Mansfield, R. (ed.) *Frontiers of Management*, Routledge, London.

Pitt, M. (1990) Crisis Modes of Strategic Transformation: a New Metaphor for Managing Technological Innovation, in Loveridge, R. and Pitt, M. (eds) *The Strategic Management of Technological Innovation*, Wiley, Chichester.

Pitt, M., Bull, A. and Szarka, J. (1991) Executive Characteristics, Strategic Choices and Small Firm Development: a Three-country Study of Small Textiles and Clothing Firms, *International Small Business Journal*, **9**(3), 11–30.

Plessy, B. and Challet, L. (1987) *La Vie quotidienne des canuts, passementiers et moulinières au XIXe siècle*, Hachette, Paris.

Ponson, B. (1985) Entreprise familiale et théorie de la firme: une introduction, ESCP document de travail 85–69, Paris.

Pontarollo, E. and Martini, G. (1989) Distretti industriali e tessuti economici circostanti: il caso di Como, in Gobbo, F. (ed.) *Distretti e sistemi produttivi alle soglie degli anni '90*, Angeli, Milan.

Porter, M. (1990) *The Competitive Advantage of Nations*, Macmillan, London.

Pyke, F. (1988) Cooperative Practices among Small and Medium-sized Establishments, *Work, Employment and Society*, **2**(3), 352–65.

Rainnie, A. (1989) *Industrial Relations in Small Firms: Small Is Not Beautiful*, Croom Helm, London.

Raveyre, M. -F. and Saglio, J. (1984) Les systèmes industriels localisés: éléments pour une analyse sociologique des ensembles de PME industriels, *Sociologie du travail*, **2**, 157–76.

Regini, M. and Sabel, C. (eds) (1989) *Strategie di riaggiustamento industriale*, Il Mulino, Bologna.

Riva, A. (1983) *Sviluppo e innovazione nella piccola e media impresa, IRER*, Angeli, Milan.

Rizzoni, A. (1991) Technological Innovation and Small Firms: a Taxonomy, *International Small Business Journal*, **9**(3), 31-42.

Robert-Diard, P. (1987) Lyon: adaptation et formation ont permis aux industries textiles de développer leurs marchés, *Le Monde*, 3 February, p. 18.

Robinson, R., Pearce, J., Vozikis, G. and Mescon, T. (1984) The Relationship between Stage of Development and Small Firm Planning and Performance, *Journal of Small Business Management*, **22**(2), 45–52.

Rothwell, R. and Beesley, M. (1989) The Importance of Technology Transfer, in Barber, J. *et al.* (eds) *Barriers to Growth in Small Firms*, Routledge, London.

Rothwell, R. and Zegweld, W. (1982) *Innovation in the Small and Medium Sized Firm*, Pinter, London.

Roux, J. and de Banville, E. (1979) Internationalisation et région: le cas de l'industrie en Rhône-Alpes, CRESAL, Saint-Etienne.

Sabel C. (1989) Flexible Specialization and Regions, in Hirst, P. and Zeitlin, J. (eds) *Reversing Industrial Decline?*, Berg, Oxford.

Sabel, C. and Zeitlin, J. (1985) Historical Alternatives to Mass Production: Politics, Markets and Technology in Nineteenth-century Industrialization, *Past and Present*, **108**, 133–76.

Saglio, J. *et al.* (1983) Les systèmes industriels localisés, GLYSI, Lyon.

Sallez, A. (1980) La dynamique des PME apprehendée à travers les problèmes de la sous-traitance et de l'internationalisation, CERESSEC, Cergy.

Samuels, J. and Morrish, P. (1984) An Analysis of Concentration, in Levicki, C., (ed.) *Small Business: Theory and Practice*, Croom Helm, London.

Scase, R. and Goffee, R. (1980, 2nd edn 1987) *The Real World of the Small Business Owner*, Croom Helm, London.

Schein, E. (1983) The Role of the Founder in Creating Organizational Culture, *Organizational Dynamics*, **12**(1), 13–28.

Schermerhorn, J. (1980) Interfirm Cooperation as a Resource for Small Business Development, *Journal of Small Business Management*, **18**(2), 48–54.

Scott, M., Gibb, A., Faulkner, T. and Lewis, J. (eds) (1986) *Small Firms' Growth and Development*, Gower, Aldershot.

Sengenberger, W., Loveman, G. and Piore, M. (1990) (eds) *The Re-emergence of Small Enterprises: Industrial Restructuring in Industrialised Countries*, International Institute for Labour Studies, Geneva.

Sforzi, F. (1987) L'identificazione spaziale, in Becattini, G. (ed.) *Mercato e forze locali: il distretto industriale*, Il Mulino, Bologna; also in Bamford, J., Goodman, E. and Saynor, P. (eds) *Small Firms and Industrial Districts in Italy*, Routledge, London, 1989.

Shailor, G. (1989) The Predictability of Small Enterprise Failure: Evidence and Issues, *International Small Business Journal*, **7**(4), 54–8.

Shepherd, G. (1983) Textiles: New Ways of Surviving in an Old Industry in Shepherd, G., Duchêne, F. and Saunders, C. (eds) *Europe's Industries. Public and Private Strategies for Change*, Pinter, London.

Shutt, J. and Whittington, R. (1987) Fragmentation Strategies and the Rise of Small Units, Cases from the North-West, *Regional Studies*, **21**, 13–23.

Silbertson, A. (1991) The Consequences of Abolishing the MFA, *Textile Outlook International*, May, 62–70.

Silly, J. (1961) La disparition de la petite métallurgie rurale, *Revue d'histoire de la sidérurgie*, 47–61.

Smilor, R. and Gill, M. (1986) *The New Business Incubator: Linking Talent, Technology, Capital and Know-How*, D.C. Heath, Lexington, Mass.

Smith, N. (1967) *The Entrepreneur and his Firm: the Relationship between Type of Man and Type of Company*, Michigan State University Press, East Lansing, Mass.

Spender, J.-C. (1983) Recipes and the Business Policy Problem, in Lamb, R. (ed.) *Advances in Strategic Management*, JAI Press, Greenwich, Conn., Vol 2.

Spender, J.-C. (1989) *Industry Recipes: the Nature and Sources of Managerial Judgement*, Blackwell, Oxford.

Stanworth, J. and Curran, J. (1976) Growth and the Small Firm – an Alternative View, *Journal of Management Studies*, **13**(2), 95–110.

Stanworth, J. and Curran, J. (1986) Growth and the Small Firm, in Curran, J., Stanworth, J. and Watkins, D. (1986) (eds.) *The Survival of the Small Firm*, Gower, Aldershot, Vol 2.

Stanworth, J., Curran, J. and Hough, J. (1984) The Franchised Small Enterprise: Formal and Operational Dimensions of Independence, in Lewis, J., Stanworth, J. and Gibb, A. (eds) *Success and Failure in Small Businesses*, Gower, Aldershot.

Stopford, J. M. and Baden-Fuller, C. (1990) Flexible Strategies – the Key to Success in knitwear, *Long Range Planning*, **23**(6), 56–62.

Storey, D. (1983) Introduction: Advanced Industrial Economies, in Storey, D. (ed.) *The Small Firm: an International Survey*, Croom Helm, London.

Storey, D. (ed.) (1985) *Small Firms in Regional Economic Development*, Cambridge University Press, Cambridge.

Storey, D., Keasey, K., Watson, R. and Wynarczyk, P. (1987) *The Performance of Small Firms: Profits, Jobs and Failures*, Croom Helm, London.

Swords-Isherwood, N. (1980) British Management Compared, in Pavitt, K. (ed.) *Technical Innovation and British Economic Performance*, Macmillan, London.

Szarka, J. (1990) Networking and Small Firms, *International Small Business Journal*, **8**(2), 10–22.

Szarka, J. (1991) Exchange Networks in the Textiles-Clothing Industry, *Gestion 2000*, **1**, 85–102.

Target 1992 (1992) RETEX: Help for Textile and Clothing SMEs, *Target 1992*, February, 4.

Textile Outlook International (1991) Consumer Spending on Clothing and Footwear in the EC, *Textile Outlook International*, November, 30–43.

Textile World (1989) Textiles Rank Sixth in Toxic Waste, *Textile World*, August, 23–5.

Thorelli, H. B. (1986) Networks: Between Markets and Hierarchies, *Strategic Management Journal*, **7**, 37-51

Thurley, K. and Wirdenius, H. (1989) *Towards European Management*, Pitman, London.

Toyne, B. *et al.* (1984) *The Global Textile Industry*, Allen and Unwin, London.

Trela, I. and Whalley, J. (1990) Unravelling the Threads of the MFA, in Hamilton, C. B. (ed.) *Textiles Trade and the Developing Countries. Eliminating the Multi-Fibre Arrangement in the 1990s*, World Bank, Washington, DC.

Trigilia, C. (1986) *Grandi partiti e piccole imprese. Comunisti e democristiani nelle regioni a economia diffusa*, Il Mulino, Bologna.

Tuloup, A. (1987) *Stratégies performantes dans les industries de la mode*, Editions de l'ADIDO, Paris.

Unioncamere-Istituto Tagliacarne-Censis (1991) *Rapporto 1990 sull'impresa, il sistema pubblico e le economie locali. L'impresa italiana e il mercato unico europeo*, Angeli, Milan.

Unione Industriali di Como (1983) *Como distretto tessile*, Edizioni Consulenze Industriali, Como.

United Nations Centre on Transnational Corporations (1987) *Transnational Corporations in the Man-Made Fibre, Textile and Clothing Industries*, United Nations, New York.

Utili, G. (1989), Mutamenti organizzativi nei distretti industriali: osservazioni su due casi, in Gobbo, F. (ed.) *Distretti e sistemi produttivi alle soglie degli anni' 90*, Angeli, Milan.

Utton, M. (1984) Concentration, Competition and the Small Firm, in Levicki, C., (ed.) *Small Business: Theory and Practice*, Croom Helm, London.

Vant, André (1974) L'industrie du cycle dans la région stéphanoise, *Revue de Géographie de Lyon*, **4**, 155–84.

Verret, R. (1989) From Labour Intensiveness to Capital Intensiveness: the Impact of Technology on the Textiles Industry, *Textile Leader*, **4**, 90–4.

Vroom, V. and Yetton, P. (1973) *Leadership and Decision Making*, Feffer and Simons University of Pittsburg Press, London.

Ward, R. and Jenkins, R. (eds) (1984) *Communities in Business*, Cambridge University Press, Cambridge.

Ward, R., Randall, R., and Krcmar, K. (1986) Small Firms in the Clothing Industry: the Growth of Minority Enterprise, *International Small Business Journal*, **4**(3), 46–56.

Watkins, D. and Horley, G. (1986) Transferring Technology from Large to Small Firms: the Role of Intermediaries, in Beaver, G. *et al.* (eds) *Readings in Small Business*, Gower, Aldershot.

Watkins, J. and Watkins, D. (1984) The Female Entrepreneur: Background and Determinants of Business Choice – some British Data *International Small Business Journal*, **2**(4), 21–31.

Watson, J. (1991) *Textiles and the Environment*, Economist Intelligence Unit Special Report No. 2150, London.

Weisz, R. and Anselme, M. (1981) L'Industrie de l'habillement en région Provence-Alpes-Côtes d'Azur. Stratégies d'entreprises et organisation de la production, Centre d'Etudes, de recherches et de formation institutionnelles du Sud-Est.

Wells, F. (1972) *The British Hosiery and Knitwear Industry*, David and Charles, Newton Abbot.

Welsch, H. and Young, E. (1984) Male and Female Entrepreneurial Characteristics and Behaviours: a Profile of Similarities and Differences, *International Small Business Journal*, **2**(4), 11–20.

Williams, A. (1985) Stress and the Entrepreneurial Role, *International Small Business Journal*, **3**(4), 11–25.

Williamson, O. (1975) *Markets and Hierarchies: Analysis and Antitrust Implications*, The Free Press, New York.

Williamson, O. (1979) Transaction Cost Economics: the Governance of Contractual Relations, *Journal of Law and Economics*, **22**(2), 233–61.

Williamson, O. (1981), The Economics of Organization: the Transaction Costs Approach, *American Journal of Sociology*, **87**, 548–77.

Williamson, O. (1985), *The Economic Institutions of Capitalism*, The Free Press, New York.

Wilson, P. and Stanworth, J. (1987) The Social and Economic Factors in the Development of Small Black Minority Firms: Asian and Afro-Caribbean Business in Brent 1982 and 1984 Compared, in O'Neill, K., Bhambri, R., Cannon, T. and Faulkner, T. (eds) *Small Business Development: Some Current Issues*, Gower, Aldershot.

Winter, S. (1987) Knowledge and Competence as Strategic Assets, in Teece, D. (ed.) *The Competitive Challenge: Strategies for Industrial Innovation and Renewal*, Ballinger, Cambridge, Mass.

Zaleznik, A. (1977) Managers and Leaders: Are they Different?, *Harvard Business Review*, May–June, 67–78.

References

Zeitlin, J. (1985) Markets, Technology and Collective Services: a Strategy for Local Government Intervention in the London Clothing Industry, in Greater London Council, *The London Clothing Strategy: A Debate*, Economic Policy Group Strategy Document No. 39.

Zeitlin, J. and Totterdill, P. (1989) Markets, Technology and Local Intervention: the Case of Clothing, in Hirst, P. & Zeitlin, J. (eds) *Reversing Industrial Decline?*, Berg, Oxford.

Index

DATE DUE

DEMCO, INC. 38-2971